The Greatest Fleecing of America:

VETERANS DISABILITY COMPENSATION

S. D. Price

ISBN: 1725106922
ISBN-13: 978-1725106925

DEDICATION

For America's truly battle-injured veterans, for America's taxpayers,
and for President Trump who inspires me with his indefatigable efforts and
unwavering courage to say and do what he believes is best for our country.

Contents

Preface ix

Prologue xi

(1) DEAR MR. PRESIDENT 1

(2) SERVICEMEN OR VETERANS 6

(3) IS VA COMPENSATION A MILITARY PERK? 11

(4) WHAT'S WRONG WITH VA COMPENSATION? 15

    CONDITIONS NOT CAUSED BY SERVICE 29

    EVALUATIONS TOO HIGH FOR NON-DISABLED 36

    SOME VETERANS DO NOT DESERVE BENEFITS 43

    FRIVOLOUS AND FRAUDULENT CLAIMS 48

    ABUSE OF INDIVIDUAL UNEMPLOYABILITY (IU) 56

    REVOLVING DOOR 61

    APPEALS 64

(5) TRUE WAR INJURIES 66

(6) HOW MUCH I$ THE FLEECING ? 71

(7) IS THE GULF WAR TO BLAME? 78

(8) MAD INCREASE IN CLAIMS AND BENEFITS 82

(9) BUT WHY HAVE CLAIMS INCREASED? 88

(10) HOW MUCH WILL A VETERAN RECEIVE? 91

(11) ENTITLEMENT REFORM – BRING IT ON 94

(12) HISTORY OF VETERANS' COMPENSATION 98

(13) HONORABLE PROGRAM, GONE AWRY 103

(14) OTHER AFFECTED VETERANS' ISSUES 114

    NONSERVICE-CONNECTED PENSION 114

    HOMELESS VETERANS 116

    VA MEDICATIONS AND OPIOID ABUSE 117

    UNFAIRNESS FOR SOME MILITARY RETIREES 118

    VA HOSPITALS AFFECTED BY DISABILITY CLAIMS 120

(15) THE CLAIMS PROCESS 127

    WHAT IS A VA DISABILITY CLAIM? 127

    WHAT DISABILITIES CAN THEY CLAIM? 133

    TYPICAL CLAIMED ISSUES 135

    TYPES OF CLAIMS 137

        EXAMPLES OF ORIGINAL CLAIMS 140

        EXAMPLES OF INCREASE CLAIMS 141

        EXAMPLES OF REOPEN CLAIMS 143

        DEPENDENTS' INDEMNITY COMPENSATION 145

    WHERE ARE CLAIMS PROCESSED? 147

    THE RATING SCHEDULE 149

(16) PROBLEMS IN THE RATING PROCESS 154

    PROBLEMS WITH VA EXAMS 154

    PROBLEMS WITH MEDICAL OPINIONS 163

    PROBLEMS WITH EVALUATION BUILDERS 165

    PROBLEMS WITH INTENT TO FILE 170

(17) SPECIFIC MEDICAL ISSUES 172

    AUDOLOGY PROBLEMS 173

        HEARING LOSS 174

        TINNITUS 180

INCREASE CLAIMS FOR AUDIO CONDITIONS 183

MENTAL DISORDERS 187

POSTTRAUMATIC STRESS DISORDER (PTSD) 187

MILITARY SEXUAL TRAUMA (MST) 217

OTHER MENTAL CONDITIONS 224

VIETNAM WAR AND AGENT ORANGE CLAIMS 235

AGENT ORANGE – WHAT IS IT? 235

AGENT ORANGE LITIGATION AND LEGISLATION 238

THE AGENT ORANGE DEBACLE 244

DIABETES MELLITUS TYPE II 246

PROSTATE CANCER 248

PARKINSON'S DISEASE 251

ISCHEMIC HEART DISEASE 252

SUMMARY OF HERBICIDE-PRESUMPTIVES 253

EFFECT ON DEFICIT DUE TO AGENT ORANGE 256

NEHMER IMPACT 258

"THE VIETNAM EFFECT" 259

GULF WAR CLAIMS 271

BREATHING COMPLAINTS 274

GASTROINTESTINAL COMPLAINTS 275

OIL WELL FIRES AND BURN PITS 276

GULF WAR SYNDROME 277

CHRONIC FATIGUE SYNDROME 277

FIBROMYALGIA 278

CAMP LEJEUNE CONTAMINATED WATER 282

SLEEP APNEA 283

TRAUMATIC BRAIN INJURY (TBI).. 290

HEADACHES.. 293

JOINTS, FUNCTIONAL LOSS, & PAINFUL MOTION............................ 296

BACK CONDITIONS... 305

FOOT CONDITIONS 308

PERIPHERAL NERVE CONDITIONS 310

SKIN CONDITIONS.. 311

RESPIRATORY CONDITIONS 314

HYPERTENSION AND HEART DISEASE 317

SURGERY IN SERVICE 320

AMYOTROPHIC LATERAL SCLEROSIS (ALS).................................. 322

SEXUAL DYSFUNCTION (ED, SMC-K, AND FSAD) 325

MALE ERECTILE DYSFUNCTION 325

SPECIAL MONTHLY COMPENSATION (SMC) - K........................... 326

FEMALE SEXUAL AROUSAL DISORDER (FSAD)............................ 328

SUMMARY OF SEXUAL DYSFUNCTION 329

(18) FIXES HAVE MADE THINGS WORSE 330

(19) WHAT CAN BE DONE? 337

(20) CHANGES IN ATTITUDES & POLICIES 341

(21) CHANGES IN FEDERAL REGULATIONS 348

(22) JOINT EFFORTS NEEDED 354

References 361

Preface

The Fleecing of America is a book Senator William Proxmire wrote in 1980 to expose hundreds of wasteful federal spending programs. "Fleecing" is the shearing of a lamb, i.e., the American taxpayer, and Proxmire used the term to describe "a smooth, legalized theft from the taxpayers." This book is not about any of the programs mentioned by Proxmire and I don't intend to implicate or associate him in any way to the content herein. I've borrowed his term "fleecing of America" in reference to another federal program which I consider to be *the greatest fleecing of them all*, the worst ongoing and rapidly increasing waste, abuse and misappropriation of American tax dollars, the Veterans Affairs benefits program known as *Disability Compensation*.

This book is *not* about war-injured veterans; I gladly pay my share to provide them with every possible benefit. They are truly "our great veterans." But the once-honorable program designed to benefit our war heroes is now greatly abused and misused, not just by non-injured veterans but by the VA administration due to current claims processing policies, automations, and quirky interpretations of regulations.

This book is written for the enlightenment of American taxpayers, the President, top officials in the Department of Veterans Affairs, the Government Accountability Office, all Congressmen, and anyone in a position to influence or decide how our federal tax dollars are spent. Unfortunately, the President, Congressmen, and highest appointees in the Department of Veterans Affairs have never worked in the lower echelons of Veterans Affairs so they have no idea what a nightmare of government waste and fraud exists and why it is increasing tremendously each year. Not only is this abused entitlement program a financial disgrace to our nation, a misappropriation of hard-earned taxpayer dollars, and a slap in the face to truly disabled war veterans, the perpetuance of VA "over-compensation" is crushing the morality and integrity of our veterans. It is destroying the will of our young veterans to work and support themselves and inhibits them from developing pride and self-respect in themselves and for their country.

Prologue

FEDERAL GOVERNMENT WASTE

In the 1970's I ran away from a lot of troubles and joined the Army. As promised, the military gave me three hots a day, a roof over my head, free medical care, free clothing, free training, free travel, and exposure to other cultures home and abroad. I will forever be indebted; it was the best thing that ever happened to me. I couldn't believe how much money is invested in every single soldier. There is no easier job, with no greater fringe benefits, than what the military has to offer, thanks to the American taxpayer dollars. But my eyes were quickly opened to government waste when I worked in an Army warehouse. We stocked many items that would sit on the warehouse shelf for a while then would simply be "properly disposed of" because they have a shelf life. Some items really do disintegrate such as adhesives and batteries, but some have to be disposed of just to make room for new ones because government contractor factories have to stay in business in case there's a war.

When I finished my military commitment, the GI bill paid for my college degree, a full four years at the college of my choice and allowance for housing for me and my family while I attended college, and nothing to repay! I would have re-entered service as an officer after college but the federal government civilians got to me first and made me offers I couldn't refuse, so I had a civil service job waiting the day after graduation.

In the 1980's I worked in Defense Contracts Administration as an inspector in many defense contractor production facilities. I saw contractors pulling the wool over the eyes of naïve federal inspectors. I heard plenty about bribes, threats, and improper handling of government materials. But the biggest shock to me was again the waste of government-purchased products or services. I worked in contractor facilities where highly combustible ammunitions and end items with combustibles had to be maintained/stored at the construction facilities rather than shipped over to government storage. They were held in the contractor's inventory and shipped as needed to various war or training exercises. When these items had been held for a specified period of time, they had to be destroyed, as in taken out to the bunkers at the factory and blown to bits. Meanwhile, new products, exactly like the ones destroyed, continued to be produced. Millions of dollars paid for items that were destroyed simply due to shelf life and/or ongoing continuous production of the items, although there was no war and no need for the items. Government contracts take about five years from idea to production. It takes so long to get allocations approved, budgeted, contracts awarded, jobs announced, and research and development done, that by the time the item is actually produced and ready to ship, the design is either obsolete or no longer needed. But once a contract is issued it must be full-filled, and paid for, regardless of whether the military will ever use the item or not.

As for government construction projects, I've been told by construction workers that when a job is finished, they dig a big hole with their bulldozer, throw in all the left over brand new tools, supplies, and materials and cover it with dirt, then pave it. This is easier than going through the process of returning any excess for credit to a government account, and it assures the allocations for the next project won't be reduced. Whenever I've expressed dismay over things like this I've been told, "Don't worry. It's just a drop in the bucket of defense spending."

So many things about the government bothered my conscience, so I resigned. I always felt that if the government could be run like a private business, we would save billions of taxpayer dollars. But the problem is there is no "owner", no CEO, no investors, and no group who cares about government waste. A single-bodied concerned peon like myself can do nothing. Except resign. So I resigned several times, whenever I got too disgusted with the government. But I always came back because I just couldn't resist the high pay and the benefits. And once you have career status they will always take you back with priority over new applicants.

In the early 1990's, I experienced tremendous waste when participating in the closure of a large military base under the Base Realignment and Closure Act (BRAC). The post where I worked had a brand-new family housing development with houses less than two years old. In fact some were still pending construction when the BRAC closure began but of course the construction had to continue. Those beautiful homes had to be boarded up and left to decay, when so many in the private community could have enjoyed them. Military equipment as much as possible was shipped to other military bases, but there was a tremendous waste of buildings and excess equipment and supplies that had to auctioned or destroyed.

In late 1990's, I again worked in contracts administration at a government contractor facility, this one making munitions. Politicians from the House of Representatives visited fairly often. I'll never forget my shock the day I overheard the plant manager say to one of them, "We've got to have a new war to keep this contract going and to keep these people employed." It was the largest employer in our area. So, I resolved not to fight the issuance of new contracts. I'm glad people can be employed even if many of them can't sleep at night for thinking of who might be killed by those munitions they're building and packing. But wouldn't it be much better if our government could help put people to work in factories to produce clothing, furniture, and basic necessities of life rather than of death, at the same time returning our country to self-sufficiency. Hopefully President Trump is leading in that direction.

At that same facility in the late '90s, I uncovered overpayments to the contractor of *millions* of dollars, which occurred simply because there was no program, no ledger or computer spreadsheet, in place to monitor whether contractor shipments actually matched the contractor billings that were being paid. I thoroughly documented my findings and brought this to the attention of my superiors and the contractor, but nothing was done about it. I was so frustrated I resigned again.

After a few years of running my own businesses, I returned again to the federal government. I wanted those vacation days, sick days, and future retirement which I wasn't likely ever to get in my private businesses. This time I tried a new venue, The Department of Veterans Affairs, hereafter referred to as "VA." After working there for 10 years, I have again withdrawn myself from the nightmare. I thoroughly enjoyed the type of work I was doing, using a computer, reading records, filling out decisions, every case unique from the last, and the work facilities were great. They even let me work at home 4 days a week. They paid me outrageously for the work I did and for all the overtime I could handle. I truly believe I did my job well and I left on good terms. But I took early retirement because I just couldn't stand it anymore. I hated being an accomplice to this fraud, waste and abuse.

Despite all the waste I have seen in federal agencies over the past 40 years, nothing compares to the atrocities of the VA. I'm not talking about federal employees wasting money on traveling to foolish conventions and using charter planes when federal ones were available. There's plenty of that in any federal agency, but that sort of waste goes on in any private business too; that's just business. I'm not talking about the medical centers keeping separate lists of appointments to hide the fact that appointments were being scheduled so far out that veterans were dying before they could be seen. I'm not even talking about the hundreds of VA claims files that were found hidden under ceiling tiles and tucked away in desk drawers because they were the "dog" cases and there just wasn't time to waste on them due to the claims backlog and production quotas. What I *am* talking about are actions being taken in the VA benefits offices that are done every day in accordance with current policies and current interpretations of regulations! These regulations and policies must be changed!

(1) DEAR MR. PRESIDENT

Dear Mr. President, Secretary of Veterans Affairs, VA Under Secretary for Benefits, Director of the Office of Management and Budget, Senate Budget Committee, House Veterans Affairs Committee, VA Advisory Committee on Disability Compensation, Government Accountability Office, any interested members of Congress, and all American taxpayers:

I'm writing to tell you how to save taxpayer dollars, how to cut out a big waste of government spending and fraud. The 5th general principle of Government Ethics is to "Disclose waste, fraud, abuse, and corruption to appropriate authorities" and that is my intent. I'm sorry I couldn't do it while I was still employed by the VA; I would have been fired.

The biggest "fleecing of America" in the 21st century is the payment of *veterans disability compensation.* The payout of VA compensation will be about $90 billion for 2018, and that's just in paychecks to the recipients, aside from the billions spent on administration of the program, and aside from medical care. The current unfunded liabilities our children will be paying for this single veterans' benefit alone, even if there was never another claim granted, is *2.8 trillion dollars* and this is increasing at a ridiculous rate each year. The amount of federal spending is not an issue if the cause is just, but the problem here is that many veterans are being paid up to 100 percent disability compensation (more than $3,000 per month for life) when they don't have a single condition impairing their ability to work or function in society, and if they do have actual disabilities, those disabilities were not incurred in war or caused by any function of military service. This is a slap in the face of every truly disabled war veteran, it's a disservice to every American taxpayer, it's creating a whole new sector of social welfare and presumed entitlement, and it's contributing to the financial downfall of our country.

Before I provide the details of the wasteful spending, complete with suggestions for correction and improvement, I'll explain why I feel qualified to address the issue. I am a veteran myself and I spent most of the past 40 years working with and around soldiers and veterans. After active duty Army, I worked as a civil service employee for the Department of the Army, Defense Logistics Agency, and Department of Veterans Affairs. I've spent time in VA hospitals, clinics, and American Legion halls.

I personally have never filed a claim for VA disability benefits. For one thing, I choose to be healthy rather than spending my life in bogus medical appointments. Secondly, I won't file a disability claim because the government has already given me all the military and veteran's benefits they promised. I'm proud to say I have worked all my life and never sought to receive any social welfare benefits. But I must admit it's hard to resist that dangling carrot, and who knows, maybe one day I'll also succumb to the temptation of an extra fat paycheck every month, just because I'm a veteran.

I have the utmost respect for our military and I recommend that every American teenager, male and female, should enlist and serve at least two years. For me it was a wonderful (while difficult and challenging) four years during which the Army fed me, clothed me, housed me, provided free health care, traveled me, trained me in skills that would lead to future employment, and paid me supplemental allowances to take care of my family expenses. As an "employee" of the Army (a soldier) I was fully compensated and well taken care of. The Army was good to me, took me to Europe and all over the U.S. I saw much of the world and I learned a lot about people from all different walks of life. Although I was raised in the prejudiced "south" I learned a new respect for all Americans by wearing the same uniform and doing the same jobs.

When I finished my service commitment I collected my "veteran's benefits" as promised. I received four years of college paid for by the GI Bill which lead to a BA degree in the field of my choice. I used a VA home loan twice to buy homes with good interest rates and no money down. With my Army discharge papers and my government-funded college degree I was given "veteran's preference" for employment and was immediately hired by the federal government to work as a civil servant. I continued to receive great employee benefits such as good pay, vacation and sick days, health insurance, and retirement benefits, in exchange for working hard. However, since leaving active duty military, I have never expected the federal government to provide social welfare to me and my family for the rest of our lives simply because I'm a veteran.

I'm writing this book for the president and legislators of America because I want to expose the atrocities of the current VA compensation program. Not only is the system wasting our tax dollars by erroneously issuing billions of dollars inappropriately, but it is spiraling out of control and affecting the future of American prosperity, specifically affecting the American workforce. Millions of young American veterans who would once have been the most experienced, educated, physically fit, worldly, well-rounded, ambitious, flexible, disciplined, in short, the most desirable entry-level employees to any American businesses, are simply no longer available to work, because instead of working they are choosing to join the social welfare rolls of America. They are *not* disabled but they are working the system; they can sit home and draw a fat check from the VA without working. VA disability compensation has become America's premier "entitlement" program.

There are many problems with the VA disability compensation system that will be detailed in the coming chapters but there are *three* main reasons this program has to be investigated and revamped. First is the abuse of the American taxpayers, unfair distribution of hard-earned income, in a country already 21 trillion dollars in debt. If the current administration is serious about taking on "entitlement reform" then this is the first program they should review!

Secondly and more important is the affect this give-away is having on the current young people of our country who should be the backbone of the future economy. The people who should become the primary wage-earners, developers, entrepreneurs of our country in coming years, instead will become part of America's social-welfare-dependent community because the system is making it so easy for them to get paid just for asking, when they are not disabled at all. These are able-bodied, normal, healthy, strong, intelligent, experienced, and often well-educated people who the rest of our society will support as though they were mentally deranged incompetents.

Another large group of payees are the over-62 crowd who file their claims immediately after retirement, decades after military service, just to supplement their retirement and social security income; they are not disabled, or if they are, it's not due to service.

The third reason this program must be investigated is because it will explain one real cause of the downfall and failure of our VA medical centers which have been blasted in the news in recent years. The VA medical centers are wasting valuable time and resources by filling up their schedules with veterans who are simply trying to beef up their medical records to support a grant of service connection, and by providing endless ridiculous examinations to support increased evaluations, instead of treating sick patients.

Early in my career at the VA, after reviewing a typical claim, it appeared that I should grant 100% disability to a veteran who was about 28 years old, college-educated, happily married with two young children, and working full-time in a decent job. I told my trainer, *"This is not right, I don't see how I can grant this."*

She looked at me scornfully and in a most intimidating voice said, *"You don't decide who gets what rating. You grant based on what the exam and evaluation builder show you. You need to have empathy for these veterans. I'm a veteran and I know how it feels. You need to do your job the way you were trained and stopping putting your personal opinion into it."*

I looked her straight in the eye and never faltered when I said, *"I'm a veteran too! That's why this bothers me so much. This veteran (in the case I was working) is clearly not disabled and was clearly lying to the doctor on his VA exam (based on other evidence), and we will reward his dishonesty and pay him 100 percent disability? This is a slap in the face to any veteran who was truly injured in battle and who truly is too disabled to work."*

I never forgot that claim, my moral discomfort in granting it, and I vowed I would do something to correct this system if ever I could gain enough experience and knowledge to elucidate the problems as well as possible solutions.

The examples I provide in this book are real. I've never written down any veteran's name or SSN or other PII (personally identifiable information), so I would not be able to provide that in order to have any of these cases verified, even if I were tortured. At one time I considered soliciting extreme examples from VA rating specialists all over America, and that would make one interesting unbelievable book! But, no, this book is not about the extreme rare examples; it's about the *everyday run-of-the-mill* claims and decisions being processed at the VA benefits offices. If any committee wants to verify anything I say, they can simply pull a random selection of veterans claims files and read them! They could also try polling VA raters because most if not all of them feel the same disgust and discomfort with this system as I do; but they also know there's no true anonymity in federal surveys, so they're not likely to risk their jobs by negatively commenting on VA policies.

I don't believe it's right for one to complain or criticize unless he has a better way or viable solution to the problem. I do have ideas for how this program can be changed to stop the spiraling increasing misuse of our taxpayer dollars and I expound on these solutions in the following chapters.

(2) SERVICEMEN OR VETERANS

Most Americans want a strong military to defend our country, even though many don't agree with defending abroad; we want our soldiers to have great equipment, training, healthcare and a good life for their families. We also want to honor our servicemen and women after they leave active duty service and there are multiple benefits offered them to include GI bill college education funds, VA home loans, insurance, and military discounts in all sorts of stores, restaurants, travel and recreational ventures.

It is important to know the difference between an active duty serviceman (soldier, airman, sailor, marine, guardsman) and a "veteran" because these terms are used interchangeably, wrongly, in all public arenas. "Soldier" is really only applicable to Army personnel, and military servicepersons in all branches can be male or female so they are more properly and correctly called servicemen and servicewomen. So I apologize in advance, but in this book I have taken the liberty to use the word "serviceman" or "soldier" when referring to any man, woman, or transgender who is serving in either the US Army, US Air Force, US Navy, US Marine Corps, or US Coast Guard.

It's important to understand that a *veteran* is a person who served in any of these military branches but who is *no longer* in active duty military service. Some go in and out while serving in Reserves or National Guard; they may be deployed numerous times into an active duty status, and when they come back from tour they are again discharged and resume being a veteran. A few government benefits are actually applicable to both active duty servicemen and veterans, such as home loan, education, and vocational rehabilitation benefits. But this book is about disability compensation, a monetary benefit paid only to *veterans* who have served a period of honorable active duty service and are no longer on active duty.

Veterans are persons who have already left the military either because they retired, or completed the obligated tour they signed up for, or they got kicked out for any number of reasons. After discharge, they are *veterans*, whether they served in a war or not, whether they completed their tour or not, whether they retired after 40 years or whether they were kicked out during basic training as unable to adapt to a military lifestyle. Disability compensation is only paid to veterans, never to servicemen still on active duty. I sometimes see news reports of our president or congressmen visiting the "veterans" up at Walter Reed National Military Medical Center, but Walter Reed is not a VA hospital, it is a "military" hospital, and the patients they visit there, recently returned from war, are not veterans. They are still on active duty status, still receiving military pay, and will not be eligible to receive veterans' benefits until they become veterans, which is after they are discharged from Walter Reed and from the service.

While on the subject of Walter Reed, I cannot stress loudly enough that I *fully support* the payment of disability compensation (after military discharge) to almost every soldier you will find in a hospital room at Walter Reed. The vast majority of these inpatients are soldiers who have "borne the battle" or at the very least have been injured seriously in the line of duty. They have been transferred there from Iraq or Afghanistan or sometimes even from a stateside post because their injuries are so severe. In most cases these soldiers in the beds at Walter Reed will not be returning to the field. They have severe injuries such as brain injuries, internal injuries, or loss of limbs. Their claims will be initiated by a VA representative at Walter Reed and will be case-managed (hand-carried) throughout the claims process. The soldiers will remain at Walter Reed until they are well enough to be released to their homes or to a VA long-term care facility. At that point they will be discharged from the military and will become veterans. If processing goes as it should, they will stop receiving military pay and start receiving their veteran's disability compensation during the same month. Servicemen who have been severely injured in battle certainly deserve the maximum benefit possible and they will receive it. They will get a monthly compensation check of several thousand dollars, and if they have lost limbs or eyesight they will also get special monthly compensation (SMC) and will qualify for housing adaptations and vehicle adaptations.

The TV commercials soliciting money for the "Wounded Warriors" program are extremely deceptive and misleading. They would have you believe that these veterans are not getting any help unless you give it. In reality, a truly wounded warrior, missing limbs as shown on the commercials, is receiving from the VA everything they could possibly desire short of getting their real limbs back: thousands of dollars monthly for the rest of their lives, modified housing, modified automobiles, clothing allowances, artificial limbs, lifetime medical care, college educations for their wives and children, and continued benefits for dependents after the veteran's death. I am glad they are getting all of this and I don't mind if the government wants to give them even more. They are truly impaired and their lives will never be normal, all due to injuries "incurred in service."

In the past, many persons who served honorably or their surviving spouses have failed to apply for VA benefits because they didn't understand that they were entitled. After I started work at the VA I asked one of my older relatives whether he'd ever filed a claim. He said, "No, I was never injured in combat." If I hadn't worked for the VA I wouldn't know better either. But new veterans know they can be paid for issues not caused by combat and even if they never served during a war period. Some of the confusion stems from there being two different disability programs, nonservice-connected pension, generally referred to as "pension," and service-connected compensation, generally known as "compensation." From the origin of VA, the difference between pension and compensation has rarely been clearly understood by veterans and even by some who work for the VA.

Pension can be paid to a veteran who served during war-time even if his current disability was not incurred in service, so long as he meets certain age and income/net worth limitations. For many decades veterans have been denied "pension" because they had no war-time service, and the general public, especially older generations, have come to believe that Veterans Affairs services, specifically hospital care and benefit payments, are only for those who served in combat, or whom were actually wounded in combat. The fact is that even if you lost a leg due to a punji stick in Vietnam, you cannot draw "pension" if you have plenty of money or high net worth from other sources. But you can draw disability "compensation."

"Compensation" can be paid to any veteran, any age, who served anywhere, for any little period of time, war or no war, no matter how rich they now are, no matter that they are fully employed, so long as their current disability was deemed to be *incurred in or caused by military service.* With the technological advances of internet and social media today, current day servicemen are well aware of VA benefits and they begin preparing for and applying for those benefits even before they leave active duty.

The older veterans are increasingly learning about VA benefits from their local offices of Veterans of Foreign Wars (VFW), American Legion (AL), American Veterans (AMVETS), and dozens of other Veterans Services Organizations (VSOs) which are *not* federal government agencies and are *not* part of the VA. The people who work at these VSOs are assigned on the veteran's request as Power of Attorney (POA) for the veterans they represent, but despite what many veterans believe, these people are *not* "attorneys" at all. They have usually filed a claim of their own in the past, learned how to manipulate the system, and are eager to share that knowledge. They will help a veteran get his claim submitted and will help the veteran communicate with the VA benefits office. Some veterans hire private attorneys to help them with their claims especially after one has been denied, but that is a foolish waste of money since there is plenty of free help from the VSOs. If they don't like one, there's another one around the corner.

But the fact is that the Veterans Benefits Administration (VBA) office will provide the best help and information the veteran can receive. They are on his side and their mission is to grant him as many issues and as much money as they possibly can. In recent years many of the older veterans have received letters from the VBA inviting them to submit claims for posttraumatic stress disorder (PTSD) or Vietnam/Agent Orange related illnesses or Camp LeJeune water-related illnesses. Therefore, a great number of claims are still being received daily from veterans who have been out of service for 20, or 40, or even 60 years. There is currently no time limit on submitting or granting a service-related claim for compensation.

(3) IS VA COMPENSATION A MILITARY PERK?

Our U.S. government has done and is doing a great job in taking care of our active duty military personnel. The equipment is somewhat antiquated and broken or insufficient, and our current administration is trying to put money into fixing that long overdue problem. But the military soldiers themselves have a good life. Military servicemen and servicewomen are *paid* a salary, not a lot of money, but certainly enough to buy the things they want and provide a good life for their families. They really don't have to spend their salary on anything they *need*, it's all for the things they *want*. They could serve without a salary and would be well cared for. If they live in barracks they get three very good meals a day, comfortable lodging with heat and plumbing, and clothing for all seasons, even an allowance for their underwear and running shoes. If they have a spouse and/or child, they may live with their family in free on-post government housing, all rent and utilities paid. Or they may opt to receive special allowances, in addition to their salary, to pay for food and housing (rent or purchase, and utilities) for an off-post home for their family. If they live in barracks and their family is in another state or country, then the soldier is provided benefits accordingly, a meal card for himself and a special allowance he can send to the wife to support the family home. In addition to the basics of living, meals and a comfortable home, a soldier gets excellent free training for a career he may take to the outside. He has ample opportunities to expand that training if he wants to work on a degree to move up in service or perhaps take college courses in an entirely different field in preparation for an after-service career. The soldier has great opportunities for free or reduced rates on traveling the world, including special tour rates and exclusive military recreation areas worldwide. Soldiers have great free healthcare for themselves and their families, at great military hospitals and clinics worldwide.

You won't hear active duty soldiers complain about health care and there's no complaint about *military* health care in the news. The health care problems in the news are with regard to Veterans Affairs (VA) facilities and medical care for *veterans*. But this book is not so much about VA hospitals or VA health care, other than to note that medical records are a part of the evidence to review in deciding a disability claim, and there is one chapter on the effect claims may have on the overuse/abuse of health care programs.

Veterans' health care is managed by the Veterans Health Administration (VHA) but this book is about Service-Connected Compensation, managed by the Veterans Benefits Administration (VBA). The VHA cannot grant or deny a claim. The VBA cannot recommend or demand that a veteran seek treatment. The VBA will review VHA treatment records, if available, and will request Compensation and Pension (C&P) examinations to be done at the VHA in support of claims. Otherwise, these are two different non-communicating agencies.

So soldiers, airmen, sailors, marines, and guardsmen on active duty are taken care of, and they get a salary to use as they please. It is well deserved because of the lifestyle they have to live. They're on call 24 hours a day and sometimes do work long days for days on end without a break. They sometimes have to be apart from their families, meanwhile living in close quarters and spending time on and off duty with people they'd not choose as friends. They sometimes have difficult stressful jobs, and they can't just quit when they get upset with the boss.

But don't forget, America has an *all-volunteer* military. Every individual presently serving is there because he or she chose to be there. We haven't had a draft since 1973, and if any of those draftees are still in service, their mandatory tour ended over 40 years ago, and they could have retired with full benefits 25 years ago. Why did the current force volunteer? Maybe they wanted to see more of the world, or to get the free training, or the educational benefits. Maybe they enjoy fighting and using weapons. Maybe it was the easiest way to get out of town or the boondocks, or maybe they chose service in lieu of going to jail. I actually met a lot of those jail-dodgers in the 1970's before the military required a high school equivalency. In any case, they volunteered, and they will get what they signed up for. If they serve honorably each one will come out a smarter, stronger, more disciplined person, with a world of education and employment opportunities handed to him in the form of a DD 214.

Unfortunately, there's a new twist to military benefits, a new perceived benefit, being promoted from within the military departments, and being pushed by the Department of Veterans Affairs onto every serviceman as he exits service and enters civilian life. In short, it is the promise for *disability compensation*, a promise that the federal government, with hard-earned taxpayer dollars, will continue to pay each veteran for the rest of his life, and many of their dependents will also continue to receive benefits after the veteran's death. This is a tax-free, monthly check in the bank, regardless of whether there is any obvious or medically documented service-related impairment, regardless of whether the veteran is working or not. This is available to any veteran who will ask for it and who is willing to play the game, i.e., willing to lie, steal, and cheat to get it. These are our great holy deserving veterans, and their integrity will not be questioned.

As you read this book you may think, "Wow, the writer is telling veterans all the ways they can get over on the system."

You're right, veterans who read it may certainly learn a few tricks. But most of it is things they can already learn from the VFW or American Legion, or from their fellow veterans in the waiting room at the VA medical center, or in current times things they are learning from their military superiors before discharge. All these people and agencies are in on it and they strongly encourage every veteran to file, file, file. Get all you can get! The VA also encourages the same. The VA wants to grant all it possibly can. The VA even sends out invitation letters to veterans, encouraging them to file claims for things they would never have dreamed of claiming, such as exposures in Vietnam 50 years ago, and exposures to water in Camp LeJeune 40 years ago.

If you listen to the top-level VA speeches you'll hear how proud they are that the claims numbers have increased and that the dollars issued each year are continually increasing. They present it as though the more they can pay out the better job they are doing for veterans. It's true, they are loving the veterans, but the fact is they are screwing the American public taxpayers, and they are doing a moral disservice to the non-injured veterans whom they are paying.

(4) WHAT'S WRONG WITH VA COMPENSATION?

In a nutshell, the VA disability compensation program is wrought with fraud and abuse from veterans, proliferated by the VA's unreasonable policies of over-granting benefits. It's a vicious cycle; the laxer VA becomes, and the more ridiculous the claims they grant, the more veterans are encouraged to submit more fraudulent new and increase claims. Too many veterans are being paid too much for too many conditions that were not really caused by their military service. It's costing American taxpayers $90 billion a year (just in payments to veterans) and the unfunded liability (future payments already committed) for compensation payments alone is *$2.8 trillion*. These figures do not include VA medical care and do not include salaries, facilities, or any overhead costs of administering the programs, some of which will be detailed in a subsequent chapter.

If a veteran submits his first claim before discharge or within a year after discharge the benefits will be granted effective the day after discharge, so he goes right from getting his military pay to getting his VA compensation. These days, many original claims are lengthy enough (with 50 to 100 medical issues listed) such that 100 percent disability is granted right away.   Frequently, a veteran is a young 20-something year old man or woman, who would appear to be in top condition. He is not limping, he is not obese, he is not a drug addict, and he may not be taking a single medication for any condition! Yet he will claim pain in both knees, both ankles, both feet, both wrists, both hands, both elbows, both shoulders, cervical spine (neck), thoracolumbar spine (mid/lower back), acid reflux, sleep apnea, headaches, and PTSD (or anxiety/depression). He may claim subjective conditions such as fibromyalgia or chronic fatigue syndrome which can't even be diagnosed. The VA examiner will provide a diagnosis for each claimed issue, and considering that even the slightest complaint of pain will warrant 10 percent for each joint, all this stuff will easily add up to 100 percent disability.

It is preposterous that a veteran can get 100 percent disability compensation granted based on the scenario above, and then he can go ahead and attend college, get a federal agency job, or work wherever in the world he wants to, and it doesn't matter! He still gets to keep his 100 percent disability paycheck of thousands per month, and he can work all he wants to. That's disgusting because obviously if he is able to work we should not be wasting all this "disability" money on him.

Sometimes a veteran gets a little sloppy with his claim, or he's unlucky enough to hook up with an incompetent VSO/POA (veterans service organization/power of attorney, i.e. his representative at the VFW), as quite a few of them know little about claims and they give terrible advice. So perhaps the veteran did not get a lot of minor injuries documented in his service records because he served many years ago before all this cheating became the norm, or perhaps he's been ill-advised by his VSO/POA; for whatever reason VA doesn't grant all his claimed issues. Or maybe VA has granted issues with severity totaling only 30 percent.   Now, the game is on. The veteran must, and will, submit a new claim (new issues not claimed before), or a reopen claim (reconsideration of issues denied before), or just ask for increases in the conditions that were granted. VA has to address all issues whether they've already been denied or not. The veteran has a chance to send in additional new or old medical records, or statements from people who knew him in service, or just more sob stories (lay statements) of his own. VA sends him to more exams, gets more evidence, and again grants everything they can, as well as granting increases in any possible issues. This time maybe it will all total up to 50 percent. But the veteran will not be satisfied with that for long. He must continue submitting new claims, reopen claims, and increase claims, over and over, year after year, for the rest of his life until he finally gets a 60 percent single evaluation or until his total compensation evaluation is up to at least 70 percent! That's the magic number he is striving for. He'd prefer to have 100 percent, but 70 percent will do equally well. Now he qualifies for Individual Unemployabilty (IU)!

IU is a benefit paid to a veteran who has less than 100 percent disability (per the calculations) but who still "cannot work" due to his service-connected conditions. If IU is granted, the veteran receives the 100 percent pay! The same as if he was at 100 percent schedular. Now there is one catch to this, and it's perhaps more distressing than the fact that many veterans are drawing 100 percent and still working full time high-paying jobs! Those who are granted IU are not allowed to work! By definition, he is getting the IU payment (100%) because he cannot work. VA sends him a form every year on which he has to re-affirm that he is not working. If he obtains "gainful employment" he will have to give up the IU payment (although he can still draw the 70 percent disability check). That would actually be in his best interest if he wanted the most possible money, to work and draw a 70 percent check. But in my years, I never saw a case where a veteran said he had found a job and was giving up the IU. They're just not smart enough to figure that out and no one, certainly no VA employee, will tell them. No VA employee would ever be permitted to encourage a veteran to give up a benefit. So the veterans choose to get the 100 percent disability then sit on their asses, take drugs, get fat, drive their spouses crazy, whatever. They are non-productive, and they become lazy losers. Many of these veterans drawing IU are in their 20's!! There is nothing wrong with them. They just gained the system.   America just lost a well-trained strong viable employee! The person just committed himself to a life of misery.

There is no better feeling and healthier living than that of working hard, succeeding, accomplishing a job no matter how difficult, but these veterans will not have that experience. Instead they will develop big habits they eventually can't afford, become truly physically out of shape (sick) and within 5 or 10 years the rest of their life is hopeless. They couldn't go back to work then if they wanted to. So the government (we taxpayers) will support them and their families for the next 50 years. When the veteran dies, we will continue to pay the spouse and dependent children, even if the spouse is independently wealthy.

***

Veteran X is 19 years old.   He spent only 6 months in service before he was kicked out for failing to adjust to military life, but he was given an "under honorable conditions" discharge which is acceptable to the VA for full VA benefits.   He sprained the left ankle in basic training and also was diagnosed with asthma and was issued an inhaler. Due to his "lack of respect for authority" and "failure to obey commands" he was sent for psychiatric evaluation where he was diagnosed with depression because he missed home and wished he'd never joined the service, so the military psychiatrist recommended his release from service.

Immediately after discharge he filed a claim for the left ankle condition, asthma, and depression. He was provided a full general medical exam on which he reported ongoing left ankle pain. The X-rays and range of motion testing were negative for objective evidence of any chronic ankle condition, so the examiner diagnosed left ankle *sprain*. "Sprain" or "strain" are the diagnoses given when there is no real evidence of any chronic condition. The fact is that strains and sprains are most often *not* chronic; they usually heal completely and do not continue to be symptomatic forever.

On exam, the veteran tells the examiner that he had asthma during childhood and that it flared up again when he was over-exerted during basic training. Pre-existing conditions should not be

18

granted unless they were worsened by service. This case could be considered as worsened by service because it flared up again during service. But this time the condition is granted as caused by service because there was no mention on the entrance exam, so the veteran was accepted as "whole" and without any disability on entrance to service, no matter what he tells later. The general examiner diagnosed asthma based on the in-service diagnosis and prescription for inhalers.

The mental examiner diagnosed depression based on answers the veteran provided on the mental exam. It does not matter that the thing causing depression (military) has now been resolved since he's not in service anymore. Now he's depressed because he got kicked out of service.

So this 19 year old is granted 10% for the ankle, 30% for the asthma, and 30% for depression. His total is 60% and he'll draw over $1000 per month even if he has no dependents. He can now begin filing his claims for increase. By age 25 he will likely have his total up to 100%. He will also be married and have three kids by then, so he'll be drawing about $3500 per month, tax-free, for the rest of his life, plus annual cost-of-living increases.

My problems with this? First, I don't like paying a veteran who only served six months and failed to complete his military commitment because he didn't want to complete it, not because he became too disabled due to a military injury. Some soldiers are seriously injured within a few months of activation and those I firmly support. In this case there was no true evidence of a "chronic" ankle condition. His asthma was present pre-service and not caused by service. His mental condition should be resolved now that he is out of service. I see nothing incurred in service and no reason to support this veteran with disability compensation.

***

Veteran X was a good soldier who served 20 years before retiring from the military at age 38. During the first 5 years of service he experienced many minor injuries to multiple joints, but no breaks or dislocations. The knee, back, and foot conditions were treated as "overuse injuries" and they apparently resolved because they were never mentioned again in the service records over the last 15 years of service. In the latter years he was diagnosed with and treated for obstructive sleep apnea, acid reflux, migraine headaches, and hyperthyroidism. A few years before discharge he went through a divorce after some physical altercations with his wife, so he received in-service counseling where he was diagnosed with bi-polar disorder.

He filed his VA claim a month before discharge so he was given a full VA general medical exam and mental exam which eliminate the need for post-service medical treatment evidence. The exams continued his in-service diagnoses for all claimed issues. He was granted 50% for sleep apnea (controlled by a CPAP machine), 30% for gastroesophageal reflux disease (GERD) (controlled with daily omeprazole), 50% for migraines (purely subjective), 10% for hyperthyroidism (fully controlled by Synthroid with no symptoms), 30% for bi-polar disorder (diagnosis continued since one anger incident 10 years ago), 10% for left knee strain (purely subjective), 10% for right knee strain (subjective), 10% for lumbar strain (subjective), 30% for pes planus (flat feet) (not necessarily an impairment), 0% for erectile dysfunction (subjective), plus special monthly compensation (additional $106 per month) for loss of use of a creative organ due to erectile dysfunction. This totals 100% disability and he will receive $3,079 per month if he has no wife or dependent children, much more if he does have dependents. He will also draw his military retirement of over $2,000 per month. He will immediately seek employment since he is only 38 years old, and there will be numerous federal agencies and government contractors vying to have him work for them, so he'll probably earn anywhere from $70K to $200K per year over the next 25 years until he retires from the 3rd source and also begins to draw Social Security. He does not have to tell his new employer about "disabilities" and they'll probably never know since none of his conditions are truly "disabling" or will hinder his work performance in any way. He is allowed to work and earn as much as he wants and it will not affect his receipt of tax-free service-connected compensation.

My problems with this? I don't believe he truly has any chronic knee, back, or foot condition. I don't believe sleep apnea, GERD, migraines, hyperthyroidism, erectile dysfunction, or bi-polar disorder are caused by military service. Even though they were first diagnosed during service, if they do exist, I believe he would have had those conditions in any walk of life, and they should not be considered as the result of him having "borne a battle." He was never in war. At age 65 he'll be drawing four significant sources of income: military retirement, private or federal work retirement, VA compensation, and Social Security, close to $10,000 a month. VA compensation payments to someone like this, not injured in battle, is a waste of taxpayer dollars that could be spent on so many other deserving projects.

***

Veteran X was 70 years old when he filed his first claim. He served 2 years as a cook in the Army from 1966 to 1968 and the last year of that was spent in Vietnam. After service he worked 40 years at an automobile manufacturing plant and he retired at age 65 with a private pension and Social Security, so he is living comfortably. He has recently been diagnosed with diabetes and heart disease, and he was encouraged by a fellow veteran at his church to go to the VFW for help with submitting a VA claim for these issues and for potential hearing loss as well. His father and two brothers also had diabetes and heart disease, but that doesn't matter, these conditions have been recognized as "herbicide-presumptives" so service connection will be granted.

The diabetes warrants 20% based on the fact he takes Metformin daily. He also has secondary diabetic conditions of peripheral neuropathy of both lower extremities, 10% each, and erectile dysfunction 0% plus special monthly compensation (SMC-K) due to loss of use of a creative organ (although his grandchildren are now teenagers and he has no intent to procreate again). The VA exam also shows renal failure warranting 60% based on lab reports although he is having no symptoms and didn't even know he had the problem. Neuropathy problems, kidney problems, erectile dysfunction and even some eye conditions are all considered common complications of diabetes so if they are present they will be granted even if not claimed, and even if there is some other possible reason for the condition. Aside from the diabetic issues, this veteran is granted 30% for his ischemic heart condition, based on hypertrophy shown on cardiac testing, although he has had no symptoms. He is also granted 10% for hearing loss which by VA medical opinion has been linked to his year spent in a war zone, even though the hearing loss was not shown in service or on any hearing test until about a year ago, 50 years after service. His total is 80% disability.

But the veteran is not working (since he retired) and he qualifies (on a "schedular" basis) for Individual Unemployability (IU) because he has at least one issue at 40% or more and his total is at least 70%. All he has to do is claim IU and say he can't work due to one or more of these service-connected conditions. A grant is supposed to require "evidence that he cannot work" but I have never seen an IU claim denied for a veteran who meets the schedular requirement and is not working. A grant for IU means he will receive the same rate of compensation as if his total evaluation was 100%. The only catch is that he must submit a form VA Form 21-4140 each year to certify that he is still not working. He is not going to work anyway, as he is 70 years old, already drawing retirement and social security. Now he's drawing an extra $3200 a month, courtesy of you and me.

My problems with this? I don't believe he is disabled, and if he is disabled it's not due to any battle he bore in service. I believe that the "herbicide-presumptive" laws were established for political reasons (to reward Vietnam veterans) and that "causation" has not been established by medical facts; only "correlations" have been established, as I discuss further in the Agent Orange chapter.

***

Veteran X has been service connected at 10% for his left knee sprain since he left military service in 1976. It never prevented him from working or playing backyard football, and he never had a VA future review exam because review exams are not required for 10% issues.

After many years of working as a carpet installer (severely bad on the knees), in 2006 he filed for an increase in his left knee condition. He was automatically given a review exam and was not required to provide any treatment records. The exam showed his left knee was impaired to a degree of 20% disability, so he was granted this increase, with no question of whether or not it was in fact the same condition from service. Even a medical opinion was not required since he is already service connected for the issue. Furthermore, on the review exam his other knee was equally impaired. That in itself should be evidence of "intercurrent cause" of the current knee conditions because both knees are the same and only one was injured in service, but to suggest such a thing and to request a medical opinion would be "developing to deny" which is prohibited.

Five years later the service-connected left knee has worsened to the point that he has had a total left knee replacement so he files another increase claim for the left knee. He also files for service-connection of the right knee as secondary to the left knee. In other words, he is claiming that his right knee condition has been caused by compensating for the left knee pain. Five years ago his exam had showed that both knees were equally bad (after a career of carpet laying) and in fact he is now also scheduled for a right knee replacement after the left knee replacement heals. VA requests a medical opinion regarding whether the current right knee condition may have been caused by the left knee condition. No history is provided to the examiner, so he knows nothing of the work history, and he doesn't have time for small talk during this quickie exam. He is asked to review one current medical record tabbed in the electronic file which shows both knees are bad. The examiner opines "Yes" the right likely resulted from the left condition because he has been service-connected for the left since 1976, so he likely had years of compensating by putting more weight on the right. The VA grants service connection for the right knee, 20% disabling.

The veteran is granted 100% disability for a period of 13 months of convalescence following the left knee replacement, after which the minimum evaluation for the left knee will be 30% for the rest of his life. After the right knee replacement, he is granted another 13 months of 100% compensation for convalescence, followed by a minimum of 30% for the right knee. If he claims to have continued pain or other impairment after either knee replacement he will be increased to 60% for that knee. He will also be granted for the surgical scars on the legs and if any scar is painful or unstable it will warrant 10%, or higher for more scars. Even one knee at 60% will be enough to qualify for IU, which will pay 100%.

My problems with this? The left knee in service was not a "chronic" condition. If it had been, he would not have been able to even undertake the subsequent career in carpet laying. The condition of both knees was clearly caused by his job as a carpet layer. The right knee was clearly not incurred in service and not caused by the left knee. The problem with the system is that once some issue gets granted, all the veteran has to do is keep coming back in with increase claims, year after year if he wants to, and his evaluations will keep going up, sometimes slowly, sometimes fast, but they will keep going up. No condition ever gets "better" in VA records, regardless of treatments, medication, or surgeries. Conditions just keep getting worse (he claims), and the veteran keeps asking for and easily obtaining increases until he reaches 100%. We cannot pay $3000 a month to every veteran who ever had a knee sprain in service. I know from medical literature and personal experience that knee and ankle and wrist and back strains/sprains usually heal without residual disability. Joint problems late in life are generally due to the type of work the person has done for decades, or due to age-related osteoarthritis and failure to maintain an active lifestyle.

***

Veteran X filed a claim three years after discharge. Although he had a knee strain in service, he provided no post-service medical records with his claim and did not mention having had any treatment after service. Every soldier gets a detailed medical exam prior to separation. His military separation exam showed no knee problem or any other chronic disability.

His VA claim is initially denied because he has no post-service medical evidence. He waited too long after service (more than a year) to file, so he didn't get an automatic general medical exam for evidence. The denial letter explains to him that he needs current evidence of the condition. So he goes to his local VA Medical Center and reports that he needs treatment for his knee so that he can file a claim. The examiner sees no swelling, no problem with range of motion for the knee, and obtains an X-ray which shows the knee to be completely normal. This record serves as post-service evidence of a "complaint." A veteran is considered competent to report his own symptom of pain, even if he cannot diagnose himself. He submits the claim again and this is a "reopen" claim. Now the evidence includes a complaint in service medical records and a documented complaint in post-service VA records. An exam and medical opinion is then obtained through a VA doctor or contracted doctor. The examiner again finds no objective evidence of a knee condition so he diagnoses it as knee "strain" and opines that it is at least as likely as not (a 50% probability) that this is the same problem he complained of in service. Therefore, service connection is granted at 10% disability. Future exams are not established for 10% issues, so he will receive the 10% payment forever, and it will never be reviewed unless he comes back in with a claim for increase.

My problems with this? The in-service condition was subjective, not chronic. The post-service condition was subjective, not chronic. The man has wasted VA medical center resources to create a phony medical record, and subsequently more resources (medical staff and X-rays) were wasted on an exam. A medical opinion, 50/50 probability, by a doctor who has never treated the

25

veteran and who has nothing more than this evidence to review, is ridiculous. A VA rater should be allowed and required to make a decision on this claim based on the evidence of record, specifically the lack of any evidence to show that this claimed condition has impaired his occupational or social functioning. Thirty years ago this claim would have been simply *denied* because there was no chronic condition shown in service. To reopen the claim would have required the veteran to show some impairment of functioning. Now VA is totally ignoring the regulation that says decisions should be based on impairment of functioning.

***

Veteran X is a 27-year-old female. She claims she has PTSD because she had husband problems during service and he left her with the kids and the debts, so her depression started in service and has continued after service. Although she didn't claim any work-related stressor, the examiner diagnosed PTSD based on her MOS (military occupational specialty) because she worked in a military hospital where she saw amputees and dead soldiers. It doesn't matter that she signed up for that MOS and performed well in it. The PTSD examiner noted that since discharge from service she is currently in college, doing well, studying for a degree in elementary education. She is also in the National Guard for which she serves one weekend per month. She says she has "no problems." The examiner says she has "no functional impairment."

Even though the examiner has diagnosed PTSD, this should be a 0 percent evaluation if there is *no* functional impairment. But the examiner checked off enough boxes of symptoms such that the evaluation for PTSD is 50 percent disability!

On her general medical exam, the examiner noted she has "moderate" radiculopathy of both arms, and that results in 40 percent for the right (major) arm and 30 percent for the left arm. Then she claimed to have occasional pain in all her joints so she gets 10 percent for each shoulder, each elbow, and each wrist. These are separate and additional to the evaluation for radiculopathy of the arms because that is a nerve condition, and these others are considered to be joint conditions. There is no abnormality shown the X-rays, and there is no limitation of motion shown on range-of-motion testing. She claims pain in the neck and back also and there is nothing seen on X-ray so the diagnosis is "cervicalgia" for the neck and "lumbago" for the back.   These are simply pain, and supposedly *pain in and of itself* is not a diagnosed chronic disability. However, these conditions are each granted 10 percent disabling.

Then she has an anal fissure which resulted from childbirth in service; finally, an actual objectively seen disability. But really, wouldn't this have also resulted if the child had been delivered outside of military service? So how can it be service-related? She should be happy she was able to have all her children delivered during service expense-free while normal civilians go in debt over having babies.

The veteran also has plantar fasciitis of both feet, which is diagnosed simply based on subjective pain, and that is 10 percent for each foot. Her knee complaints of pain also warrant 10 percent for each knee. The veteran really claimed nothing except occasional pain in all these body parts (just like every normal body has occasional pain in our various body parts.)

My problems with this?   This veteran is in perfectly fine condition to go to work, to college, and to serve in the National Guard on weekends, and yet we are paying this woman 100 percent disability compensation.   The VA documents her as totally and permanently disabled, and that should only apply to someone who cannot work and can't be helped with a vocational rehabilitation program.   But this woman will finish college and she will work. She will earn a normal American living as a school teacher.   But she will have the added bonus of $3,500 per month for the rest of her life, courtesy of the VA, paid for by you and me, our federal tax dollars.

There are many problems with this scenario, many ways the VA system is screwed up. First is that obviously too many of the issues being granted are not really chronic disabilities. Then there's the VA exams or DBQs (Disability Benefits Questionnaires) which are just checklists for the examiners to run through and quickly check off boxes. But they have no idea the compensation results that are coming from these DBQs. If you were to ask an examiner for his personal opinion of the level of disability, I'm sure it would be nowhere near what the VA "evaluation builder" system of determining an evaluation based on these checked boxes. The examiner said that this veteran has right arm radiculopathy (which was all subjective, there was no nerve test done to show any nerve impairment) and he indicated it was "moderate" which he probably thought was not very severe. But "moderate" impairment of the major arm is a 40 percent disability. This is the same evaluation one would get for having a foot amputated! There is an amputation rule that prevents VA from granting more than 90% percent for the entire arm (hand, wrist, elbow, and shoulder joints); but the nerve condition doesn't apply to that. So she could get 20% for the hand, 10% for the wrist joint, 50% for the elbow joint, and 40% for the shoulder joint, combined not to exceed 90%, but then an additional 40% for nerves, all for the right arm.

The VA rating specialist can see the whole record but cannot make the correct decision. An astute rater could easily sum up this veteran's condition and grant her 50 percent total (which would be very liberal, even excessive), and could justify it the way SSA does their decisions, but no, that's not the VA way.

When General Hickey, Under Secretary for Benefits at the VA, came to every VA Regional Office in America in 2014/2015, she made it very clear that raters should not dispute the VA examiners. Just go with it. Don't argue and don't return exams to the examiners. She stressed the three rules of rating are: (1) Grant if you can, (2) Deny only if you must, and (3) Never develop to deny. In other words, if it looks a little fishy and perhaps a little more information would indicate that the condition is not as severe as it looks, don't you dare go asking for that information, just grant with what you have. But if additional information would help you grant, then you must develop for it.

CONDITIONS NOT CAUSED BY SERVICE

When American soldiers *die* in battle, their families receive death benefits including Dependents' Indemnity Compensation (DIC), a separate type of VA compensation, fully deserved and undisputed. Military reports show that about 200,000 American service members have been injured, but not killed, in battles from the start of the Vietnam War to present (from about 1965 to 2018). Many of those have died over the past 50 years, at which time their disability compensation was stopped and their survivors then qualified for DIC, again not a part of VA Disability Compensation funds. So from 200,000 subtract the thousands who have died, then add a few hundred still alive who may have been injured in World War II or the Korean War. Now consider there are about 5 *million* veterans currently receiving disability compensation, and about 600,000 of those are rated as 100% disabled. Who are they? The majority of them were not injured in battle.

One of the main things wrong with the VA disability program is that compensation is being paid for conditions that were not incurred in battle and were not even caused by military service. For example, Veteran X was in a status of processing out of service in October, pending a discharge date in November. He'd already had all his separation exams and for all intents and purposes his military file was closed out. However, like many separating soldiers he had several weeks of leave accrued so he left the military post in Hawaii and went home early to Florida to get a jumpstart on civilian life while still on the military payroll. At home in Florida he was playing flag football and ruptured his left Achilles tendon. After initial triage at the local hospital, he was sent back to his last duty station in Hawaii to undergo surgery and was kept in the military for two more months until it was healed. He was subsequently granted service-connection for the left ankle condition because it "was incurred during service." Yes, he was on the service payrolls, but I contend that this is not a proper interpretation of "in service" when it comes to disability compensation. I don't think it is what

President Lincoln had in mind when he said we would support "those who have borne the battle."

I interpret "incurred in service" to be a disability that resulted from doing some military action such as performing the duties of his MOS (military occupational specialty) or jogging with his platoon during daily PT (physical training), or while fighting in a battle.

The majority of all rated joint disabilities, if they actually even started while the claimant was in service, were incurred during the process of playing sports. I don't mean the Army or Navy football team. I mean just after-duty-hours playing basketball in the gym. Of course, the military is considered a 24-hour job, but unless he is on a battlefield, the soldier only works 8 or 10 hours a day then goes home to his family, or goes out to the local bars, or works out at the gym. It is during these after-duty hours and on weekends that most of the injuries occur and they have nothing to do with the military service.

Another large number of musculoskeletal and head injuries are the result of private automobile and motorcycle accidents that occur not in the line-of-duty but occur while the soldier is driving around on the weekend, and most often when he's in a leave status nowhere near his duty station.

Other injuries result from fist fighting, some on duty, some in bars after duty, some while home on leave. Then there are gunshot wounds, non-war-related, and some self-inflicted. Then there are injuries from falling down stairs, slipping on ice, stepping in a hole, and working with mechanical equipment or hand tools (all off duty).

It is true that many minor musculoskeletal injuries are incurred during basic training. Such an intense fast-paced training program is stressful on the average recruit who has not been doing much physical activity prior to service. Many will have shin splints or they'll step in a hole and twist an ankle while doing a run. But these are acute injuries that heal before the soldier even finishes basic training. If they didn't heal, he would be put out of service at that point. If there is no X-ray evidence of a fracture or critical injury, and if there was no further treatment needed in the umpteen years after the injury healed, specifically no disability found on the military separation exam, then it just should not be granted. It's that simple.

These veterans often spend 20 years walking a beat as a policeman or delivering mail or squatting as a brick layer, and then claim their aches in old age are due to the little injuries they had during basic training. It's just not true. I have personally had several breaks and sprains many years ago, and these conditions healed leaving no residuals. Look at race car drivers and professional skate boarders who've broken or sprained almost every joint in their body, and they just heal and go back out to work. These wimpy veterans would have us to believe that because they twisted an ankle in basic training 40 years ago, they now at age 65 suddenly cannot work due to that ankle injury. It's fraud.

When it comes to diseases or medical conditions other than musculoskeletal, it is even more likely that the condition was not caused by service. Just because it first manifested or was first treated in service, VA will grant it, but I contend that is not the proper interpretation of "incurred in service" or "caused by service" or "borne the battle." If all the veteran's family members are also experiencing diabetes or heart disease, those conditions were not likely caused by service. If the veteran has HIV or AIDS, that was not caused by his military duties, but still it is granted because it was "incurred in service" meaning it was first diagnosed in service or within a year after service. If a woman has a scar from a C-section done while she was on active duty, that scar was not "incurred in service." The latter part of this book includes many examples of specific conditions that VA is paying compensation for that I think should not be considered as "incurred in or caused by service."

***

Veteran X was treated during service in 1968 for urethritis (urinary infection). His service treatment records state that the condition was "not misconduct" and "not incurred in the line of duty." In that era the military records would list any condition treated and would clarify whether it was related to military duties/combat. Now, in 2018, *everything* found in the military personnel file or military service treatment records is considered "in the line of duty" and that should not be.

***

Veteran X was an officer, 0-3, who served 25 years. On the day of discharge, he was in perfect health and had been earning $89,760 per year. The day after discharge he filed a claim for 20 issues, every part of his body, and none related to any in-service injury or disease. For the issue of Meniere's syndrome, which was diagnosed totally on subjective symptoms of dizziness, he was granted 60%. For sleep apnea (fully treated by CPAP and not caused by service) he was granted 50%. For PTSD (after 25 years with no complaint) he was granted 50%. For migraines (totally subjective, no log of headaches) he was granted 30%. For gastroesophageal reflux disease (GERD) (totally subjective complaints, no ECG done) he was granted 10%, and a selection of multiple petty other little aches and pains, for which each was granted 0 or 10%. Immediately upon receipt of his rating decision, which already granted him 100%, but with future exams scheduled, he submitted a claim for IU. VA examined all the issues again (thousands of dollars of exam expense for nothing). The result is still 100% but this time is he granted Permanent and Total so that he won't have to have any future exams. Also, his wife or children (regardless of how mediocre they may be as students or how motivated they are to attend college) will receive free educational benefits (yes 100 percent college tuition) because this veteran is "unable" to work and pay for their college expenses. Never mind that he is receiving $4,500 in military retirement and $4,500 per month in VA benefits. And not to mention that if he wants to he *can* work and earn even more income, without affecting his current retirement and VA income. He can earn another $100,000 a year if he wants to, and we will still pay for college for his mediocre kids, while so many truly poor but truly deservingly brilliant kids out there cannot attend college in America.

***

Veteran X served as a clerk in Vietnam from 1965 to 1967, never saw combat, just did clerical duties. He claims PTSD and on VA exam he reports that he had a poor but happy childhood and graduated high school in 1963 before he was drafted into service. After service he worked as a jail administrator for 4 years, a prison guard for 12 years, then Director of a Judicial District for 3 years. After that he worked as a courier and semi-driver for FedEx and retired after 23 years with FedEx. He was married to the same woman for 48 years, has grown children and grown grandchildren. He reports that he has PTSD because he is stressed out about how his daughter and her husband are always borrowing money from him and being irresponsible with their money. Is he granted service-connected PTSD for this? Of course he is, because he is a Vietnam veteran and everything possible will be given to a Vietnam veteran. For those who were in combat a PTSD stressor is automatically conceded. I contend that if their current condition did not result from that war, and they have no symptoms related to the war such as nightmares or hypervigilance, then even PTSD should not be granted.

***

Veteran X had a documented personality problem before entering service. She had also abused drugs and alcohol, and attempted suicide prior to service. In service she did great, went up the ladder quickly to E-7 in just 8 years, while several husbands divorced her due to her infidelity during that time. After service she went straight into a government job and was still working full time when she filed her VA claim for mental disability. Based on her C&P exam and the VA evaluation builder, her condition warrants 100% due to her history of attempted suicide, which the examiner included even though that was pre-service. She shouldn't even have a current mental diagnosis, certainly not one caused by service.

In my opinion, no veteran should be getting 100% for a mental issue unless they are totally out of their mind, psychotic, and locked up in a mental institution, and it somehow started during service.

***

Veteran X spent almost the entire 3 years she was in service just having surgeries and recuperating from surgeries. The records show that on entrance to service she had a bilateral knee condition of "knock knees", with both knees turned inward, which was noted as "congenital" which means she was born with it, not caused by service. She was allowed into service and apparently made it through basic training with no problem. In 2010, less than one year after entering service, she was working as a mechanic and got hit in the knee with a tool and chipped a bone fragment. Since she had to undergo a surgery to remove the bone fragment, the military went ahead and did surgery on both legs to correct the knock knee condition, by correctly aligning her femur and tibia. As soon as she recovered from the surgeries she was discharged from service, at age 23, on "permanent retirement" which means the military is paying her a retirement. That doesn't stop her from getting VA benefits as well. By the time of her VA claim she had had 11 surgeries at military expense (several after discharge as a retiree). When she got out in 2013 she was in receipt of military retirement pay of $1,200 per month.

She then filed her VA claim for IU. In addition to her knees, she claimed other disabilities and was granted a total of 80% disability due to petty issues. None were caused by service because she spent her whole service in hospitals or convalescence. A few of the more trivial claims were denied, including "female infertility." She was 23 years old, never yet married at the time of her claim for infertility. Then she claimed depression (not PTSD) and depression was conceded because it started in service in relation to the knee surgeries. On mental exam, based on things she told the doctor, he conducted a PTSD exam and diagnosed PTSD on top of her depression disorder. She had not provided a stressor statement with her claim, but the examiner extracted three stressors from her. The PTSD diagnosis was based on sexual assault by her uncle when she was 9 years old. The 2nd stressor for PTSD was she reported that some pilot died in an accident while she was on a ship. She didn't know him, didn't witness his death, and she herself was never in any danger. The 3rd stressor was that she was in a motor vehicle accident (MVA). The examiner tied her PTSD to all these stressors. He never bothered to look at the military records to see that the knee surgeries were prior to the accident and she had no injuries at all from the claimed MVA. PTSD should not have been granted because there is no verified in-service stressor for PTSD. It doesn't really matter because she is conceded the "depression" related to knee surgeries, and all mental conditions will be granted together. She would have received the same evaluation even if she didn't have the PTSD diagnosis. All the symptoms were considered as part of her depression.

***

Veteran X served many years in the Reserves but he has not been on active duty since 1995. In 2009, while away from home for a period of refresher Reserves training, he was in a car accident, hit from the rear. He was seen by medics on the scene and he was fine, no unconsciousness, no cuts or scrapes or bruises, no complaints. Later that night he felt worse so he went to the ER where he was diagnosed with neck and back strain (whiplash). He did not mention any headaches, and x-rays were all negative. The VA granted him service-connection for the pain in his back and neck. Five years later he requested an increase, says he's had headaches since the accident. A medical opinion is obtained and the examiner says yes, he has cervicogenic headaches due to this cervical injury so that is granted secondary. What's wrong with this story? The Reserves trip was *not active duty*. Service connection would be warranted if the soldier was on the rifle range or drill field or jogging with his platoon when he suffered an injury. This would be an "in the line of duty" injury if he were injured while doing actual military training. But this was a car accident off post, it just happened to have occurred while he was away at training. It was written up as in the line of duty, so VA took it and ran with it. The regulations do provide that if a soldier is on his way to or from active duty training, then service connection is warranted, because he is then actually in an active duty status. If he's stationed in Hawaii and gets in a car accident while he's home in Texas during Christmas vacation, that would be service-connected, ridiculous but legal. But a person who is not in an active duty status, should not qualify for service connection for things that happen unless they are actually training-incurred. Few people understand the meaning of "in-the-line-of-duty."

Should even the ones who are on active duty status be granted for injuries that were not related to their training or performance of their job? If they fall off a ladder while trying to patch the top of a 5-ton, yes that's a service-related injury. If they catch malaria due to hiking through a swamp in Vietnam that should be service-connected, because it is not something he would have been subjected to if he hadn't been drafted! But what if a soldier is downtown in bar and gets beat up, or he wrecks his motorcycle on the weekend, or he twists his ankle playing basketball in the YMCA one evening after work. These things in my opinion should not be service-connected. A great majority of the service-connected conditions are exactly that, things that did not happen "in the line of duty." The VA regulations need to be changed to clarify that injuries not related to one's actual military training or performance of his MOS, are not subject to "service-connection." Military hospitals will still treat the conditions while he is in service because that is a military benefit, free healthcare for him and his family, for all medical conditions. But once he is out of service, and military benefits end, he should not use VA medical centers for treatment of such conditions, and he should not be paid for the rest of his life for his non-military-related injury.

EVALUATIONS TOO HIGH FOR NON-DISABLED

Fully functioning veterans should not be receiving 100% disability payments. Numerous veterans employed at the VA and other federal agencies are earning $60K to $200K each year in their jobs and also receiving *100%* disability compensation. Many others are working for government contractors in Afghanistan, making $200K+ a year, and receiving *100%* disability from VA. This just is not right. A 100% disability is supposed to mean that the veteran is totally functionally impaired such that he is unable to perform any sort of gainful occupation.

Many are getting 100% disability pay, by qualifying for statutory Individual Unemployability (IU). VA regulations provide that even a 60% disability, for a single issue, or 70% disability including one at least 40%, is enough to support a claim for permanent and total disability and/or qualify for IU so in reality anyone meeting this 60% or 70% criteria should not be fully employed. I'm not saying they shouldn't work. If they can work successfully then they should be working! But if they can work they should not be awarded such high levels of compensation!

Even 30% or 50% is too high if you can't see anything physically wrong with the person and he is able to work a technical job, a job dealing with people, or any job that requires skill and endurance. The rating schedule was set up to represent that a person receiving 50% disability pay can only do 50% as much or earn 50% as much as he could have if he was not injured.

I recently shopped at my local home improvement store and when I asked for my 10% military discount the sales associate starting talking about *his* military service. He started bragging about how he is receiving compensation for his PTSD and sleep apnea, totaling 90% and that the VA pays him "two thousand, two hundred dollars per month!" I wanted to slap his face and say, "No, it's actually me and this humped over 90-year old co-worker of yours that pays you that!" Here he was, a healthy looking young man, 22 years old, able to lift at least 50 pounds, able to drive the forklift and/or climb a ladder to take things off the highest shelf, able to write up the special order, schedule my delivery, and process my payment. In other words, he was totally functioning, with no apparent limitations, and obviously able to support himself. Meanwhile, the little old male co-worker standing nearby looked much too old and decrepit to be doing this or any kind of work, and yet he obviously *has* to work for the rest of his life to make ends meet. The unfairness of the situation was bad enough, but I couldn't believe the veteran was bragging out loud in the presence of the old man, and felt no shame.

The problem, and solution, is that VA disability ratings are obviously too high and the disability system needs an overhaul. If the rating specialist was allowed to make a logical decision and evaluation based on all evidence, specifically evidence regarding functional impairment, these dichotomies of working-disabled veterans would not exist.

***

Veteran X served 9 months in the Navy from 1971 to 1972. He injured his left wrist in service and the military determined it was a chronic disability so they discharged him with 10% disability. He filed a claim with the VA and VA granted him 60% for the same issue, and later increased it to 80%. This is more than a person would get if half his arm was amputated! During the time that he was drawing 60% for the left wrist condition, he worked 37 years for USPS. It seems to me he could not have been hired or held any post office job if he had limited use of one arm. During that time, he also was married 30 years to the same woman and raised 7 children. He retired at age 65 and claimed IU (cannot work) so he was granted IU (100% compensation payment). Then he wrote his congressman to complain how poorly VA is treating veterans. Then he applied for Vocational Rehabilitation at age 67. Go figure. It was just something else to ask for, without even researching what he was asking for. He continues to receive federal retirement in excess of $2,500 per month plus VA disability of $1,700 per month.

***

Veteran X filed his original claim within one year after discharge, at age 46. He had served from 1988 to 2015, fully successfully, and then retired. He had no combat service and no significant injuries during service. There were no disabilities noted on his military separation exam. The following issues were claimed and denied: chronic fatigue syndrome, dry eye syndrome, hyperlipidemia, viral syndrome, cardiovascular condition, dermatitis, and traumatic brain injury. The following issues were granted: sleep apnea 50%, bilateral pes planus 30%, migraines 30%, PTSD 30%, prostate hypertrophy 20%, right knee strain 10%, left knee strain 10%, right shoulder strain 10%, left shoulder strain 10%, cervical spine strain 10%, thoracolumbar spine strain 10%, right hip strain 10%, left hip strain10%, tinnitus 10%, left lower extremity radiculopathy 10%, right lower extremity radiculopathy 10%, residual of pinky finger fracture 0%, GERD (acid reflux) 0%, and right knee scar 0%. This totals for a 100% compensation evaluation.

This man was able to raise a family and to work for as many years as he wanted to, in the job he wanted, without limitations, and he will now draw $65,000 per year in military retirement from that job. That's fine and deserving; however, he will draw an additional $42,000 ($3,500 per month) of tax-free income from the VA. There is nothing visibly wrong with this man. If you see him walking down the street or on the golf course you will not discern any of the issues he has been granted. He is a fraud. What an insult to truly injured veterans! Since he is rated 100% P&T (permanent and total) his wife and children also quality for free college education, and when the veteran dies the wife (and dependent children) will continue to receive compensation if they apply for Dependent Indemnification Compensation (DIC).

Now imagine a young soldier who gets his entire arm blown off by an IED on the battlefield. He will never be able to work with two hands again, hug his wife or children with two normal arms. He will work, but jobs will be limited because he can't type or lift things and he will even have difficulty with dressing himself (it generally takes 2 hands to button a shirt, zip up pants, pull on socks, and tie shoes). But for this truly service-connected significant battle injury he will not receive 100% disability, and unless he reaches the 100% with other combined conditions, his wife and children will not qualify for the DIC benefits.

***

Veteran X is a perfectly healthy veteran who reportedly works full-time, jogs, and works out at a gym regularly. He is granted service connection 30% for asthma because it was diagnosed in service and because he reportedly uses an "inhalational anti-inflammatory medication." The DBQ does not say he requires it daily, but notes "intermittent use" which could be as rarely as once a year or less, who knows, because the exam doesn't ask. He probably has not used any since service. He was in a motorcycle wreck during service and required surgery on his clavicle. He is now service connected 20% for that shoulder even though there was no pain shown on the range of motion testing, but he reported that with flareups (however infrequent) he may have pain. He injured a knee in service playing basketball and now reports that after excessive running his knee will sometimes have a painful flareup, so he gets 10% for that. He also gets 30% for a cardiac arrhythmia because "tachycardia" was shown on a Halter monitor test in service. This is all wrong because tachycardia just means a heartbeat is "slower" than normal, and it is a common finding in athletes because they intentionally train their hearts to beat slower to endure more. He has also been awarded numerous other petty issues at 0% each which will likely be increased the first time he asks for an increase. These are rhinitis, sinusitis, and GERD, all with totally subjective symptoms, nothing shown on exam or on any diagnosis testing. For now, his conditions are totaling 70% disability. He continues working, making $100K per year, and drawing the additional 70% disability ($20,000 per year). He will keep on working out at the gym and jogging every day to stay fit.

***

Veteran X is a female who spent 4 years in service. She had a BA degree before entering and the Navy paid off $55,000 in student loans in exchange for her enlistment. She had excellent health during service with no treatment for any medical problems, but she filed her claim shortly before discharge and the following issues were diagnosed on her general medical exam. Polycystic ovarian syndrome, based on symptoms of reportedly heavy painful menstrual cycles, never treated by a gynecologist. Migraines, subjective only, no logs kept, noted as related to her monthly periods. Anemia, noted as documented once during a heavy menstruation. "Adjustment-like disorder" claimed as depression. The examiner describes her mental condition as "very mild; a condition is noted but the symptoms cause little or no impairment and is well-controlled by medication." But because the doctor clicked a box indicating "disturbances of motivation and mood" the VA evaluation builder generates 50% for the mental disability. She is also granted 30% for the gynecological issues, and 30% for migraines, all based on subjective complaints with no treatment history, but because they were reported on the pre-discharge VA exam. Her total was 80% which met the schedular criteria for IU, so she filed a new claim for IU, noting she had not worked since discharge from service. And that's all she needed; she is not working and she meets the schedular criteria. This woman is 26 years old with a college degree and should be entering the work force, but instead she will sit home and watch soaps for the rest of her life, at our expense. If she does decide to go to work, she can, and it won't affect her compensation payments.

***

Veteran X retired as an E-8 so he'll draw a monthly retirement of at least $2,500 a month in addition to social security benefits. He went to work for a government contractor within one month after discharge. Within a year after discharge, he filed a VA claim so he was given a full general medical exam for all claimed conditions, as well as a mental exam, without any need for showing prior treatment of any chronic disorders.

There were no diagnoses of record of any serious injuries or chronic disabilities either on his retirement exam or in the months following service before the claim. Two months before discharge, on recommendation of his command, he had undergone a sleep study and was diagnosed with obstructive sleep apnea, and was prescribed a CPAP, but this condition has not impaired his ability to

41

work, during or after service. Throughout the 20 years of service he had incidents of minor joint complaints and headaches, just like everybody. In the military, treatment is free, and it gets you time off from work, so the soldiers report to sick call on a regular basis.

On the respected advice of his POA, the veteran claimed everything he could find in his service medical file. He claimed bilateral shoulders, bilateral ankles, bilateral elbows, bilateral knees, bilateral wrists, and bilateral feet, rhinitis/sinusitis, headache, sleep apnea, sleep disturbances, and depression/anxiety due to leaving service and entering civilian life. The mental examiner provided a diagnosis of "adjustment disorder" and the examiner opined that the condition is due to anxieties of entering civilian life after serving 20 years. He was also awarded 10 percent for each claimed joint, 50 percent for sleep apnea, 30 percent for headaches, in addition to 50 percent for the mental illness, totaling 100 percent compensation.

IF he was so sick and disabled, why did we allow him to stay in the military receiving pay all those years when someone more physically able could have been doing his job? If he's afraid of civilian life, why not stay in the military for another 10 years, then retire for a lot more money and social security to boot. Why? Because now he can draw a big federal paycheck from the contractor, as well as his military retirement check, and also a big VA entitlement check. He can enjoy his fancy home cinema, new truck, boat, and vacation home. Whenever he gets tired of working his civilian job he can quit, then spend his days traveling, fishing, sailing, or golfing, and still be receiving from VA as much income as an average working man might receive, in addition to his military retirement pay and social security benefits.

***

Veteran X, during service, was diagnosed with diabetes and HIV (blood test finding only, no symptoms). Since discharge in 1986 he has been rated 70% disabled due to HIV, diabetes, and depression related to HIV. He is now claiming AIDS and "failure to climax." He has received 70% (up to $1,500 a month) from the VA from 1986 to 2016 (for 30 years) while he worked full time for the post office. His condition progressed to AIDS along the way but he kept working. He then retired from the USPS at exactly 30 years and filed a VA claim for IU (a claim that he cannot work due to service-connected disabilities). He had become an alcoholic over those years and had developed kidney disease. He reportedly was drinking 10 pints of Brandy per day.   The kidney disease was of course most likely related to the alcohol consumption; but it is a well-known complication of AIDS and diabetes, so kidney disease and erectile dysfunction were granted secondary to diabetes, and alcoholism was granted secondary to depression which was secondary to AIDS. The kidney disease alone was 60% but his total evaluation was still just 90% so he was granted IU.

All the VA evaluations are supposed to be based on the degree to which the conditions cause functional impairment affecting one's ability to work, and IU is only to be assigned when the evaluations don't total 100 but the conditions are preventing him from working. This man retired after 30 years at USPS!   His conditions were not caused by service anyway, just happened to be diagnosed during service. But besides that, his employment was never affected by his conditions. He has always received paychecks from the federal government: first the military, then USPS, then federal retirement, but he has double-dipped and triple-dipped with payments from the VA.

SOME VETERANS DO NOT DESERVE BENEFITS

Over and over we are granting benefits to bad soldiers, veterans whose discharge documents say "dishonorable" and "bad conduct" but for whom one single lowest-level claims examiner has decided that his service "was honorable for VA purposes" and so we must pay him for life. Other bad soldiers were discharged "under honorable conditions" or the DD 214 may even say "honorable" but the reason for discharge prior to completion of his commitment is noted as "unsatisfactory performance," "bad conduct," or "substance abuse." These veterans do not deserve VA benefits. The military has noted that they did not properly fulfill their commitment of service and had to be discharged before completing their term.

The claimant has now filed a law suit (disability claim) against the federal government, and it should be reviewed in a court-like fashion. My first choice would be to simply deny any veteran if the military has not given him an honorable discharge, without further review by the VA. But if the VA must make a decision of their own, this should be done by someone with some "judicial" knowledge and experience, preferably an attorney. And even if the military has indicated some sort of honorable discharge on the DD 214, if the reason for early discharge was bad conduct and non-performance, then the VA should also send these for review by an attorney. In most cases, these people should not be paid veterans' benefits.

***

Veteran X started active duty in 1960 and developed financial problems in the first 4 years. He was writing bad checks and accumulating debts impossible to repay on a soldier's salary. He was brought to military court and they considered kicking him out of service but he blamed it all on his wife and he divorced her. He remarried and remained in service. In February 1966 he shot himself in a fit of rage because he was angry at a superior officer. The military determined the injury was due to misconduct and was *not* in the line-of-duty. That was eventually overruled by the VA and they paid compensation for the residuals of the gunshot wound.

The soldier was sent to Vietnam in August 1967 and he immediately began requesting a hardship relocation due to his wife's pregnancy so within four months they had sent him home. He will get any Agent Orange related benefits even though he shirked his Vietnam duty.

By 1977 he had become a First Sergeant. He assigned one of his own men to police duties so that he could go and have an affair with that man's wife. On multiple occasions he met the woman at local motels, all verified by investigation. The woman was only 17, and it was considered statutory rape by state law, but under the Code of Military Justice (UCMJ) it's not statutory rape unless she was under 16, and that prevailed in his case. When a crime is committed during service, the military has the option of prosecuting under UCMJ or letting it be done in the civilian sector, and they will generally choose to do it by UCMJ so that it won't hit the civilian news and make the military look bad. In the military courtroom the military officers attempted to embellish this sergeant's great character, while calling the woman a whore because she reported she had been raped 7 times while hitchhiking and they said she was asking for it.

But it also came out in investigation that the sergeant had falsified his college degree documents. He reported having attended two colleges, both of which denied having any knowledge of him. Financial investigation showed he had been overpaid for 7 years because he falsified his date of entering active duty, and also revealed that he owed the IRS several thousand dollars. The IRS had tried for many years to collect and were unable to find him. His addresses on the tax forms were all false, no such address. IRS eventually wrote it all off as uncollectable.

The same year that the sex charges came against him, he reported that he had served 20 years of active duty and was therefore due to retire, so the military went easy on him. In processing his retirement, it was discovered that he had claimed more years of service that he actually did have because he claimed 3 years that were just Reserve service starting in 1957, and the DD214's showed that he entered active duty in 1960; but somewhere along the line the records (total years) had been adjusted, no doubt by a Private taking the word of a 1st Sergeant. The military ultimately decided not to prosecute the soldier because they "didn't want the community to find out about the sex scandal." This is all documented in his military file.

It is a typical example of numerous military files I read about horrible soldiers who were protected and enabled by the military for years, and after retirement, the VA jumped right in and continued to support him with a separate fat paycheck for the rest of his life. He should have been given a dishonorable discharge early in service and should not even be eligible for VA benefits.

***

Veteran X was discharged after 6 months in service "under honorable conditions" for reasons of "misconduct – serious offense." He cannot continue in or rejoin the military; however, he can be paid by the VA for the rest of his life for *not* working. In VA regulations, he is treated the same as "honorable."

The veteran's military personnel file shows that he had a "poor attitude, poor performance, and apathy towards the military." His discharge documents note "inability to adapt to military environment." He had received DUI's in two towns where he was not supposed to be. He had disobeyed orders and had left base without authority. His military dress appearance was "poor" and he was not shaving.

Several years after service he applied for and received VA education benefits in 1984. His wife claimed an apportionment of his education money because he was providing no support to her or his kids. Within a few months the veteran was terminated from college due to "poor attendance" (same as the Army) but he never told the VA so he was grossly overpaid educational benefits. He still owed the money to VA in 2015, more than 30 years later, and it was only discovered when he filed his first compensation claim for a whole list of problems. He was granted 50% for PTSD, 30% for migraines, and 10% each for miscellaneous joint problems, for a total of 90% disability. His educational debt was "waivered."

***

Veteran X joined the Marines in 1974. Military records show that after 2 months and 8 days in basic training he was discharged honorably due to "unsuitability for the Marines." The discharge records noted that he had failed the 8th grade twice and could not read higher than a 2nd grade level. He admitted that he had failed the military entrance exam 3 times, then paid a friend to pass it for him on the 4th try. As a juvenile he had been in trouble for burglary and had troubles at school. After 2 weeks in Marine training, he was transferred to a medical platoon because he was "incapable of learning due to mental deficiency." From there he was transferred to the "Academic Rehabilitation Platoon" for remedial academic training to help catch up his academic skills, but after 2 weeks he was still doing poorly and could not read or understand the training materials, so he was discharged from service. After discharge he spent multiple years in prison. In the 70's it was for homicide, in the 80's for robbery and kidnapping, and in the 90's for drug possession with intent to distribute. In 2000 he submitted a claim for service-connection for mental issues including PTSD and schizophrenia. He said his PTSD and other mental problems resulted because his drill sergeant spit in his face and told him he wasn't fit for the Marines. VA should never be subjected to rating these claims from someone who never made it through basic training due to mental deficiency, and no injury ever incurred in service.

***

Veteran X spent 29 days in service, after which he claimed service connection for mental issues due to service. He says he was sexually assaulted by his superiors when they found out he was homosexual, and that he was discharged for homosexuality. His discharge papers show nothing about homosexuality (there is a code for that) but show he was discharged due to misconduct. He had a criminal record prior to service and he reported that he had been regularly using heroin since age 12. After service he was diagnosed with bipolar disorder and alcohol and heroin abuse. The examiner said that his bipolar condition had existed prior to service but was aggravated by his 29 days of service, so VA pays him. Again, VA should not be spending time or money on a dishonorable veteran who served less than a month and was not injured in service.

FRIVOLOUS AND FRAUDULENT CLAIMS

Veteran X served a little over 90 days in the Army. Prior to service he shot himself in the leg at age 16. This was fully discussed and documented on his military entrance exam, and there was no chronic disability noted. After service he claimed service connection for the leg wound, saying that it happened during service. It was denied as a pre-existing condition and he appealed. The denial was continued at the local level but was eventually granted by the Board of Veterans Appeals (BVA), based on a VA exam on which the veteran insinuated that the condition had been incurred in service. BVA apparently had not read the other evidence of record, specifically not the military entrance exam. It's bad enough when pre-existing conditions are granted because they were not mentioned or evidenced on the military entrance exam, but this was clearly stated as pre-existing.

Once BVA makes a decision, the lower offices will not refute or dispute it. I actually tried on several occasions, noting that BVA employees are only human and can make mistakes, but I was never allowed to dispute a BVA decision. In fact, I was not even allowed to dispute an in-house Appeals Department decision, and the people making those decisions were less experienced than I was! I was told that they have the authority to make decisions outside-the-box, not within the same realm of government regulations that I had to abide by, and there is no internal affairs office checking their work.

So once this veteran's left leg had been granted by BVA, he filed for the right leg and for his back, both as secondary to the left leg. Both of these conditions were granted as well as PTSD which was deemed to have developed due to the "in-service" injury of the left leg. The veteran received 100% compensation plus Special Monthly Compensation, Aid and Attendance, and housing allowance (to modify the home for handicap) due to loss of *use* of both of his legs (although he was still walking on them).

His compensation payments alone are more than $7,000 per month, for a condition that did not happen in his measly three months of service! I kid you not, I did not make this case up, and I was required to grant *increases* for these fraudulently-claimed and erroneously-granted issues. By the time the claim came to me, the primary issues had all been granted for several years and I was directed to leave that alone and to look only at increasing the evaluations if the conditions had worsened.

The regulations *do* allow severance if the grant has been in effect less than 10 years, and allow a reduction of evaluation, so long as it has not been in effect more than 20 years, and regulations allow severance or reduction at any time if the grant was based on fraud. But in fact, despite seeing plenty of fraud and erroneously granted conditions, I have *never* seen a severance.

The only reductions (without severing) I ever saw were for evaluations that had been in effect less than 5 years, and those are actually rare to come by as well. The regulations say you can reduce if the "evidence shows sustained improvement." I believe this proof could be in any manner of form, such as proof he is using the legs for work or for playing basketball, or medical records showing treatment for other problems and making no mention of any leg complaint. But the real VA ignores that regulation or makes their own interpretation of it, such that reduction cannot be done unless there are two consecutive VA exams within a five-year period, both showing improvement. You can't reduce based on anything other than a VA exam, not actual treatment records, but simply an exam template with boxes checked off by some examiner who has never treated the veteran and who has seen the veteran only once in his life. The exam is based almost entirely on whatever the veteran wants to answer on the day of exam, how far over he wants to bend, how many episodes of pain he wants to claim he has experienced, how much medicine he wants to report that he has taken, and with no supporting documented proof of any of it.

Do you see why I had to write this book? The people at the lower echelons of the VA who are actually developing and granting these claims have no authority and no permission to use any common sense or to apply any morality to the claim at hand. They are told there is no time to "nit-pick" the claims. "Just grant it and move on!" Do not question the veteran. Do not question the doctor. Do not question or try to reverse any decision made before yours. If it has never been granted, grant it; if it's already granted, increase it. If you can't, then tell the veteran what you'll need to see in order to increase it, so he can reopen the claim, again.

Occasionally a VA examiner will make the following remark on an exam. "Findings on ROM (range of motion) testing are most likely fictitious and should not be used to support any level of functional impairment." In many cases the examiner sees that there was an exam or medical record a month or so earlier which showed that the ROM was perfectly normal. Now it is grossly exaggerated to the point that it would warrant a 40% disability (same as if it was amputated). Unfortunately, if the examiner just logs the measurements and does not make a remark, the rater has to grant, and cannot use his common sense. The rater cannot reference the prior medical records and cannot reference the fact that the claimant remarked on a separate PTSD exam that he is regularly golfing or bicycling or jogging.

Most of the veterans receiving big payments are indeed members of fitness centers where they work out regularly (despite claimed disabilities) because this gives them something to spend their days doing since they are not working. The federal government should be more like the insurance companies investigating workers' compensation claims. When someone files a big injury claim, an agent is assigned to snoop around and see if the person is indeed handicapped, or if he's just faking it on exam. They are able to deny many claims when the truth is evident. But not VA. It is against VA policy to develop for evidence that would deny or reduce benefits.

VA makes no effort to weed out the lying cheating thieves who are taking our hard-earned tax dollars. Although there is a person in each VA office assigned as the "fraud investigator" most employees cannot tell you who that person is or how to report what looks like a fraudulent claim. VA would rather just pay it than to waste time and resources to fight the frauders. On the rare occasion that fraud becomes evident because a veteran clearly admits to working while receiving a benefit based on "can't work" such as Pension or IU, all the veteran has to do is plead financial hardship and the overpayment will be forgiven/waivered. I think it's time the VA started actively confronting the clearly fraudulent claimants and make examples out of them so the problems will be reduced in the future rather than to continue exploding as it is at present.

***

Veteran X served 20 years in Armor brigades including 5 tours to southeast Asia. He'd seen plenty of combat and had received a Purple Heart (issued for injury in combat). He had legitimate service-connected mental and physical injuries. He was enrolled in a PTSD group therapy program at the VAMC when he told his doctor he didn't want to come to any more sessions and the doctor asked him why not. The doctor quoted the veteran as stating, "I don't want to be part of this. It's so disrespectful. We got guys out there losing their lives and we got guys in here fabricating stories."

***

Veteran X has obtained a copy of his service treatment records (STRS) and searched them to find any symptom noted in service that he might possibly claim now. He filed for a right arm condition and left arm condition, but both issues were denied. The "right arm condition" reference was simply a note on his military entrance exam documenting that he had a tattoo on his right arm. The left arm condition was simply a note during a routine exam that the blood pressure had been checked by placing a cuff on his left arm. So many hours are spent on developing and rating bogus claims like this, but the devious claimant doesn't even get spanked with a wet 4spaghetti noodle. He just gets an apologetic letter about how greatly we regret being unable to grant the claim.

***

Veteran X is a 22-year-old who spent 3 years in service and got out on a "under honorable conditions" due to drug use. He had a VA exam prior to discharge and another VA exam after discharge. Different issues were claimed on his pre-discharge claim than were claimed after service. The two exams showed different symptoms, findings, and diagnoses, despite being only 6 months apart. The pre-discharge exam showed no hearing loss, and on the post-discharge exam the audiologist said he could not evaluate the condition because the veteran was "inconsistent, unreliable, and failed to cooperate on the speech discrimination portion of the exam." He told the veteran to come back another day for an exam with a different audiologist. On the mental exam one month after discharge, the claimant reported that he has been to 2 job interviews and believes he will be offered both jobs. When asked about his military service he said he "did really well, succeeded in everything, got awards and promotions." When asked how he'd been doing during this month since discharge, he said he was functioning "good" and that he was actively seeking employment and planning to attend college starting next semester. He was living with his wife, and maintaining good relationships with his parents and siblings now that they are living closer together. He said he has plenty of friends, likes to shoot, hunt, camp, and do anything outdoors. With the wife he likes to go to movies, the mall, go on dates, and do outdoors stuff too. He made no mention of any mental problems. So why is he claiming "anxiety, depression, and PTSD"? And why will the VA grant it?

***

Veteran X served from 1966 to 1969. He filed his first claim in 2012, listing 44 issues. Forty-three of the issues were denied and one was granted. He kept coming back in after that with new and different issues. When he finally couldn't think of any more issues to claim, he filed an "1151 claim" for illnesses and injuries caused by medications prescribed by VA physicians for his *nonservice-*connected conditions. If people like him could be stopped after their 3rd or 4th frivolous unsupported claim, the VA claims department could be cut in half. But there is no recourse for the VA claims developers. They have to keep on sending more letters and requesting more records, often duplicates or unrelated to anything shown in service. Then the raters waste more time denying the same old issues or new issues that have nothing to do with military service.

***

Veteran X is drawing 90% disability compensation. He achieved a rank of E-8 in service so he draws plenty of military retirement pay. After retiring from service, he immediately went to work for a defense contractor for which he does IT work from his home! He told the VA examiner he will quit that job "as soon as I can afford to." Since he's still working he knows he cannot get IU, so he is claiming an "increase" to try to get his 90% up to 100% schedular.

***

Veteran X is 22 years old, served 3 years. He claims "finger" and explains "I just woke up one day and my right index seemed swollen." He said it is not painful now, but he still feels that it "seems larger than the left one." (Aren't the right-hand fingers usually larger than the left for any person who is right-handed?) The examiner gave no diagnosis of a finger condition. The veteran also claims his right shoulder hurts if he runs a lot (he runs!), and his lower spine and right knee both hurt hurts if he skates a lot (he skates!) The examiner found nothing. I call these frivolous and fraudulent claims.

***

Veteran X served 2 whole months in the military in 1984. Within 2 weeks she was found "unfit for service" so she was discharged as expeditiously as possible but it took 2 months. Thirty-three years later in 2017 she filed a claim for a heart condition which had recently been diagnosed. When she was denied VA benefits she went on a rampage at the VA and wrote letters to two congressmen, the secretary of the VA, and President Trump. Most of the VA-related letters congressmen get are from people like this, or from prisoners who have nothing better to do than write letters.

***

Veteran X, in 1976, was off duty, hiking in Hawaii, carrying a machete when he slipped and lacerated his right hand. Upon discharge he filed a claim and was granted 0% for the scar because it was incurred in service. Now, 40 years later, after he has had a full career of working with his hands as an auto mechanic, at age 62 he files a claim for a right hand numbness condition. Although all symptoms were subjective (no evidence on any testing) he was granted 20% for nerve impingement of the right hand, and the scar was increased to 10% for reportedly "painful scar." Raters are not doctors, but even raters know that a 40-year old "scar" that is not unstable is not painful. The condition underneath the scar could be painful but that would be a muscle, bone, or nerve condition, not a painful scar. In this case he has already been granted for the nerve condition, so compensation for the scar is duplicative and wrong. Compensation for the nerve condition should also be disallowed unless there is some deficiency shown on an electromyography (EMG). For some complaints there are no tests, but this condition can be tested. It is not logical to accept subjective evidence to support an evaluation for a condition that supposedly started 40 years ago and yet has not been treated or tested in 40 years, and when records of evidence show the ability to work with the hands has never been impaired! (Besides the fact that the condition was not caused by any military activity.) But raters are not permitted to bring logic into a rating.

***

Veteran X submits a frivolous increase claim for 3 issues, requiring 3 more VA exams. First, he had a lymph node removed from his left arm pit 25 years ago. The scar cannot be seen anymore, there are no symptoms, he takes no meds for it, he has no anemia or residuals from the condition. On exam he admits, "it has remained the same." So the 0% he always had is continued. Secondly, he has a scar one-inch long on his left middle finger, residual of a laceration in service 25 years ago. It is not painful or unstable, so the 0% is continued. His 3rd issue is a cervical strain that he has had since 1991. The exam shows no reduction in range of motion and no pain on motion. It should be rated 0%, but he's already 10% for it, so the 10% is continued. The 10% cannot be reduced unless there are two consecutive VA exams within 5 years both showing improvement. Another routine future exam will be diaried for 18 months. At that time, if the exam shows the same thing this one did, VA will notify the veteran of a "proposal to reduce" the 10% to 0% and will give him 60 days to respond. Upon receipt of that letter he will need to go to any doctor and report that his neck is painful and get that report in his file. Another rating will be done and the current evaluation will be continued. If he does not respond to the proposal letter by sending new medical records, a rating decision will reduce the evaluation to 0%, effective the first of the third month after notification. During the next two months he will dispute the reduction by sending in statements or more treatment records, or he'll ask for another VA exam to confirm that he is still having neck pain. VA will order another exam and this time the exam will show that he reported "pain" and a new rating will continue the 10%. Another routine future exam will not be diaried for this 10% disability because all VA needs is a subjective comment of "pain" in order to continue or resume the 10%.

If a million veterans have a single 10% evaluation that is allowed to continue for 50 years unquestioned (granted at age 25, until death at 75), over the period of 50 years that will be about $82,000 per veteran, for a total of 82 *billion* dollars (actually much more than that with the future cost-of-living increases).

ABUSE OF INDIVIDUAL UNEMPLOYABILITY (IU)

Individual Unemployability (IU) is paid to a veteran whose total compensation evaluation is less than 100%, but because he is reportedly unable to work, he is paid 100% compensation anyway. After all, compensation is supposed to be based on functional/occupational impairment.

The veteran may qualify for IU with as little as 60% disability if he has one condition of that severity, and this 60% can be made up of several conditions if they are of the same disease process; for example, diabetes at 20% plus 20% for diabetic neuropathy of each arm and 10% for diabetic neuropathy of each leg would total 60% and would qualify for schedular IU. Otherwise, he will qualify for schedular IU at 70% total compensation so long as at least one condition is 40% or more. But in fact, IU can be paid to someone with any little degree of disability if the evidence clearly shows he cannot work due to the condition. This is called non-schedular and it must be approved by the Service Center Manager at the office granting the claim, a little more work, but happens all the time. A veteran receiving IU gets 100% disability payments and most of the time he will be granted permanent and total status at the same time, just as if he had been given a 100% schedular evaluation, so no future exams will be required.

The first difficulty of the IU claim is that to be granted IU the claimant cannot be gainfully employed (he can work a little, but not a regular 40-hour week) and the medical exams must indicate that the service-connected conditions are functionally impairing his ability to work full time. The examiner is not supposed to state whether the veteran can work or not; that is supposed to be up to the rater to decide. But the rater can't use logic such as analysis of the veteran's social life, or when the veteran last worked, or why the veteran quit his last job. The rater must base the decision on what the physician provided, so the physician might as well be making the statement.

IU cannot be paid to a person who is working. If he is working, the claim is simply denied on that basis. Then the claimant quits his job and resubmits the claim. And VA works it again and grants it.

The second difficulty for the IU claimant is that once he is granted IU, he must submit a form (VA Form 21-4140) to VA every year, verifying that he still is not working. It's just a signature and one check box. The VA doesn't get much credit for the time spent on these "non-rating" issues so they are generally backed up several years for review. Those who do not submit a timely response will be sent a rating decision threatening to discontinue the IU; then the form will be returned by the veteran and another rating will be done to state that the IU benefit is continued. A lot of time and resources are wasted on this issue.

The only "verification" VA has that the recipient of IU is truly not working, is the *Income Verification Match* (IVM) computer program which allows VA to match their records with IRS (Internal Revenue) and SSA (Social Security) records once per year. This is used by the VA to check on veterans receiving Pension or IU, both income-based benefits. The most recent data I found on the effectiveness of this IVM program was a quite old Office of Inspector General (OIG) report, *Audit of Veterans Benefits Administration's (VBA) Income Verification Match (IVM) Results, November 8, 2000,* which reviewed the records for a 5-year period of 1995-1999. It reported quite a lot of overpayments and mismatches of income, as well as many records unable to match. The potential monetary impact was noted as "significant" in that about $300 million in beneficiary overpayments involving potential fraud had not been referred to OIG for investigation, and $921 million in IVM related overpayments were not recovered for the 5-year period. Many cases of mismatch showing veterans had been overpaid were simply "waivered" for financial hardship, even if they were determined to have resulted from fraud such as under-reporting their or their spouse's income. Several recommendations were made by the OIG, including that the VA must "refer potential fraud cases to OIG" and "assure that accounts receivable be established to recover IVM related debts from beneficiaries." I was unable to find any follow-up report to indicate any improvements ever resulted from the OIG investigation, and no report of any further investigation done since 2000.

There are plenty of OIG studies on the internet available for review for practically every aspect of the VA world. The OIG is the "government's watchdog" and they will find problems and discrepancies, fraud and abuse, anywhere they want to look. But is anything ever done about the things they find? I don't know. But I guess that's another book.

***

Veteran X is claiming an increase in his PTSD to include a grant of IU. He spent one year in service and got out early due to misconduct because he was living with a girl while he was married to someone else. He now lives with a girlfriend who has 2 babies, a one-year-old and a 3-month-old. They live in a trailer which is paid for, and he has a car. He got out of service in 2015 with no disability noted in service but was granted 50% for PTSD because he claimed it within a year of discharge. Within 6 months he reopened his claim to request IU. He had worked two factory jobs during that time and never missed a day of work, so the claim for IU was denied because he was working. He then quit the job for no reason (per the employers) and resubmitted the claim for IU based on PTSD. This veteran is 25 years old and nothing is wrong with him. According to his own report, he is "tired, lazy, overweight, and doesn't feel like doing anything." He wants us to believe those are symptoms of PTSD and he cannot work due to those PTSD symptoms. Yet the records show he has no problems with relationships and making babies, and he has no problem doing work if he is willing to work, which he is not.

***

Veteran X was a SFC, E-7, when he retired from service after 20 years with an honorable discharge and he had no disability noted in the military records. Within a year after retiring he filed a claim for IU and stated that he cannot work due to "adjustment disorder."

He says he can't adjust to civilian life, but he's only been out a few months. Has he tried? He obviously had no mental or physical disability shown at discharge, so whatever problems he has now were not incurred in service. We (American taxpayers) are paying for his military retirement. We should not also be asked to pay him a disability check for something not incurred in battle.

***

Veteran X is claiming IU based on PTSD and a prostate condition. His prostate condition evaluation, based on voiding dysfunction, is currently 40% and his PTSD is 70% but this only calculates to 80% and he wants IU or 100%. VA provides him with review exams for the two conditions which he says prevent him from working. The new exams show his voiding condition now warrants only 10% and his PTSD now warrants only 10%, a total of 20%, not qualifying for IU. Will VA reduce him? Of course not. The rating decision simply states that "although improvement was shown on the recent exams, sustained improvement has not been shown" and all current evaluations are continued. Another routine future exam will be established for about 18 months up the road, and he will never be reduced because he will go into that exam ready to answer the questions correctly this time to warrant the higher evaluations, and he will be granted IU.

***

Veteran X worked as a mechanic for Grumman at the Newport News Shipyard for 37 years with pay in excess of $60K per year before he took a normal retirement from them. He then started his own delivery service business which he operated until he could take full social security retirement at age 65. Now he draws his retirement of $1,700 per month plus SSA of $1,900 per month and his wife also draws SSA. At age 65 he submitted a claim for IU, noting that he cannot work due to a mental condition that was caused by his one year of military service from 1971 to 1972. He worked successfully for 37 years after service! How can we humor such a claim?

***

Veteran X is a 25-year-old woman who is claiming IU. She has 3 children under the age of 5 and she says she doesn't want to have to pay babysitters. She is physically able to generate, deliver, and care for babies (not easy work), and yet she says that her back condition prevents her from working. The same thing is frequently seen on IU claims from men. They have made numerous babies, sometimes from several different mothers, and the more babies you have the more your benefits increase, but these guys can't "work" due to their back conditions.

***

Veteran X appears to be a well-adjusted person based on his reported social activities and past work history although he has recently retired. He is granted 50% for a mental condition, 10% for his back, 10% for the right knee, and 10% for the left knee. All the claimed joints have osteoarthritis which is just age-related arthritis and the examiner diagnosed it despite all the X-rays being normal. The conditions total 70% so he meets the schedular criteria for IU and will receive 100% compensation.

***

Veteran X served 3 months in 1974, strained his back in basic training, and got released from service. There was no fracture or ruptured disc, only subjective symptoms and the degree to which he claimed he could bend over warranted him a 20% evaluation from the VA. After service, he never worked in his life. At age 61 he applied for social security disability and was denied because they found that he was not too disabled to work. He then applied for IU from VA. The VA examiner conceded that he cannot work due to his back and radiculopathy of both legs secondary to the back condition, so he is granted IU. This despite the fact that the records show he has diabetes (nonservice-connected) and that his leg condition is actually peripheral neuropathy, a common complication of diabetes!

***

Veteran X worked more than 20 years as a corrections officer, retired at age 62, and promptly submitted a claim for IU.   If you pull 100 case files that have granted IU, you'll see about 80% of them were filed at age 62 or 65, within a few months after retirement.   Before this they could not be granted IU, because you cannot receive IU if you are gainfully employed.   "Retirement" at retirement age, is not evidence that you *cannot* work. Many people continue working until their 80's *if they want to* (Just look at the U.S. Congress). This is fraud and abuse of the VA system. A claim for IU is a law suit against the federal government claiming that one is unable to work due to injuries sustained during military service, and it needs to be addressed as such. Those who file such fraudulent suits against the government should be made to pay the government for time and resources wasted, like paying court costs when you lose a civil case.

REVOLVING DOOR

It doesn't take a claimant very long to discover the "revolving door" of VA benefits. More, more, more. After they file their first claim, they keep coming back in again and again for the rest of their life. If denied, they'll keep reopening and then appealing until they get granted. If granted, they'll want a higher percent. If they've maxed out the percent for all particular ailments, they ask for Individual Unemployability (IU). After being granted IU, they are getting compensation at the 100% rate, but they still try to get the 100% total evaluation so they can get DEA (Dependents Educational Assistance) and also so they won't have to send in the annual statement attesting they are still unable to work. Once they get the total 100% evaluation they can actually go back to work and earn an income in addition to their 100% disability compensation!

Even after they have been granted 100 percent disability they keep coming back. They can't understand how 20% for the back, plus 70% for PTSD, plus 30% for GERD doesn't equal 120%, and they want 120%. A person cannot be more than 100 percent disabled, so 100% compensation is the limit; however, the veteran then starts claiming supplemental benefits such as Special Monthly Compensation (SMC) and ancillary benefits that can be paid to veterans with certain serious manifestations. For example, Aid and Attendance is an additional SMC benefit paid to one who needs help with activities of daily living such as dressing, eating, or using the bathroom. SMC for loss of use of extremities is paid to one who has lost an extremity or lost use of an extremity. Such a loss will also entitle him to Special Housing Allowance so his house can be handicap-modified, and Auto Allowance so his vehicle can be modified.

Over and over, veterans send in letters to the VA, their congressmen, and the President saying, "I'm not looking for a handout. I just want what I deserve." Really?

***

Veteran X served from 1990 to 1994 and had a car accident in service in 1994. Two years after service, in 1996, he filed a VA claim and was granted 10% for right knee residuals, noting no other problems from the accident. Five years later, in 2001, he claimed numerous other symptoms related to the car accident, and was granted 0% for lumbar strain, 0% for cervical strain, 10% for bunions on the feet (not sure how this resulted from a car accident!), and 10% for head injury, so with the knee 10% his total was up to 30%. Although these other conditions were not shown in service, the car accident was shown in service, so he was deemed to have the required "in-service event" and the required "post-service complaints." He continued to file increases over the years, getting his back evaluation up to 40% and neck up to 30%, and getting granted for PTSD and Traumatic Brain Injury (TBI) related to the accident, so his total went up to 100%, and he was granted permanent and total (P&T) disability, so VA would not require any more reviews or exams.

In 2017 he again claimed an increase in everything, including many issues previously denied, for a total of 30 issues. Although he was at 100%, already P&T, exams had to be done because there was the potential that he might qualify for the Aid and Attendance benefit (Special Monthly Compensation). All of the exams showed improvement in all issues, but nothing could be done. It had been more than 5 years since the prior exam, so lacking two consecutive exams in 5 years, he could not be reduced on one exam. Routine future exams are not ordered for people over 55, and since he would turn 55 before another 18 months passed, no more future exams could be diaried for him. Even if the back and neck were reduced as they should be, his total would still be 100% because his PTSD was 70% and a separate evaluation for TBI was 40%. Did he need Aid and Attendance? No, he was doing fine, still riding motorcycles, with all these back and neck problems! At age 54, he had been living with his mother since service until she recently kicked him out because he was dating a married woman she didn't approve of. So suddenly he was on his own and needed more money.

Not only have claimants like him totally abused the system by taking our tax dollars for themselves, the amount of cost involved in processing such claims is horrendous. Many VA workers, VSRs and Raters spent dozens of hours developing his cases, thousands in VA salaries, plus thousands on just the most recent exams which were for naught, and not to mention the overheads for the VA offices and medical facilities. Thousands of cases like his every day add up to a major financial burden for the U.S. If these jokers were not in the system, if they could be cut off at the start, or never granted anything in the first place, then the VA budget could probably be cut by 80%.

The VA regulations must be revised to put time limits on submitting claims (timely submittal after service or after diagnosis). There should be limits on reopening claims (number of times and how long after denials). Increases could be handled by automatic review exams (every 5 or 10 years) and automatic re-evaluation, not based on increase claims submitted by veterans. If the claimant notifies VA that a significant worsening has occurred, such as required surgery or hemodialysis or hospitalization, then VA could initiate an increase claim in those cases.

APPEALS

If a claimant doesn't like the rating decision he receives, within one year after he receives the decision he can request a "reconsideration" of the decision, without submitting any new evidence, and the claim will be re-rated. If he's still unhappy, within one year of the last decision date, he can file an "Appeal" with or without submitting new evidence, and the case will be addressed by the Appeals Department. If he doesn't like their decision, he can opt to have his file sent to the Board of Veterans Appeals (BVA) in Washington DC. If he doesn't reopen or appeal within a year but wants to submit new evidence more than a year after the denial then it's a "reopen claim" and will go through the same local rating procedures again.

The Board of Veterans Appeals (BVA) can grant anything they want, without reasonable rationale. The decision will be lengthy, wordy, and full of legal jargon. The work of the BVA is not scrutinized by anyone, and their decisions are not to be questioned by anyone at the regional office level. That may not be dictated by law, but it is certainly the way a low-level rater is trained. Do not question BVA! In fact, even the DROs (decision review officers) on the Appeals Team at the regional office are not to be questioned. Why can't VA accept that BVA members are only human, they do make human errors, and they are not all geniuses? Also they are not above the law, and therefore should be held to the law. It is not uncommon for BVA to grant sleep apnea secondary to allergic rhinitis, sleep apnea secondary to asthma, and sleep apnea secondary to PTSD, none of which is medically reasonable. This has caused many other veterans to appeal their own denials based on the prior case decisions which are all over the internet. I have also seen BVA grant many conditions that were *not* present during service, but they are able to grant just based on lay statements from the veterans. The word is out, and the VA is being smothered in appealed cases. Every veteran who is denied is now being encouraged to request reconsideration and if still not granted, then appeal! Nothing to lose, everything to gain.

(5) TRUE WAR INJURIES

If you are a war-injured veteran, this book is not about *you*, but it is written *for* you. Other than in this chapter I don't discuss veterans with real war injuries, what their evaluations are, or how much compensation they receive. I hope they are receiving the maximum benefits available because their lives will never be the same as they would have been without the war injury. Many amputees and seriously injured veterans do go on to fully gainful employment and do marry and have families, but still they have been changed, and they have to adapt to a life with handicaps or deficiencies. The VA disability compensation program was created for them, and I am happy to support them with my tax dollars.

David Wood's "Beyond the Battlefield" series done for the *Huffington Post* described some horrific injuries experienced by soldiers in Iraq. The soldiers are going on foot patrol and stepping on IEDs (improvised explosive devices), bombs that have been rigged underground. Wood says it's basically a bucket of cruel explosives along with whatever nasty stuff they can find to put in the bucket. When a soldier steps on one of these and it blows, it either rips off one leg, or rips him up between the legs, destroying his sexual organs and usually ripping all way into his lower abdomen. All this nasty stuff from the bucket is likely to cause infection and the doctors spend days just trying to clean all this stuff out of the bottom of his body. Soldiers live in fear daily that they may step on one of these and it will cause them to be dismembered. Wood gave an example of a soldier who is still recovering. When he stepped on the IED he lost at the same moment both legs and his right arm. Fortunately, a field medic with him when it happened was able to save the injured man's life by applying tourniquets to all three limbs to stop the bleeding and therefore was able to save the brain and the torso.

Wood's example is a real veteran who has "borne the battle" and who fully deserves the maximum of VA benefits. He deserves to be paid well now, to be given the best medical care, and he should receive the full benefits available to his family members, including educational benefits, because obviously he will not likely be able to work and take care of them. Anyone missing three limbs should not be expected to work. He also deserves to receive special monthly compensation and this is what special monthly compensation was developed for, people who have lost or lost the use of their legs or their arms and/or have lost use of their sexual/reproductive organs.

It must be so humiliating or disturbing for one of these veterans who is so severely injured, so fully deserving and meeting the regulation requirements for such a payment, to then see some perfectly normal healthy veteran also getting 100% disability when there's obviously not a thing wrong with him. This is the problem I have with the VA system. We are paying any veteran who comes asking for it. I wish I could have provided my own example of a serious injury case, but in my 10 years of processing claims for the VA I never once processed a claim or rated a claim based on serious battle injuries. Such cases are rated by a small group of VA specialists, while thousands of claims processors and raters at 56 Veterans Benefits Offices spend millions of hours on claims for non-serious and mostly non-battle-incurred issues.

Many veterans are paid for "loss of use" of their legs because they can't walk like they used to. Some claim neuropathy or claudication of the legs due to diabetes. But most of them are grossly obese and that's why they cannot walk and must use a wheelchair. I'm sorry they have ruined their own lives by being lazy and becoming so obese that they can no longer move the way the body was intended. But this is not the responsibility of the government and the taxpayers who do get off their butt to work each day. The working people should not have to pay (without choice) for those who are riding around on their scooters (by choice). If you visit a VA medical center several times in the same month you will see the "regulars" who spend their lives in the clinics and in the emergency room or in the hospital, just wasting taxpayer dollars. Some have nothing else to do and they enjoy the attention they get from the medical providers and other veterans. It's one big social club in the lobby and waiting areas. Why not hang out there when it costs them little or nothing for the medical care, and the records of their visits will support their future claims for increase?

Meanwhile, there are veterans truly suffering from things that happened to them in a warzone, and they're not faking it in a wheelchair so they'll never be granted. There are some veterans from the Vietnam War and even some left over from the Korean War who have never been properly rewarded for problems that they have had to live with as result of conditions in Korea and Vietnam. These wars were hard on their bodies, physically and mentally. They didn't have the comforts of home that Gulf War soldiers have, and when they were sick or injured they often did not get prompt and adequate medical attention.

In Vietnam, from walking through swamps and rice paddies, the soldiers developed all sorts of rotting of the body including "trench foot." Their feet got wet and they had to keep wearing the wet socks and boots. Their skin rotted and all sorts of organisms/parasites inhabited their bodies. An average human being has up to 30 million organisms crawling in and over him throughout the body at any given time and these are normal in order to keep our bodies in healthy balance. But the Vietnam soldiers were exposed to an environment that was unnatural to them as they were taken out of the realm of their normal habitat organisms. They were infested with organisms on their bodies or in their bodies that scientists have not even yet fully investigated and come to understand. These veterans have itches and rashes and recurring sores that will continue for the rest of their lives. Symptoms may go away for a few months but then are triggered again by some unknown source. They wake up and have the outbreak again. Some have unique little spots all over their bodies. They go to the dermatologist and are given all sorts of creams but none of it works. One diagnoses it as eczema, the next diagnoses shingles, and the next diagnoses it as tinea versicolor. The doctors often write it up as a new condition, never acknowledging that it's the same problem diagnosed before as something else. These veterans are older, and grew up in tougher times, so they often learn to live with these problems and don't let the symptoms prevent them from working. However, the symptoms do affect that person's life and they should be compensated because something has happened to them that would not have happened to them in the normal American environment. This is an actual battle injury! Unfortunately, I have had to deny cases like this because even although I believed their complaints, the symptoms were not present on the day of examination, and the doctor did not read the history, and my opinion as a non-physician did not matter.

Similarly, Korean War veterans should be compensated for residuals of frostbite, for which the symptoms sometimes only occur during new exposures to cold weather. If they have symptoms that could be residual of a frostbite history, and no other intermediary cause, it should be granted. That was an actual war injury! The medical records from that era were very little to begin with, then many of them were destroyed in a St. Louis records warehouse fire of 1973, so many veterans are currently out of luck with such issues. Those claims require evidence, while Gulf War exposure claims and many mental claims require practically no objective evidence for granting.

Those veterans who have been to Iraq and Afghanistan have also been exposed to heat, sand, and burn pits. *If* it can be shown by objective medical evidence that they do have actual manifestations of any condition related to those exposures, then they should be compensated for it. But in no case should a veteran be compensated just because he went to a certain location. He has already been compensated for being there by the military while he was there; he received either combat pay, imminent danger pay, hostile fire pay, hazardous duty incentive pay, or hardship duty pay. Laws are in place to fairly compensate these veterans for any long-term effects of such exposures and if the symptomology is shown in medical treatment records, then they should be compensated. Service medical records these days are electronic and very extensive, so there's no reason to have to guess about any condition not shown in those records. Gulf War issues are discussed further in a subsequent chapter.

(6) HOW MUCH I$ THE FLEECING ?

Senator William Proxmire's book, *The Fleecing of America,* 1980, is filled with examples of wasteful federal spending, mis-use of hard-earned taxpayer dollars. Most of the examples are short-term contracts that were issued to develop useless products, or to research foolish ideas, of no long-term consequence. They are projects that began and ended, and the money spent was actually "just a drop in the bucket" when considering the federal expense of maintaining a great country like the U.S.A.   Proxmire was also openly critical of many military spending programs but as far as I know he voiced no concerns with payment of veterans' disability, as it was not really being abused during his era of service. But I believe he would roll over in his grave if he could see the current VA budget submission.

The "greatest fleecing" of America, the greatest shearing of the American taxpayer, "a smooth, legalized theft from the taxpayers," is the VA's Disability Compensation program. The sad thing is, it's not a small amount of money, and it's not a short-term contract that will eventually be completed. The VA compensation program is spiraling out of control.   The wasteful fraudulent spending is escalating each year and there is no foreseeable end to it.

According to the *Department of Veterans Affairs FY 2018 Budget Congressional Submission,* in 2018 VA will provide service-connected disability compensation benefits for over 4.6 million veterans and over 420,000 survivors (spouses or children of veterans deceased due to service-connected issues). This disability program is separate from the veterans Pension benefits program (for financially needy *war* veterans) which will serve an additional 289,000 veterans and 204,000 survivors.

In accordance with current law and payment schedules, veterans who are granted service-connected disability compensation are receiving anywhere from $136 to $10,000 per month for the rest of their lives. The total amount of compensation paid out to veterans per year is tremendous, currently about ***$90 billion*** per year. But here's the scary part. Per the *Department of Veterans Affairs – FY 2017 Agency Financial Report*, the compensation *liability* is ***$2.8 trillion dollars***, increased from $2.5 trillion in 2016. The $2.8 trillion includes obligations that will be paid in future years for claims already granted, based on actuarial calculations, even if VA never granted another claim. This is 2.8 trillion dollars of taxpayer money obligated just for *Compensation* benefits, monthly compensation checks to veterans for disabilities that were supposedly incurred during military service, and which are supposedly preventing the veteran from his full employment potential.

The above figures *do not include* veterans' health care, VA hospitals, GI bills, burials, insurance programs, or even disability Pension benefits, and do not include the cost of operations, employee salaries, office leases, etc. The budgeted amount for the entire Department of Veterans Affairs (VA) for 2019 is $198.6 billion, up more than $12 billion from 2018, mostly due to compensation increases.

Additional benefits paid by the VBA in 2017 include *non*service-connected Pension (for financially needy *war* veterans) payments of $5.6 billion, and $243 million in burial benefits for deceased veterans. VA education benefits paid, including the GI Bill benefits (college expenses), and Vocational Rehabilitation and

Employment Program, were over $50 billion in fiscal year 2017, including $1.8 billion for Dependents Educational Allowance (paid to wives and children of 100 percent disabled veterans). The corresponding liabilities for these programs are $87.6 billion for pension, $4.9 billion or burials, and $50.7 billion for education. Each of these programs has problems/atrocities of its own, but the focus of this book is *Disability Service-Connected Compensation*, a benefit awarded to veterans disabled by medical conditions supposedly caused by military service. The amounts for all benefits are increasing greatly each year, as the number of all claims is increasing greatly each year, even though we have less living veterans.

According to *U.S. Veterans Eligibility Trends and Statistics, 2016, prepared by the National Center for Veterans Analysis and Statistics*, from 2007 to 2016 the total veteran population decreased from 23.6 million to 20.4 million, but the number of veterans claiming benefits rose from 38% to 48% (almost half of all veterans alive are now using benefits). Those benefits include education, home loans, and insurance, but health care and/or disability compensation accounted for 76% of the use. The cost of burial benefits remained steady and education benefits actually decreased. By 2016, 4.6 million veterans were receiving *disability* benefits. By 2020 more than 5 million will be receiving disability compensation.

The statistics show that veterans using benefits are more likely to be between the ages of 25 and 34, or over age 65. Why is that? From my personal analysis it's because age 22 to 34 is when they first get out of service and they try to continue on with federal support just because they're veterans. Age 62 to 65 is when those who work choose to retire from the real world and then ask the government to pick up the slack for them. Social security is there for them, and often private retirement funds as well, but they're asking for an additional supplement from us taxpayers just because they once served in the military.

In addition to the $2.8 trillion in obligated compensation payments to the veterans, you must also consider the cost of administering the program, thousands of employees in 56 offices developing and deciding and paying these claims. According to *Department of Veterans Affairs – FY2017 and FY2018 Agency Financial Reports*, the cost of operations for the VBA (Veterans Benefits Administration, not medical facilities) is about $4 billion a year. Rent and utilities is about $170 million including about $80 million just to rent the VBA offices. There are numerous other itemized business expenses too complicated to mention. Again, I am not talking about any medical care or facility of the Veterans Health Administration (VHA). I am only discussing the Veterans Benefits Administration (VBA) which includes 58 VBA offices, 56 of them processing compensation claims. These offices typically occupy multi-story federal buildings owned or leased by the government and maintained under GSA contracts. Each office has hundreds of non-medically-trained non-judicial-trained clerical workers clicking on computers, spitting out letters to veterans. The administrative expenses in support of just the compensation program is more than $2 billion for 2018.

The most wasteful expense of administering the program (other than the veterans' payments) is the payment of employee salaries and employee benefits. A GAO (Government Accountability Office) report to the Senate Budget Committee, GAO-4-215, *Federal Workforce: Recent Trends in Federal Civilian Employment and Compensation* dated January 2014, showed spending on pay and benefits for all VA employees increased by 10.5 billion dollars, a 53.4% increase (more than doubled) during the period of 2004 through 2012, and 94% of that increase was from 2008 to 2012. This was justified as due to "increased demand for medical and health-related services related to the wars in Iraq and Afghanistan." But these wars have been going on since 1990 and the number of injuries in this decade has been no greater than at any time in the '90s, so the increase in claims and medical care is for other reasons, to be explained later.

The VHA (*health* administration) had 334,637 employees in 2017 including doctors, nurses, other medical professionals and admin staff for the medical facilities, (aside from all the private physicians contracted to perform exams and provide medical care).

I am not suggesting any reduction in medical facilities, care, or employees; in fact, at the current rate of demand we need more health facilities and health employees. However, if some of the fraudulent and frivolous claims could be eliminated, this would reduce the number of needed health care workers, examiners, and health care facilities, and it would free up existing resources for true medical care.

But this book is about Veterans Benefits Administration (VBA) which in 2016 employed 22,152 employees, with average annual salary of $70,000, but many earning more than $100,000, all totaling $1.55 billion in salaries for that year.   The 2018 budget request projected almost $3 billion in salaries for VBA, not for people performing any medical care, but just various benefits claims processors and their supervisors.   The budget request for 2018 shows that 15,527 employees are assigned specifically for processing (or supervising) disability compensation benefits.

Each of the 56 benefits offices handling compensation claims has hundreds of Rating Specialists earning $55,000 to $95,000 per year (average $80,000 per year), hundreds of Veterans Service Representatives (claims developers), earning $35,000 to $75,000 per year, plus Claims Assistants, File Clerks, and other clerical staff assistants earning $30,000 to $60,000.   Ever since the 2012 directive to get claims processed within 125 days, overtime has been pushed and frequently mandated, so many claims Raters are earning an additional $30,000 each year for overtime worked, resulting in a six-digit annual income. $100,000 is not an extreme salary, but for a position which requires (permits) no thoughtful decision making, no creativity, no supervising, and no personal communication with clients, it is unreasonable.

Besides the actual claims processors there are at least 6 levels of Supervision in each office: dozens of team coaches and assistant coaches, several assistant service center managers, a service center manager, an assistant director and a director, and these are GS-13 to GM-15, earning from $88,000 to $150,000 per year. Then there's more at the very top, the president's cabinet and department heads, earning more than $200,000 per year.

We'll have to keep some of these employees because we need a Veterans Benefits Administration to administer benefits to the truly war-injured veterans. However, if we remove the fraud and non-war injuries, one or two offices should be enough to handle the legitimate case load, not 56 offices. The seriously-injured war veterans' claims are already processed separately from the rest; they are "case-managed." They were "hand-carried" before everything went on-line, and now they're computer red-flagged, and these claims are sped through within days of the soldier's discharge. "Case management" is done for a veteran who is seriously (SI) or very seriously injured (VSI), or who has lost a body part (SCP), or who is terminally ill. These cases are never seen at the regular VBA offices.

The VBA was set up to have one office in each state and territory, or two offices in the largest states, and an office would handle only the veterans living in that state. Now with automation, any claim can be worked by any of the 56 offices, and claims are deliberately mixed up and distributed to provide more equality in rating decisions. Therefore, all claims could technically be worked out of one or two offices anywhere. It would reduce overhead costs and would lead to more consistency in ratings.

Just what the total cost to maintain and operate a federal building to accommodate these workers is, I can't imagine, but millions of dollars are spent in ongoing projects to upgrade and maintain the buildings. In addition to property leases and construction, there are huge expenses in electricity and water, internet and telephone services, cleaning, and security.

Around 2014 the VA started allowing many of the claims developers and raters to work at home with their own computers, but at no savings to the government, as they still had to maintain a cubicle and computer in the office building and come in to work at least once a week. In 2015, a greater number were sent home and some office space was consolidated, so that the employees shared spaces, used by different ones on different days. But at the time of that program (E-CAP) the government had to issue federally-owned equipment including laptops, monitors and keyboards to each at-home employee and started paying millions for security programs and bandwidth for those employees to access the government sites through internet.

At the same time that VBA's system is becoming more automated for the claims processors, the system also now allows veterans to upload their own claims on-line and upload evidence to their own files. The 2018 budget included over $38 million for the VBMS ("the VB Mess") technology/computer system for processing claims, plus $115 million for VCIP, a new document conversion system, over $3 million for NWQ claims/records on-line system, $26 million for centralized mail, $12 million for training, etc. etc. and etc. The full budget request can be seen on line at www.va.gov/budget.

The cost of this program is almost unimaginable and unbelievable. The intent of the program is good and legitimate but it has been improperly administered until it is now mostly waste, and this money could be put to so much better use. With $2.8 trillion we could provide free community college for everyone in America who wants it! Or based on the average cost of a good private 4-year college being $30,000 per year, we could put 23 million people through all four years of college!

We are currently (in 2018) indebted to pay $2.8 trillion even if we never grant another claim. We're paying out at a rate of $90 billion per year, increasing annually. That's just the deposits to veterans' accounts, not including billions of dollars of VBA operating expenses to administer this injustice. Every year the VBA is receiving a greater number of claims and granting more and higher amounts to able-bodied veterans who are just playing the entitlement game, milking the hard-working taxpayers. The U.S. government is already in debt for 21 trillion dollars and this program is one of the reasons for it! Less revenue and more wasteful spending because veterans who should be working are being rewarded for not working!

(7) IS THE GULF WAR TO BLAME?

In *The Three Trillion Dollar War: The True Cost of the Iraq Conflict,* a book by Linda J. Bilmes and Joseph E. Stiglitz published in 2008, the authors explained that the true cost of the Iraq War was, at that time, $3 trillion and counting, rather than the $50 billion projected by the White House, because many things had not been considered, including the cost of ongoing lifelong benefits for the soldiers of that war. Some of those benefits are paid for legitimate physical or mental injuries from the war and I believe that's what they meant; they weren't even talking about unjustified spending. But in my experience, much of it is totally unjustified spending to support veterans for the rest of their lives, for either no true injury at all, or for conditions totally unrelated to their military service.   If we keep taking on new wars, keep increasing our military, and keep granting unwarranted benefits the way it is currently being done, the VA compensation system could become the hidden unsuspecting cause of the financial collapse of the US government.

Now 10 years after *The Three Trillion Dollar War*, the war is still going on, and current news reports say the Southeast Asia war has cost America over $5 trillion, with nothing to show for it. I expect this $5 trillion includes the cost of equipment and weapons for both our soldiers and the foreign country soldiers, all sorts of training expenses, construction and reconstruction expenses, and salaries and medical care of all soldiers involved. I'm not sure if this estimate includes the trillions of dollars that VA will continue paying all those soldiers when they return home. A very small number of the soldiers will actually either die or receive significant war injuries for which they will certainly deserve every benefit we can possibly provide. But almost every single Gulf War veteran will claim PTSD as well as chronic fatigue, gastrointestinal issues and respiratory issues due to exposure to sand and burn pits. The VA regulations and policies have become so lax that practically everyone who claims these conditions will be granted, and these veterans will never "improve." They will continue to request increases until they are receiving 100% disability or IU (which is also 100%). It is a disgrace.

A *Military Times* article "Report: Wars in Iraq, Afghanistan cost almost $5 trillion so far" dated September 12, 2016 noted that $4.79 trillion had already been spent plus billions already requested for future spending on the wars. Of that total they calculated more than $1.2 trillion in increased and future costs for veterans' health care, not including other VA benefits such as education benefits and home loans. They didn't say anything about "disability compensation," only "veterans health care" as if these were one and the same, and they are not; they are entirely different appropriations. It's amazing how even "military" reports don't even recognize the compensation problem and how the military is feeding this disability-grabbing frenzy.

Disability compensation, managed/issued by the Veterans Benefits Administration (VBA), is a whole separate thing from veterans' health care which is managed by Veterans Health Administration (VHA), and, war or no war, the compensation payouts will continue to increase each year.

The *Military Times* article and others like it have quoted statistics from an independent study done by Watson Institute International & Public Affairs, Brown University, entitled "US Budgetary Costs of Wars through 2016: $4.79 Trillion and Counting, Summary of Costs of Wars in Iraq, Syria, Afghanistan and Pakistan and Homeland Security." That paper updated a similar report first released by Neta C. Crawford, Boston University, on June 25, 2014. Both reports noted that about 2 million of the 2.75 million people who have been deployed to the war zones, have left the military and entered the VA system, and that about 52,000 were officially wounded in action in Afghanistan and Iraq or were evacuated from the war zones due to disease or non-hostile injuries. So what are the other 1.9 million of them claiming? The updated report noted that due to a great increase in veterans' claims, the VA had nearly doubled in size from 2001 to 2016, now up to 350,000 VA workers (including VHA, VBA, and VCA) and that number of staffers was projected to grow over the next several years to keep up with the increasing claims.

The report states that GWOT (Gulf War) veterans have been making more claims for injury and illness than earlier veterans because they have a higher rate of service-connected disability than veterans of previous wars. I'm not so sure of that. It's true that they are more likely to submit claims, and that more service-connection has been granted, yes, but medical evidence of more war injuries, not really.

Specifically, the report said that more than 1600 soldiers in the post-911 wars have had battle injuries requiring major limb amputations as of late 2015. I am fully in support of those 1600 veterans! I fully concur with paying those veterans 100 percent disability, even if they are able to work, as many amputees do, some even run races, or return to battle, and many otherwise function well with artificial limbs. I fully agree with giving them the maximum benefit to include the highest payments, housing modifications, automobile modifications, and educational benefits for their wives and children. But even if you give every one of them a million dollars that is still only $1.6 billion, a drop in the bucket of the VA compensation payments total, currently $90 billion per year.

The report says that these Gulf War veterans have greater incidence of skeletal injury, posttraumatic stress disorder (PTSD), and traumatic brain injury (TBI) than has been shown in other wars. It says that as of 2014, about 700,000 GWOT veterans had been classified as 30 percent or more disabled, and that more than 327,000 GWOT veterans have been diagnosed with TBI. What those report-writers don't realize is that a TBI diagnosis is almost always based on totally subjective symptoms, not requiring any documented head injury, as discussed in my future chapter on TBI.

The report estimated that *war related* spending from FY 2001 through 2016 was for VA medical care about $37.4 billion, and for VA disability benefits about $53.7 billion, in addition to social security disability payments of $6.5 billion. Even if those were the "war related" costs of Gulf War injuries and illnesses over a period of 16 years, that is very small compared to the total amount of disability benefits paid over that period of time, mostly paid for non-war-related conditions.

So, no, there is no evidence to support that the drastic increase in disability benefits paid is due to actual Gulf War injuries.

(8) MAD INCREASE IN CLAIMS AND BENEFITS

From 2000 to 2014, the population of living veterans fell by about 17 percent, but the number of veterans receiving compensation climbed by 55 percent, and VA disability payments tripled during that 14 years from $20 billion to $60 billion per year. Now 4 years later, the payments have risen to $90 billion per year. According to the VA's *2016 Annual Benefits Report,* in just 4 years from 2012 to 2016, the number of compensation recipients rose from 3.5 million to 4.4 million.

More alarming is how the level of claimed disability is rising for individual veterans, resulting in higher amounts paid to each claimant. In just one year, from 2015 to 2016, the number of veterans receiving 80% disability rose 10%, receiving 90% disability rose 14%, and receiving 100% disability rose 10%.

The number of veterans being granted Individual Unemployability (IU), payment at the 100% rate because they cannot work, is rising ridiculously, and VA doesn't even have an adequate system for verifying a veteran's income. A review by the

Government Accountability Office in 2015 found that from fiscal years 2009 through 2013, there was a 22% increase in IU granted, with a 73% increase in recipients aged 75 or older! Of the new beneficiaries in 2013 (first granted in 2013) about 2,800 of them were over 75 years old, and more than 400 of them were over 90 years old! Of course they're not working; should they be? This is totally out of the realm of what IU is meant to be. It was intended to pay a veteran who would be working if he hadn't been rendered incapable of work due to military injuries. I'm sure the data for the past 3 years would be even more shocking, but it doesn't seem to be readily accessible, despite VA's proclaimed "transparency."

Another ridiculous increase is the number of veterans receiving Special Monthly Compensation (SMC) based on "statutory housebound" which is granted automatically to anyone meeting the criteria. To qualify for this, a veteran needs one disability evaluated 100% and at least one other condition evaluated at 50% or more. That sounds pretty serious but in fact there are plenty of fully functioning working veterans receiving this benefit because it doesn't take much to get evaluated 100% for a heart condition or for PTSD, and then if you have sleep apnea at 50%, you get the SMC. This added benefit *doubles* the amount of compensation one receives. A veteran with no family would receive about $2,974 for a 100% total evaluation, but with this SMC he receives $6,303 per month!   A veteran with wife and 3 children would receive about $3,426 for his 100%, but add the SMC and he gets $7,207 per month! Add hundreds more to that if he has more kids or dependent parents or kids in college or if his wife needs A&A. It's an unfathomable payment to someone who might be also receiving a normal paycheck for full-time work, or a retirement annuity and social security.

The cost of the compensation program annual increase is only minutely due to annual cost of living increases; that is really not an issue. The annual VA compensation obligations are increasing significantly because each year a larger number of new claims are received, the average number of issues on each claim is going up, more increase claims are being received and granted, and more veterans are being granted for issues that were never granted in the past. This chapter is about the numbers, the increase in number of granted claims and amounts of disability being granted. This information is derived from the VA annual congressional budget submissions. The last 10 years of budget submissions are readily available for anyone's review on the VA website, *https://www.va.gov/budget/products.asp.*

The *VA 2017 Budget Request* reported that the number of veterans receiving VA disability service-connected compensation had increased over 78% since 1999, from just over 2.3 million in 1999 to over 4.1 million in 2015, and that total VA funding had grown by nearly 86% from 2009. The number receiving compensation in 2018 is about 5 million, reflecting an increasing number of claims and higher percentage of grants.

The average level of disability and corresponding higher individual payments is also increasing each year. The average degree of disability has risen from 43.5% in 2011 to 51.5% in 2017. That is in part due to more claims for increase each year. In 2017, 6.5% of those already receiving compensation received increases, up from 5.9% receiving increases the previous year. The average amount of increase also continuously rises; the average increased rating in 2016 was up to 72% disability, and by 2017 the average increased rating was up to 73.3% disability. The amount being paid to veterans receiving Individual Unemployability (100% payments for a lesser level of disability) rose from $282.5 million in 2011 to $348.5 million in 2017. The amounts being paid to veterans receiving special monthly compensation (in addition to 100%) rose from $402.8 million in 2011 to $648.3 million in 2017. In 2018, compensation payments range from $136 to $10,000 a month or more, averaging $16,700 per year, and that's up from an average of $12,600 per year just 10 years ago.

The *VA Congressional Submission, FY 2019,* reported that "The VA budget has grown far faster than federal spending or GDP over the past 10 years." A close look at the details of the past 10 annual budget submissions reveals significant annual increases in the *compensation* portion of the budgets. The whole VA budget for

2019 is almost $200 billion dollars, including medical care and administrative costs for all the multiple VA programs. Just the compensation pay-out-to-veterans portion of that obligation is $93.4 billion, up from $37.7 billion in 2008. Compensation obligations for the period of 1990 to present (18 years since Gulf War began) is greater than all the compensation paid from WWII, Korean Conflict, Vietnam Era, and all peacetimes combined.

The amount of compensation a veteran receives has nothing to do with how many years he spent in service, nor what rank he attained in service, nor whether he works, nor how wealthy he may be. It only depends on the level of disability he has been granted by the VA benefits office, and how many dependents the veteran has. For example, a veteran who is single with no dependents and has only one service-connected condition rated 10% would only be receiving $136 a month in 2018. A veteran with one severe condition 100 percent disabling, or with multiple service-connection conditions totaling 100 percent, and receiving high levels of Special Monthly Compensation, and who has several dependents such as a wife, dependent parents, college-kids, or small children, can be receiving as much as $10,000 a month from VA for the rest of his life. He may also qualify for such ancillary benefits as Housing Allowance or Housing Adaptation Grant, Automobile Allowance, and Clothing Allowance. The wife or children may continue to receive payments (Dependents Indemnity Compensation) after his death, and his dependents are also entitled to free education (Dependents Educational Allowance).

The *2018 VA Congressional Submission* provides the following explanation for why in 2019 the compensation obligations will increase by $5.9 billion more than 2018. Quotations indicate direct quotes from the report; parenthesis and italics were added by me. For one thing, VA reported that "claim production levels will remain high through 2019 due to the efficiency gains realized from the transformational process changes and technological advances" and that this will result in an "increased veteran caseload" (more veterans being paid). Meanwhile, VA noted that based on historical data, the 'average degree of disability' is forecasted to continue increasing as it has been doing each year. VA reported that the average degree of disability for a veteran increased from 48.9% in 2015 to 50.1% in 2016, and that this is "consistent with the average rate of increase since 2010." They further explained that "additional regulations, legislation, and the increasing number of completed claims as well as *number of issues per claim* have contributed to *rising disability ratings" (rising total evaluation or total degree of disability assigned to each veteran)*. Therefore, the increase in budget is needed due to the "increasing average degree of disability" and "increases in average degree of disability cause significant increases in average payments." They don't bother to explain *why* the average disability level is higher, but I am trying to explain it.

The *VA Congressional Submission (Budget), FY 2012* reported that the number of veterans receiving compensation has increased by more than 39 percent since 1999, from just over 2.3 million veteran recipients in 1999 to nearly 3.2 million veterans in 2010. VA authority attributed the increase to the ongoing Gulf War (although it had already been going on for 9 years in 1999) and the ongoing addition of new Agent Orange presumptive conditions (yes that is one valid reason). VA anticipates that *reopened* claims for *increased* benefits will also continue to grow as the veterans get older and their conditions worsen. During 2010, *reopened* disability compensation claims, including previously already denied or claims for increase, comprised 59 percent of all disability claims received. The total number of disability claims received increased from 674,219 in 2001 to 1,192,346 during 2010, while *original* disability claims with *eight or more claimed issues* increased from 22,776 in 2001 to 70,620 during 2010.

The *VA Congressional Submissions, FY 2017, FY 2018 and FY 2019*, showed that VBA has completed over a million disability claims per year for the last eight consecutive years, including about 1.4 million compensation and pension claims for each of the last few years.

The number of people receiving compensation (veterans and survivors) in 2011 was 3.3 million. By 2018, there were about 5 million recipients, averaging $16,700 per year. It is estimated that in 2019 there will be about 5.3 million recipients, with average payment of $17,200, and in 2020 about 5.5 million will receive payments averaging $17,900 per year. (A separate 469,000 veterans and survivors will receive pension payments averaging $12,000 per year.)

The *VA Congressional Submission, FY 2019*, shows that compensation paid in 2017 was about $80 billion, projected for 2018 is $86.2 billion, projected for 2019 is $93.4 billion, and projected for 2020 is $101 billion.

The Veterans Benefits Administration (VBA) processes and pays many other types of veterans claims and even though compensation is by far the biggest and most wasteful program, on budget reports those dollar figures are tucked in amongst all the lesser programs. A quick review of the annual budget request is impossible; you'll likely get bored and give up before you reach the end of the section on the Veterans Cemetery Administration (VCA) which always comes first. If you do reach the VBA section, ignore the education, housing, and insurance benefit portions. When you reach the "Compensation and Pension" section which puts both programs in the same charts, you must pick out the parts that apply to compensation versus burial and pension benefits (two much smaller programs).

The budget reports show that VBA paid *non*service-connected Pension (for financially needy *war* veterans) about $5.4 billion in 2017, about $5.5 billion in 2018, and it's expected to be about $5.6 billion in 2019 and $5.8 billion in 2020. Those pension benefits were paid to about 290,000 veterans and 204,000 surviving spouses or children in 2018. The number of *pension* recipients is expected to *decrease* in 2019, and further decrease in 2020 as the World War II and Vietnam Veterans who took this benefit are gradually dying. The benefit is out there just the same as always, but now all the Gulf War veterans are foregoing the pension which is a lesser benefit, as they all attempt to obtain a greater benefit through disability compensation.

(9) BUT WHY HAVE CLAIMS INCREASED?

The primary reason more claims and bigger claims are being received is not because of soldiers returning from Iraq and Afghanistan. The biggest factor is that VA laws and policies have become increasingly "liberalized," eased and slackened, essentially inviting and encouraging more claims.   In the past a condition wasn't granted unless there was proof it started in service, but now there are all sorts of medical opinions "associating" various conditions to things that *might* have happened in service. Opinions are being used to support mental conditions where there was no problem in service, current chronic conditions that *may* have resulted from an acute condition shown in service, and chronic diseases such as diabetes and cancers that *may* be related to herbicide exposures or contaminated water in service.   More veterans are filing more claims, for a greater number of issues, and are filing repetitive increase claims demanding higher evaluations.

Besides the laws making disability easier to grant, other laws (Veterans Claims Assistance Acts) have required VA to help veterans more in submitting their claims and supporting evidence. VA has even sent letters to veterans soliciting claims. They solicited claims for posttraumatic stress disorder (PTSD) when the granting criteria was loosened (fear and easing standard), and claims for herbicide-related issues from all Vietnam Era veterans, and contaminated water-related claims from soldiers who served at Camp LeJeune. They have basically invited and at the very least encouraged exposure-related claims from all soldiers who ever served in Southeast Asia (Gulf War syndromes).

One of the biggest reasons for more claims is that the veterans now have internet access where they can find dozens of websites and blogs giving them support and advice on how to "work the system." Veterans can now submit their claims and evidence on line and they can review their own files and keep track of the progress of their claims. Websites give them tips on exactly what wording to use or what symptoms to claim in order to get their claims granted.

The Veteran Service Organizations (VSOs) such as Veterans of Foreign Wars (VFW) and American Legion (these are not VA offices) are also providing veterans with "cheat sheets" giving them specific language to put on the claims. It's rather telling to see two different veterans claiming the exact same scenario happened to them in Vietnam (for PTSD), or claiming the exact same progression of symptoms have occurred from service to the present, and it is clear that this statement was copied word for word from a "template" provided by the VSO. I have even seen cases where they sent the entire template in with their claim, giving multiple scenarios and symptoms. They were only supposed to pick out a few of these things to claim, but they just sent the whole template in lieu of submitting a list of issues, and it even says "template" or "suggestions" or "examples" across the top of the page. But VA accepted this as their claim.

Another place the veterans get their ideas for their claims is from sitting in the waiting rooms at the VA hospitals and clinics. Every time I have ever been there I would overhear conversations about "what can I do to get up to 100%?" Every veteran in there has his story which he tells over and over week after week about how first the VA denied their claim, then they finally got granted because an "attorney" at the VFW argued the case for them.

The VA refers to the representatives working/volunteering at the Veterans Service Organizations as the veteran's "Power of Attorney" or "POA" so the veterans assume these are attorneys, but they are not. POAs don't even need a high school diploma to do that job. Most of them do it because they learned how to gain the system on their own claim and now they want to share the wealth. It's a power trip.

So the typical veteran's story goes that after he and his POA got the first 10% granted they put in for an increase year after year and finally it went up to 30% then up to 50% then up to 70%. Then they fought until they got Individual Unemployability (IU) so now they're getting paid the 100% rate, but they are still trying to get a Permanent and Total actual schedular 100%, because if they get that then their family will be taken care of forever! They pass this story on and on, along with tips on how to act on exam if you want to get your claim granted or your evaluation increased. For example, if it's a back exam you must only lean over a tiny bit when the examiner asked you to bend over. If it's a leg condition, you walk in with a limp or a cane and only bend the knee a little on the range-of-motion testing. If it's a mental condition you need an increase for, you go unbathed and unshaven for 3 days before the exam. You wear dirty clothes and drink a shot or two of whiskey just before you go in. If it's a hearing exam, just don't raise your hand when you hear the sounds. And no matter what the condition is, when the doctor goes down the list of symptoms, just say yes for every one of them.

So the veterans talk, and they research, and they submit claim after claim. It's a game, a challenge, to get what they believe they "deserve" because they once served in the U.S. military. They have no consideration for the middle-class taxpayers who are actually paying them these benefits and no consideration of how this abuse of appropriations adds to the pool of debt that will drown America.

(10) HOW MUCH WILL A VETERAN RECEIVE?

There was a time when I'd see a very young man driving a brand-new Cadillac or wearing $300 tennis shoes, and I would assume he was either a drug dealer or a pimp, or that he had won a big lottery or a wrongful death lawsuit.   Nowadays I realize he might be a software engineer, but the odds are this person is simply drawing a lot of VA disability compensation in addition to his regular income.

Currently in 2018, veteran disability compensation is paid at a rate of anywhere from $136 per month for 10% disability, to over $10,000 per month for 100% disability with special monthly compensation (SMC) and enough claimed dependents.   Regular 100% disability is about $3000 per month for a veteran with no wife or children and receiving no special monthly compensation (SMC). If he qualifies for SMC based on being truly housebound or by simply meeting the "statutory housebound" criteria by having one issue 100% and another issue at least 50% (and still being able to leave home, drive, work, play golf, etc), his monthly payment doubles to over *$6,000 a month*! The veteran gets extra if he has a spouse or child or dependent parent, or 8 step-children; he gets extra for every one of them. Many veterans marry a person with a horde of children from a previous marriage just to increase their VA compensation, and those kids may already be getting support from any number of other sources. He also doesn't have to live with his spouse or kids to collect based on their existence. VA has gotten so lax in recent years that the claims workers don't even have to review marriage or birth certificates, they just take the veteran's word for it over the phone.

For the most extreme example of compensation payment, based on the 2018 calculator, a veteran with 100% total evaluation and also drawing the highest level of special monthly compensation (SMC), who has a spouse, 2 dependent parents, and 1 dependent child, will draw $12,325.25 per month ($3261.10 for 100% plus $9064.15 for SMC). Each additional child under 18 will add 82.38, and each college-attending child will add $266.13 per month. If his wife also qualifies for aid and attendance that adds another $152.06. So if he has 2 kids in college and 4 kids under the age of 18, he will be receiving $13,258.71 per month, which is $159,080.52 per year, just from the VA. And that is all tax-free income; he will pay no income tax on this! Not a bad little family income. And here's a kicker. Since this 100% veteran is a military retiree, he is also drawing every penny of his earned retirement from the military department. If he retired as a high-ranking officer with 40 years of service that could be more than $15,000 a month, or $180,000 a year before taxes. Military retire pay is taxable so that might reduce his net to $135,000, but added to his VA disability he is bringing in more than *$315,000* net cash per year based only on military service. Does that make any sense at all?   Yes, this is an extreme example, showing the high end of the pay scale, but entirely possible.

The average veteran filing a claim probably served only 3 years and left service as a E-4, so he's not drawing any retirement pay from the military. But after serving only 3 years in the military he could still bring in over $150,000 a year for the rest of his life from the VA based on claimed service-related disabilities! The fact he served only a few years, or in some cases literally only a few weeks has no bearing on his payment!   Worse yet, he may have been demoted to the lowest grade of E-1 for bad conduct in service, or he may have been discharged from service before completion of his first period of service, and he will still qualify for compensation.

Most soldiers who get kicked out because they want out or because the military wants them out, still manage to be awarded a "general" discharge or "under honorable conditions" discharge and these allow payment of all benefits. The only time VA does not have to pay compensation is if the discharge reason is specifically stated as "misconduct" or "bad conduct." But even in these cases, it is often paid. Although the military service has found a soldier's conduct to be unworthy of continuing military service, the VA will review the facts of why he was discharged and prepare a "Character of Discharge" decision of their own, many times resulting in the decision that the service was "honorable for VA purposes." There is no rhyme or reason as to which cases will be considered honorable for VA purposes. It just depends on the individual doing the review and these people have no legal expertise or training in helping them make this decision. If the general public could see the history of many of these veterans they would certainly not approve of their hard-earned tax dollars going to support these bums who were a disgrace to the military.

If a veteran was truly injured in battle then, regardless of honorable service, I am all for paying all this money. He did sign up for the job. He did know the risks involved. But he did suffer and now he may not be able to fulfill in the private sector what would have been his full potential. If he has suffered loss of limbs, or had a blast to the head, or serious internal wounds from gunshots or explosions, then I am all for paying him and supporting his family. Perhaps most readers think that is what VA disability is all about. That is indeed what VA disability *should* be all about. However, the number of seriously injured veterans is negligible when considering the total number of veterans receiving disability payments.

(11) ENTITLEMENT REFORM – BRING IT ON

In 2018, "entitlement reform" is a top priority for some members of Congress who realize there is a lot of fraud and abuse in the Social Security Administration (SSA) disability program, so they want to clean that up and "get the able-bodied population back to work." News reports and mid-term election debates discuss cracking down on disability fraud, noting it's time to stop using hard-earned tax dollars to support some who are milking the SSA system instead of working to support themselves. But I haven't heard a word about reforming VA's disability entitlement programs.

An "entitlement program" by definition, per Auburn University, *A Glossary of Political Economy Terms,* is "The kind of government program that provides individuals with personal financial benefits (or sometimes special government-provided goods or services) to which an indefinite (but usually rather large) number of potential beneficiaries have a legal *right* (enforceable in court, if necessary) whenever they meet eligibility conditions that are specified by the standing law that authorizes the program" and it goes on to provide a list of examples including Veterans'

Administration programs. I propose that to tackle "entitlement reform," Congress should start with the biggest offender of them all.

The most abused entitlement program is VA disability compensation. Through this program, especially "Individual Unemployability" (IU) which is the VA's "can't work" program, millions of able-bodied veterans, aged 20 to 60, are not working because the VA is paying them 100 percent disability and they are not allowed to work while receiving IU. Many others are working full time *and* receiving 100 percent schedular compensation. That is separate from the IU issue, but also must be changed. A person working full time should not be receiving 100 percent compensation from VA, because he is obviously *not* totally disabled.

Fraud in the SSA program is mostly small stuff. Some poor people are receiving SSA benefits while not reporting some minor under-the-table earnings. Others are claiming disability and drawing a very meager SSA check when they could be working a minimum wage job, but they couldn't afford to pay for daycare, so they're better off on welfare. But the fraud in VA disability claims is huge, blatant and shameless. Veterans are paid "disability" compensation when they are clearly not disabled, even if they are working full-time in high-salaried federal jobs! Those who have been awarded Individual Unemployabilty or Pension can't legally draw the benefit if working, so they opt not to work.

I've seen some fraudulent SSA claims in the files of veterans because the VA reciprocates with SSA for veterans' records. If a veteran files for SSA disability, SSA will obtain the VA medical records for use in making their decisions. In turn the VA will obtain the SSA records for use in rating pension and unemployability. In many cases the SSA does deny the claims of malingerers and freeloaders. Their examiners will often state, "Although you have some disabilities, the evidence does not show that you are too disabled to perform some type of work."

VA pays little attention to what SSA has decided. VA will grant disability anyway based on VA exams and any lies submitted by the claimant. Ironically, once the VA has granted disability, the SSA is compelled to reverse its decision based on VA records. The veteran shows SSA that VA has found him to be totally disabled, so SSA follows suit. To straighten up the VA program would certainly lead to less abuse of the SSA program and would save this country trillions of taxpayer dollars.

Meanwhile, there are so many hard-working American couples and single parents who are not receiving any social handouts and are struggling paycheck to paycheck. They cannot qualify for any government social services help because they are "working" or "earning too much money" or "don't have a child under 6 years old" or "don't have a disabled adult in the household" despite the fact that even two adults making minimum wage do not earn enough to properly support a family in this day and age. These families cannot afford things most Americans now take for granted such as cell phones, satellite TV, internet, Christmas gifts, vacations, and new clothes. They shop at Goodwill and eat spaghetti with no meatballs. They certainly can't afford health insurance or college tuition. Many of the older generations are helping to support them, with no tax write off.   While the poorest working-class people get no help at all, we supplement the income of veterans who are earning high salaries or drawing retirement and social security. I appreciate veterans for having served and I'm all for their benefits such as VA loans and GI Bills, but they have never been promised a continuing monthly income after service and I do not approve of supporting them with my tax dollars just because they're veterans.

If all this VA expense was for the service of "battle-injured" veterans, I would have no complaint. The problem is, the large majority of this expense is just a waste.   The truly deserving and warranted cases for disability compensation could be handled by a few hundred employees in *one* office building.

A VA employee can work 10 years processing disability claims and never see a single case that involves a soldier getting a bullet wound or shrapnel wound or IED blast injury. Those injuries do happen but the claims are never seen at most of the 56 claims offices.

If a solder is seriously injured in battle he gets emergency treatment on location, sometimes even goes to a local private hospital, and then is transferred to Walter Reed National Military

Medical Center (WRNMMC) in Bethesda Maryland. He remains on the military payroll until his condition has stabilized. Meanwhile VA field representatives there begin processing the claim so that by the time the soldier is discharged (becomes a veteran) his VA benefits are ready to go into effect. He goes directly from receiving military pay to receiving VA disability compensation pay.

There are also pre-discharge programs whereby any serviceman can file a disability claim before being discharged. These claims are handled by the Winston-Salem special regional office. The other 55 VA benefits offices are handling nothing but a bunch of frivolous claims for conditions not truly caused by military service.

When President Lincoln committed our taxpayers to paying VA benefits, he said it was to provide for "those who have borne the battle" and their surviving spouses and children. This is very clear. "Those who have borne the battle." That means that if a soldier gets a leg or arm blown off in war, when he comes home, he cannot provide for his family the way he would have been able to do, so VA will compensate for that degree of disability. If he's had several limbs blown off, or brain damage, he may be truly 100 percent disabled and never expected to work again at gainful employment. If he's only lost one hand or one eye or has some internal parasitic disease from foreign swamps, he may be 50 percent disabled. This means he is expected to be able to earn only 50 percent of what he would have before the injuries, so he should go ahead and work and earn that, and the VA will pay him the other 50 percent to *compensate* for the reduction. The entire VA regulation (38 CFR, Chapters 3 and 4) regarding disability compensation, repeat over and over that the amount of disability compensation paid, or the evaluation percentage granted, is to be based on the degree of disability, specifically the degree to which the person's ability to perform work has been reduced.

Reform of this VA program requires cracking down on dishonest claims, but it also requires cracking down on the VA, to stop the improper granting of high disability payments to able-bodied working men and women, and to older veterans who have stopped working by choice, because they're retired!

(12) HISTORY OF VETERANS' COMPENSATION

***"To care for him who shall have borne the battle
and for his widow, and his orphan"***

A complete history of Veterans Affairs as well as the Veterans Benefits Administration programs can be found on www.va.gov and I don't intend to duplicate it in this book. The VA website "history" explains how our ancestors have graciously provided benefits to war veterans since 1636 under various named programs, and the U.S. government has provided benefits to war veterans since the 18th century American Revolutionary War. The official federal agency, the Veterans Administration, was established in 1930, and was upgraded to the cabinet-level Department of Veterans Affairs in 1989.

The non-surprising common thread to all the programs for almost four centuries was that the benefits were intended for "war veterans." For many years if you served in the military at all you were in a war; that's why you were drafted. Since 1973 we have had an "all volunteer" military, and actually a small percent of current day soldiers ever fight in a war. Even if they do go to serve a year in Iraq or Afghanistan, most of them do not see battle. The facilities provided on those foreign bases rival the posts in America. They have gyms, movies, air conditioning, internet service, hot meals with dessert, basically all the comforts of home, but they're getting paid bonuses due to being "activated" to an overseas hostile territory. I have spoken to and read the stories of many veterans who served in Iraq or Afghanistan who say they never saw any semblance of battle, never heard an explosion, and never feared for their life. However, anyone who served in any place where war has been declared, during the official periods of war, is considered to have been in war. They do get the benefits of war pay while they're there and they do get the advantage of having served in war when they later apply for VA disability.

In 1865, near the end of the Civil War, Abraham Lincoln vowed in his 2nd Inaugural Address that our government (i.e. American taxpayers) would ***"care for him who shall have borne the battle and for his widow, and his orphan."*** With these words President Lincoln affirmed the government's obligation to care for those *injured during war* and to provide for the families of those who *perished on the battlefield.* The statement, *which is the current official motto and mission of the Department of Veterans Affairs,* means to me that America will compensate the soldier who was severely injured in "battle", i.e. in the course of war, and injured to the extent that he could no longer work to support himself and his family, and that the government will also take care of the families of those who *died* in battle or of a battle injury.

The result of this mission statement is that the VA has developed two "disability" programs for providing a monthly paycheck to veterans. These are Nonservice-Connected Pension and Service-Connected Compensation.

Nonservice-Connected Pension is a payment for financially needy veterans who have served in war time, even if they didn't actually serve in combat, as long as they served during the years officially designated as World War I (1917-1918), World War II (1941-1946), Korean Conflict (1950-1955), Vietnam War (1961-1975), or Gulf War (1990 to present). That's right, anyone who has served any time in the past 28 years is eligible, regardless of combat experience or injury. If a war era veteran's income falls below the poverty level and he has very little net worth, and he's too disabled to work for any reason, then VA will pay him Nonservice-Connected Pension (previously called war pension) just because he has the financial need. If he's over 65, he doesn't even have to show any disability at all, and at any age the disability never has to be due to any injury or event in service. If he's drawing Social Security benefits, the VA benefit will only be the supplemental amount needed to bring the SSA amount up to the current federal poverty level (about $12,000 for a single claimant or $25,000 for a family of four in 2018). He will receive additional if he has dependent family members, and additional is warranted if he is so disabled as to be in need of regular aid and attendance with performing activities of daily living such as toileting, eating, bathing, and dressing.

The VA Pension program is also full of fraud and abuse. Pension is being paid to veterans who've been dead for years, and is being paid to many veterans who are not needy but who have transferred all their assets into the names of their children or trust funds. I don't plan to go into detail about Pension. This book is intended only to expound the problems of the *Service-connected Compensation* program, but it is important to understand that there are two separate veterans disability programs. Plenty of veterans have selected to be bums and draw VA pension because they don't want to work. But pension remains somewhat under control because it never provides a large income. Veterans try harder to get compensation which pays much more.

Pension only provides enough money to bring the claimant up to the poverty level of income. If he owns property or other assets bringing his net worth up above the poverty level or if he is working for a living he cannot qualify for pension. It is only for those not working and not having high net worth. If the claimant is drawing social security benefits because he did work at one time, the VA only pays a little pension benefit to supplement that SSA benefit and bring him up to the poverty level. If he has never worked, the pension becomes a benefit comparable to regular SSA. So while this program does support a lot of alcoholics and drug addicts, it does not make them rich, and many receiving VA pension are still homeless.

A veteran cannot receive both Pension *and* Compensation. The VA must pay the higher of the two programs, whichever will provide him the greatest benefit. A smart veteran will first exhaust all efforts to get the Service-connected Compensation, and if that is denied, then he should try for Pension which is better than nothing.

In 2018, approximately $6 billion will be paid in VA Pension to 493,184 beneficiaries, an average of $12,166 per recipient. That's minimal compared to the approximately $84.6 billion paid to over 5 million for Compensation, with an average benefit of $16,796 per recipient. This book is *not* about the problems with Pension, but it's important to understand that program and that it exists separately from Compensation. I have no intention to argue the justification for Pension, but it seems to be just a sort of reward for those who were drafted to war. It's no longer reasonable in this time of an all-volunteer military where every soldier qualifies for pension because we've been in the current "war" for 28 years and most of them have not seen a battle. Still, Pension is the program that comes closest to caring for "those who shall have borne the battle" because it's based on wartime service and financial need, while Compensation is paid to multitudes who have never seen battle nor been in financial need.

President Franklin D. Roosevelt is considered to have been a very smart man and one of the best presidents this nation has ever had. In 1930, he saw VA benefits as one of the least justified expenditures of federal funds, and he used a presidential authority to discontinue the veterans' pension program and greatly reduce the compensation benefits as one measure to bring America out of the great economic depression. Veterans revolted with the help of Veteran Service Organizations, so as soon as Roosevelt's power ended in 1935, the laws were changed to restore all the prior veterans' benefits as well as to add new ones. No doubt the VSO's will forever be a force to be reckoned with when it comes to veterans' benefits reform, but they shouldn't be feared any more than any other protest group. Many of them should be prosecuted for creating and submitting fraudulent claims for veterans.

President Lincoln was a wise and popular president and he is the one who initiated the strong veterans' benefits programs we have today. The problem is that his statement and the laws that have been based on his proclamation have been stretched way over and above what were initially intended. *VA service-connected compensation has become an abused entitlement program, a way to compensate every person who has ever served in the military, and to pay them for the rest of lives so they never have to work again.* Sometimes it takes a number of years for a veteran to maneuver his way up to receiving 100 percent disability compensation. It's a game that many veterans play and some win it earlier than others. Greater numbers are jumping into the game each year, regardless of how long ago they may have served.   Not only are we paying veterans for illnesses that were not caused by war, we are paying them for conditions that are not really disabling them at all.

The great majority of conditions being paid for are things that would have happened to the veteran whether he had ever served in the military or not. These are injuries from playing basketball and other sports, automobile and motorcycle accidents, and falling off the roof while home on leave, as well as many injuries that were actually incurred many years after service. These are diseases such as uterine fibroids, hyperthyroidism, hypertension, diabetes, heart disease, and cancers, when there is clear evidence of familial/genetic causes, smoking, drug-use, obesity, and other high risk factors. These are conditions such as residuals from elective surgeries done in service for childbirth (C-sections), vasectomies, cataracts, and deviated septums.   Worse yet, claimants are being paid for conditions not visible to the naked eye and not confirmed by any test.   These include fatigue, erectile dysfunction, constipation, headaches, tinnitus, and multiple other conditions that are usually not debilitating diseases, mostly just a bunch of bogus subjective complaints.

(13) HONORABLE PROGRAM, GONE AWRY

The VA disability regulations were written to implement President Abraham Lincoln's promise to "care for those who have borne the battle, and his widow and his orphan." The VA's mission statement is *"To fulfill President Lincoln's promise 'To care for him who shall have borne the battle, and for his widow, and his orphan' by serving and honoring the men and women who are America's veterans."* You'll see this written on the wall of every VA building, and it's the opening statement of every VA classroom training and VA speech. This is very important; this is the theme of this book, and the purpose of this book.

Unfortunately, while VA professes this to be the mission, it is not what the VA is doing. The statement clearly says "those who have borne the battle." This clearly means those who were injured in battle or died in battle. The word "widow" means a spouse and "orphan" means a dependent child, either of whom was left in need when a serviceman died in battle or later died from some injury caused by battle. For many decades, the VA *did* interpret the regulation that way, and people in America understood it.

If you interview very old people today, if they have not been corrupted by a VFW or American Legion officer, they will tell you that VA disability is for those veterans who were injured in war. Many World War II and Vietnam Era veterans still alive have never filed a VA claim because they either didn't go to the battlefield or they were not injured on the battlefield. If you read VA disability ratings that were done during the years of 1950 to 1980, you'll see that VA disability was being granted only for actual in-service injuries, specifically injuries of war. Gradually a few other odd-ball disabilities started slipping in, because in addition to a gunshot wound, the veteran was also treated for a stomach problem, or a stress disorder during service. So service-connection was granted for those as well because the issues began during service.

Historically, soldiers have been given early discharge from service due to various illnesses, injuries, or mental conditions that were disabling them to the extent that they could no longer perform their military duties. In these cases, service-connected disability compensation has been granted based on those conditions (specified on the military Medical Review Board and Physical Evaluation Board). The soldier was gainfully employed by the military and often his intent was to continue with that employment, but when the military found he could no longer physically or mentally perform his job, he was released based on disability. Sometimes the soldier is put on TDRL (temporary retirement) and draws retirement income even though he's nowhere near meeting normal retirement criteria. A few years later he is medically reviewed and may be given full retirement. The soldier may be given separation pay or severance pay of many thousands of dollars to hold that veteran over in the private sector until he can be retrained through the VA vocational rehabilitation program, or until he can be granted VA disability benefits. The military takes care of their soldiers while they serve and for the period of time they would have served if they could have fulfilled their full period of original commitment.

When a person joins the US military (Army, Navy, Marines, Air Force, or Coast Guard) he commits to a certain period of years, anywhere from 2 to 6 years. He understands that the mission of the

US military is to provide security to this nation against all enemies foreign and domestic. The person realizes he will be trained to serve in and survive *war*. Any person who has joined the US military since 1973 has done so on a voluntary basis. If he does not understand what he is signing up for, then he should surely be able to figure it out within the first week of basic training. It is very easy to get released from the service commitment during the basic training period simply by asking. The military does not want to waste time and resources on someone who does not want to be there and who is not able to pull a full load for whatever reason, whether it be attitude, aptitude, or physical problems. If a soldier makes it through basic training he goes on to advanced individual training to acquire specific skills for the job position he has been hired to fill. The US military is the best employer in the world. The soldier as an employee of the federal government is provided with free training, travel, housing, clothing, food, medical care, and he receives additional pay if he has a family to shelter and feed.

The US government/military has never promised to provide for a healthy soldier or for his family *after* discharge from service. IF a soldier is injured in battle, the Veterans Benefits Administration steps in, effective the date of discharge, because now the person is no longer a soldier but is a veteran. The military offers the individual a job and benefits in exchange for him filling that needed position as a soldier. The military benefit ends the day the soldier is discharged. Unfortunately, today's soldiers do not understand this because of the gross misapplication of VA benefits. Today's soldiers apparently think that by joining the military they will receive pay the rest of their lives, if they play their cards right! Active duty soldiers are being encouraged to fill their medical file with as much bullshit as they can in order to form a basis for receiving VA compensation after discharge.

Over the years, the interpretation of the VA disability regulations has been relaxed and expanded to include any type of physical or mental complaint a person could possibly have. The regulation is now interpreted to mean that any sort of medical condition symptom that was first noted during service can be granted now as a service-related disability. If there was no actual diagnosis in service but there were a few complaints in service, as minor as a headache or stomach ache or back ache, the VA simply requests a VA doctor to express a medical opinion and if the doctor chooses to link a current condition to that remote service, even though there's been no problem for the past 40 years, it can and must be granted. Doctors, particularly the contracted private examiners, are being trained to err in favor of the veteran, diagnose everything possible and link everything possible, so VA can grant, grant, grant!

Furthermore, the VA continues to expand the list of diseases that may be granted on a presumptive basis, when there were no symptoms in service or for 40 years after service, just based the fact that the veteran served in the country of Vietnam or drank water at Camp LeJeune. It doesn't matter that the veteran's father, mother, and both brothers all have diabetes; if this man served in Vietnam, VA will grant service-connection for his diabetes which manifested 42 years after his discharge from service, at the about the same age his father and brothers had also been diagnosed, although they never went to Vietnam. VA will grant peripheral neuropathy, kidney disease, vascular disease, eye disease, and erectile dysfunction all as "secondary" to his diabetes, and this can easily add up to 100 percent disability. If by chance it doesn't add up to 100, then he simply asks for "individual unemployability" (IU) and he will be granted the same pay as 100 percent disability.

The current VA disability compensation regulations, found in 38 CFR, Chapters 3 and 4, have been in effect since 1945 and each year they are modified slightly to add or clarify symptoms or levels of disability. But if you look at a progression of rating decisions issued over the past 70 years you'll be amazed at how interpretation of those regulations has changed. The VA Adjudication Procedures Manual, M21-1, which attempts to put the laws/regulations into working guidelines, is also undergoing continuous change, so much that the adjudicators cannot possibly keep up with the changes, and any given claim may not be decided the same by any two raters.

Unfortunately, the changes are not for the better, unless you just want to give veterans everything they ask for. It's getting to the point where the whole VBA (Veterans Benefits Administration) can and might as well be shut down. Just let the veterans enter their claims on-line, indicate what level of benefits they want to receive, and let a computer issue the monthly deposit to their account. Some higher level VA employees have actually seriously proposed this as an improvement to the system, because it would be a way to process claims faster! Those people have never actually worked claims and they no idea how dishonest many claimants can be. When you tell a person to "take whatever you want" they will take everything they possibly can!

As for the current procedure, when a disability claim is received at the VA, the rating department reviews the claimant's service medical treatment records and his personnel records if applicable, and then reviews any current medical evidence submitted, or records of his treatment at any of the VA medical centers. For most of the 20th century, if a claimed condition was not shown in the service records, it was simply denied. Usually the only conditions shown in the records were serious conditions such as actual gunshot wounds, broken legs, and hernia repairs. Those were the things the soldiers went to treatment for, and the records are quite amazing. They were kept quite well by the military departments and sent to the St. Louis federal records holding area after the soldier left service. Except for some records destroyed by the St. Louis fire in 1973, all veterans' records are now held in custody of the VA and are uploaded to the VBA's electronic claims processing system upon receipt of a disability claim. Records prior to about 1990 were usually brief; one small folder would hold all the records for even a 20-year career soldier. Around about the time that records started being uploaded and maintained electronically, in the mid 1990's, they also became more detailed and often the files contain hundreds of duplicate records, so the files got larger and larger. In the 2000's before VA started scanning the veteran's entire file into an electronic on-line file, it had gotten to the point where some veterans' files were 20 or more volumes deep, each volume a couple of inches thick. At the height of the "backlogged claims" debacle, some news stories reported that the structural integrity of some of the federal buildings was in jeopardy due to the weight of all these files. Now the veterans' files are no longer kept in the claims processing offices. They are sent to a scanning facility and the electronic files can be accessed by claims processors in any state, and many of the claims developers and raters work from laptops in their homes. Each veteran's file contains hundreds, even thousands, of scanned pages.

One reason each veteran's file is much thicker now is because in-service health care is more extensive whereas at one time a file might include nothing more than the entrance exam and the exit (separation) exam.   Now the services do many more interim exams such as at reenlistment time, or pre-deployment and post-deployment, and routine exams such as annual audiograms, routine lab tests, etc.   But the main reason the current files are so horrendously thick is that the soldiers are deliberately beefing up these files. They are feigning illness and going on sick call every possible time they can just to get "stuff" put in their medical file. If they have a little knee pain or back pain (what human doesn't from time to time?) they go to sick call and get it documented. Although the physician will likely just assess the condition as "acute back pain" or acute knee pain due to "overuse" and although the condition may never be reported again, that's ok. The deed is done. The incident has been documented. Now the veteran has a case 40 years later when his back starts hurting from old age, despite the fact that he may have worked a back-straining after-service job for 20 years, or he may have been in car accidents, or fell off a roof. VA doesn't know that. VA only knows that one time in 1980 this veteran said he had back pain during service and now he again says he has back pain. If a medical doctor will give a simple opinion that the current condition is at least as likely as not (at least 50 percent probability) incurred in service, then VA will grant the disability as service-connected.

Why are the soldiers going to great lengths to get all sorts of illnesses and injuries and symptoms noted in their medical records? Because they *know* that this will lead to money after service. This is told to them *by their military superiors*. They are *advised* to put as much medical symptoms as possible into their file so that after discharge they'll be able to claim disability and will be paid disability compensation for the rest of their lives. It's a big game the military is playing with our tax money. A person need only serve as little as 90 days for most illnesses, or even just one day if he is actually injured that first day, but it takes many weeks for the discharge paperwork to be complete, so he'll have 90 days anyway by the time he's discharged. The military departments are as guilty as VA in perpetuating this criminal activity, because they are encouraging the soldiers to go to sick call and to get every medical complaint documented that they possibly can. Many soldiers are given time off for the last 30 days of service just to get these medical records in order for discharge.

Frequently a soldier has a great medical history and has achieved flying colors for 20 years but when he gets down to that retirement exam he comes forth with reported problems of every joint in his body, although he's never had a documented injury. He claims he has headaches, stomach problems, and tinnitus, all totally subjective issues with no evident symptoms. He claims he has anxiety and depression, and it doesn't matter what is causing this. It could be marital problems because he was caught screwing around, or he could be stressing over the fact that he will soon be out of the military where he'll no longer have free clothes, free three hots a day, free lodging, and a paycheck for what is often a cheesy job. He reports that he snores and thinks he may have sleep apnea, so they give him a sleep study a week before discharge, and sure enough he qualifies for a diagnosis of sleep apnea. This assures him 50 percent disability right off the bat, for the rest of his life. The military helps him document all these complaints and can also help him file a pre-discharge claim which can be decided within six months prior to discharge, then solidified by the VA immediately after his separation from service.

After a soldier is discharged, the military has helped him all they can with his potential claim. He is now a veteran and he's turned over to the Department of Veterans Affairs (VA). He must now go to the VA medical centers for free medical treatment, unless he's a retiree, in which case he may continue to get his free health care from the military hospitals. The veteran may now report to his closest VA Benefits Office (regional offices are located one or more in each state) or he may go on-line to ebenefits.va.gov and enter his claim on-line without ever reporting to an office, or he may send in a hard-copy claim by mail.

The veteran is also advised by the military and by the VA that he may obtain free assistance from any one of a vast number of VSOs (Veteran Service Offices), by POAs (individuals with assigned Power of Attorney), veterans' representatives located in every American town. These may include Veterans of Foreign Wars (VFW), American Legion, Military Order of the Purple Heart (MOPH), and hundreds of other non-profit agencies including Department of Veterans Services in every state, which have been established to help veterans (free of charge) to file their claims and milk the federal government out of every penny possible. It's a game with them to see just how much they can get for a veteran. They file false claims for the veteran, and they embellish any claim that the veteran can come up with himself. They advise the veteran to go and get some post-service medical care documented, go to the VA medical center or to any private doctor and spit out a slew of symptoms. It won't matter if the doctor diagnoses anything or prescribes any treatment, just getting those claimed symptoms on a medical paper is enough for the VA. If a condition was reported in service and reported again after service, disability compensation will almost always be granted.

I must clarify again that that my sentiments are *not those* of the current "VA establishment." Although many employees secretly feel the way I do, no employee is allowed to openly express these feelings without being counseled and/or fired. The VA creed is that the VA will do everything in its power to grant the most it possibly can to each veteran. VA does not acknowledge fraud, abuse, or malingering (feigning or lying about sickness) on the part of veterans. VA employees are trained, "Grant if you can; deny only if you *must*." The only time you *must* deny is when the veteran is claiming that a condition started in service and there is no record of the condition in service and no way you can possibly connect the current condition to anything that may have happened in service. Still there are many conditions that can and are granted even though they weren't shown in service, because they are linked to some exposure or experience in service, and those are clarified in later sections of this book.   The regulations do say that if there is an "intermediary cause" for a condition, such as perhaps a recent auto accident or serious on-the-job injury well-documented as having occurred after discharge, then the issue should not be granted. However, I have seen many such cases that were granted, even though there was a clear intermediary cause, if there were some complaints of similar symptoms in service, because the examiner said he could only *speculate* whether or not the condition existed prior to the second incident.   When a decision is on the fence it must be decided in favor of the veteran.

I have often overheard veterans gossiping about how the VA denied them, didn't want to help them, tried to keep from paying them, but they kept on reopening their claim until they got what they rightly deserved!   But if they only knew how untrue this is and that they got granted because they finally said the right thing. The VA trains it's employees to grant, grant, grant.   The VA as an organization does not care about tax dollars. There is no "owner" or "CEO" or "stockholder" to care whether the VA is blowing money foolishly. We individual *taxpayers* are the owner, CEO, and stockholder. It is *our* money they are blowing, but the taxpayer has no say in government affairs other than to petition a congressman. Unfortunately, the general public and the congressmen have no idea about all the fraud and abuse.

The VA's Veterans Benefits Administration (VBA) goal is to grant as many claims as possible, as fast as possible, and to grant the highest possible evaluation (amount of monthly compensation) to each veteran. The more claims they grant and the more money they grant, the better the VA looks.   This bunch, the VA Benefits Administration, the VA Medical Centers, the military departments, and the VSOs, are all working to give as much money as possible to any and all veterans. There is no agency out there looking for fraud and abuse in the VA system, and looking out for the best interest of the American taxpayer.   Yes of course there is a "Fraud, Waste, and Abuse" program in the VA play book. Yes, there is a supervisor in every federal agency building whose job it is to investigate and report on any incidents of fraud brought to their attention.   Yes, there are regulations regarding fraud, but these are never read, discussed, or enforced.

As a VA employee I was never trained on the regulations regarding fraud and abuse, I was never encouraged to report fraud, and when I did try to report it anyway, I was told to shut up and do my job and have sympathy for veterans.   I was trained "grant, grant, grant."

Over and over, 38 CFR 4.23, *Attitude of the Rating Officer*, is drilled in the heads of the raters, and VA interprets it to mean that the rater must not let his personal opinion influence his rating decision.   However, the regulation simply says that the rater should not be influenced by the nasty behavior or attitude of a veteran. Specifically, the regulation says, "In the exercise of his or her functions, rating officers must not allow their personal feelings to intrude; an antagonistic, critical, or even abusive attitude on the part of a claimant should not in any instance influence the officers in the handling of the case. Fairness and courtesy must at all times be shown to applicants by all employees whose duties bring them in contact, directly or indirectly, with the Department's claimants." All this says to me is that if a claimant is very rude on the phone or in his statements (as they often are) we should not let that veteran's rudeness influence our decision. This regulation does not say to me that I must grant a case when the documented evidence clearly shows a fraudulent claim. In my more than 10 years working VA claims I saw what I felt was fraud and abuse practically every day, but I never saw or heard of a case where a veteran was charged, prosecuted, denied, or had to return compensation due to discovery of fraud.   You will hear the claims examiners whispering about cases all day long, preposterous ridiculous cases that nobody believes should be granted, and yet they *must* be granted and are granted.

Each rating office has a whole in-house staff of "Quality" specialists whose job is to review cases and make sure they were decided correctly. Then there is the "STAR" (Systematic Technical Accuracy Review) office in Nashville where higher level quality specialists are reviewing rating decisions from all the 56 rating offices. But all that any of these "quality" specialists are doing is making sure the decisions match the boxes on the DBQ's! They're just following the same rules the raters are following, and catching a few typographical or technical errors. They are not verifying that any logical decision was made on whether any claimant is truly functionally impaired by conditions truly caused by military activity.

Then there's the VA Office of Inspector General (OIG), constantly spitting out their little reports of how poorly the VA is performing in all arenas, including how poorly STAR is performing, but never even scratching the surface of fraud and abuse. Somebody needs to inspect the way VA trainers/training writers and policy manual writers are interpreting and applying the regulations.

Based on the old case files I have read, forty or fifty years ago fraud was not a serious issue. Veterans were not filing fraudulent claims, and they were not being granted undeserved benefits. Now with internet blogs and everyone hanging out at the VFW and hanging out in VA waiting rooms just for social interaction, most veterans are well educated on the process and it's just a big game to see how fast one can get to 100 percent disability.

The VA has done everything possible in recent years to get the word out to all veterans, including sending out letters to veterans, to encourage them to file claims, claims they would have never dreamed of filing, and for benefits they do not feel they actually deserve. But when some agency is begging you to take free money just for the asking, the veterans who are not jumping on board may be the foolish ones.

(14) OTHER AFFECTED VETERANS' ISSUES

The following veterans issues are discussed because they are either impacting VA compensation, or VA compensation contributes to these problems. Also, if we could reduce some of the waste of over-developing and over-granting compensation, maybe more could be done for financially needy veterans and certainly more could be done in providing actual medical and health services.

NONSERVICE-CONNECTED PENSION

Nonservice-connected pension is a totally separate VA benefit, comparable to social security disability and can supplement social security disability. Pension is paid only to war era veterans and has nothing to do with in-service injuries. This program will take care of our war veterans, "those who have borne the battle," even if they have no service-connected disabilities. The VA's mission is to serve war veterans and regardless of whether there is any combat injury, there is no reason for a war veteran to fabricate claims, to lie about disabilities and try to relate them to service, if he truly cannot work and truly needs financial help.

Many Vietnam war veterans are drawing nonservice-connected pension from the VA simply because they have never worked in their lives. They came back from the war hooked on drugs and alcohol, or became hooked shortly after returning. They had no war injuries other than perhaps shellshock but they never filed a claim for that. If they never worked and they have little to no income or net worth, they will be granted Pension to supplement whatever the Social Security Administration gives them.

The soldiers who returned from war, eked out a living, worked factory jobs or supported themselves in skilled trades, perhaps ran a machine shop, or a lawn service, or a bakery, or locksmith service, those hard workers who struggled but supported themselves and their families and paid taxes, they usually cannot get VA pension. If they reported their earnings properly, and worked until age 65, they qualify for regular Social Security benefits, and VA can only pay pension enough to supplement the SSA and bring them up to the national poverty income level.

Pension can't be paid to a veteran who's gainfully employed. No disability is required if the claimant is 65 or older, served in a war era (not necessarily in battle, just during the war years), and has little or no income (including SSA) and has low net worth   If he's not 65 yet, he can still draw pension if he's found to be too disabled to work due to any injury or disease, or even due to drug and alcohol abuse, because the disabilities for pension are not caused by or incurred in service. If the disabilities were incurred in service, the claim would be considered for service-connected compensation, which pays higher. If a veteran qualifies for both, he will be paid the higher of the two benefits. Usually compensation is higher, but if he's only 10% or 30% disabled, the pension may be higher.

In 2019 the VA will pay out over $90 billion in compensation and a separate $9 billion in pension. When you hear a veteran say, "I tried to get my military pension, but the VA denied me," this means he did not qualify for pension because he was either too young and not disabled, or never served in a war era, or already has adequate (at least above poverty-level) income through employment or receipt of retirement or social security benefits. Unfortunately many apparently believe that every veteran is entitled to a "pension" regardless of current income, just because he served a few years in the military.

An interesting fact is that the number of VA Pension recipients is expected to *decrease* in 2019, and further decrease in 2020 as the World War II and Vietnam Veterans who took this benefit are gradually dying. The benefit is out there just the same as always, and everyone who served from 1990 until the present (way more than those who have survived the older wars) will be potentially eligible for pension. But all the Gulf War veterans are foregoing pension because it's a lesser benefit, as they all attempt to obtain a greater benefit through disability compensation, whatever that may take. They will only accept pension as a last resort.

The VA pension program is full of fraud and abuse like any welfare benefit or entitlement program. Many recipients work under the table and report no income, and many have transferred all their assets into their children's names or trust funds so it looks like they have no net worth. Thousands if not millions of dollars are being paid every year to veterans who are dead and someone is still cashing those checks. But that's another book.

HOMELESS VETERANS

Many claims for submitted by "homeless" veterans have to be denied, all issues, including Pension. The veteran is truly homeless, sick, may be an alcoholic or drug addict, but nevertheless he served his time in the military. VA has to deny compensation because his service records show no disabilities were incurred during service. It's sad, but it's *right*, because veterans disability compensation is meant for people who were injured in the line of duty. But he also cannot qualify for nonservice-connected Pension because he did not serve during a time of war.

The ironical and distressing fact is that while we are not paying that homeless veteran anything, we are paying compensation to another veteran who is independently wealthy, either by private work or because he retired from military as a general officer. The compensation payment is in most cases based on conditions that were first diagnosed during his service but were not truly caused by any military activity, so is he any more deserving than the homeless veteran? I would prefer that my tax dollars help the homeless veteran than to help someone who is doing fine financially and who has no disability that was incurred during actual military activity. For that matter, I would prefer that my tax dollars help *any* homeless person, or any low income working class family, than to help a financially stable veteran who was not injured in war.

VA MEDICATIONS AND OPIOID ABUSE

The availability of free or very low cost medications from the VA medical centers is fostering serious problems with drug addiction as well as illegal drug sales and distribution. The veteran often gets the drugs by first filing a fraudulent disability claim for conditions and symptoms he doesn't have, usually either mental issues such as anxiety or depression, or any condition causing "pain."

That's right; I am accusing some veterans of being liars, thieves, and drug pushers, because I have *seen* it in their records. Thousands of veterans are abusing the free medication system at the VA, and no doubt selling the drugs. Over and again, the same veterans will report that they didn't get their medications in the mail, and the prescription will be resent to them. There is no collaboration between VA and other pharmacies so the veteran can get what he uses from CVS and sell everything he gets from the VA.

Meanwhile, many of the ones who are actually using the VA medications are becoming drug addicts because the supply is unlimited and overprescribed just for the asking.

In 2018 the Trump administration has proposed that they will do something about the current huge problem of opioids abuse in America, and the VA is a good place to start.

***

Veteran X is service connected for joint complaints for which he has been prescribed large doses of oxycodone and fentanyl (opiates).   When he filed for an increase, his review exam lab reports showed NO opiates in his system!   The lab tests were however positive for benzodiazepines (benzees) although the VA had never prescribed this. He explained that he also gets treatment from a private physician and that the private doctor prescribed the benzees.   The VA doctor puzzles over why there are no opiates in this man's system when he has had large prescriptions filled repeatedly.   The doctor BOLDS these remarks with exclamation points in the record, but no one else will ever look at it.   The doctor notes that he is reducing this medication (since he sees it's not being used anyway) and he tells the patient to start tapering off and to reduce the pills from three-a-day to one-a-day over a period of weeks.   One week later, the veteran phones the doctor, very angry. He is out of meds and wants more. So the opiate prescriptions are refilled. Period.

UNFAIRNESS FOR SOME MILITARY RETIREES

A gross inequality in the compensation program is that military *retirees* who have been granted less than a 50% total evaluation cannot receive the money unless their injuries were combat-related. Technically, the VA pays the compensation amount so that the retiree can benefit from the tax-free status of compensation income, but his retirement income is then reduced by that payment amount, so the bottom line is the veteran does not actually receive any VA compensation until he is at least 50% disabled.

Until 2004, no veteran could receive military retirement pay and VA compensation concurrently. In 2004 the law was changed so that a veteran could receive both if he was at least 50% disabled. And in 2008 it was further changed to provide that if the injuries were combat-related, then the veteran could receive both, but very few rated conditions are actually combat-related. So this issue of "concurrent receipt of retired pay and compensation" also called "the Retired Pay Restoration Act" or H.R. 303, has been hashed about by Congress for the past 15 years. First discussed in 2003, then reopened in 2005, and reopened again in January 2017, but as of July 2018 it was apparently still in committee.

So a veteran who served only a few months or years, then went on to a life-long career in any private corporation, will receive his retirement anuity from that corporation, and he will also receive the full amount of VA compensation granted, regardless of how much he has earned by working, or how much retirement he is drawing. However, a veteran who made a career of the military and retired after 20 or 30 or 40 years of service, is not allowed to draw both his retirement and VA compensation, unless the VA compensation level is 50% or higher. That's right; backwards as it sounds, the one who qualifies for more than 50% compensation (a greater amount of money) *can* draw both, while the one who qualifies for *less* compensation cannot receive any.

It makes no sense at all. For example, you have two men who both have been granted 20% due to a back injury in service. Both men are drawing retirement from the career they chose. The one who served two years in the military and made a career elsewhere after service gets the VA compensation; the military retiree (who devoted his life to service) cannot draw the VA compensation.

I don't know if this policy was supposed to save tax dollars, but it actually leads to greater expense and payout. As you can imagine, this injustice encourages the retiree to continue filing more new or increase claims to try to up his evaluation to at least 50% so that he can draw something! So the policy ends up costing the VA more because some retired veterans might would have been satisfied with less than 50% with their retirement pay. In the end, these retirees deserve the full amount they qualify for (for injuries caused by military service) regardless of how little or much it is. They most likely showed commitment and performed well for our military if they made it to retirement, and that can't be said for many VA compensation recipients. Some of the most whiney and useless soldiers are the ones now drawing the most VA compensation.

VA HOSPITALS AFFECTED BY DISABILITY CLAIMS

First to clarify again, VA disability claims are administered (received, decided, granted) by the Veterans Benefits Administration (VBA). Veterans health care is provided by a different organization, the Veterans Health Administration (VHA). Two very different and separate agencies, and unfortunately there's very little communication between the two.

The VBA (claims department) does have access (electronically/on-line) to all VA Medical Center treatment records, and these records are obtained and included in the claim files and, to the extent possible, reviewed by the raters making decisions on the claims. VBA has no authority to suggest that a veteran seek treatment, and has no control over treatments or anything going on at the VA hospitals or anything put in the VA treatment records. The VBA does enter (electronically) a request for the applicable VA exams (DBQs) which will be needed to decide the claim, and these requests will be fulfilled by either the VA medical centers, clinics, or private contracted physicians.

Meanwhile the VHA hospital physicians and staff have no control over disability claims. They don't receive claims or encourage claims, and they generally don't know about what claims are in progress or which ones have been denied before. They do have access to see what total percent of compensation a veteran is receiving and what issues the veteran has been granted service-connected compensation if they wish to look it up. But generally a VHA physician just treats the veteran for whatever he claims, and fills out whatever DBQ's he has been asked to complete. The physician does not make a decision on any claim; only the VBA rater does. A physician can pretty well bet that if he gives a positive opinion an issue will most always be granted, but he has no idea what evaluation will be issued for the condition, or how much the veteran will earn from this endeavor of a claim.

In recent years, VA hospitals have been beat to death by the media. Directors have been fired because records were hidden and falsified. Veterans were waiting months for care because the VA hospitals just simply could not accommodate and fill the demand for services. It seems that this demand has increased at a much faster rate than the hospitals were able to grow. Meanwhile, hospital employees were quitting left and right and going to the private sector. The VA cannot find enough physicians and nurses. I can't find statistics but it seems to me that more than 50% of the VA physicians are foreign nationals and that's growing. Ever wondered why we can't get and keep good doctors and staff at the VA hospitals? This book should help you understand it.

According to the American Federation of Government Employees, AFL-CIO, *The Government Standard*, September/October 2017 issue, there were more than 49,000 vacant positions in the VA, with at least 45,000 of them in the health care system. They suggested that the solution is to have more money poured into the system for hiring. But there's no shortage of money for the VA. A position wouldn't be open if money hadn't already been allocated for filling the position.

The fact is nobody wants to work for the VA. Many people do hang on to their jobs there because the benefits are great, pay is great, vacation and sick leave benefits are great, retirement pay is great. If employees could find any other job to give them equal pay and benefits, 99% of them would be out of there. I heard it whispered every day I ever reported to a VA office. But why is the work so bad? It's actually easy. The government provides very detailed regulations and policy manuals to follow, provides tons of training specialized to each position, and never makes you work more than the hours you're paid for. In most ways, the VA jobs are cushy and easier than anything comparable in the private sector. However, people have "consciences" and working for the VA is like working for a crime mob. You may get paid well but you just don't feel good about yourself and what you're doing. This book exposes many of the specific things that stress an employee working in the compensation benefits department. But for now, I'm trying to address how this has affected the VA health system, hospitals and clinics, and how it is causing their loss of employees, loss of credible health care, and general demise.

These veterans who are filing the false claims, as a means to get rich quick, or at least to never have to work again… they are destroying the VA health care system. First there are the VA general medical examinations. Whenever a veteran files his claim within six months pre-discharge or within a year after discharge, he will be given a full general medical examination, which will include specific examinations, Disability Benefits Questionnaires (DBQs) for each condition he has claimed. So depending on what he claims he'll have a knee exam, shoulder exam, wrist exam, ankle exam, foot exam, gastrointestinal exam, kidney exam, lung exam, skin exam, etc. There are more than 60 specific general medical DBQs to accompany the General Medical Review DBQ, and some veterans will need a dozen or more of them completed by the general practitioner. Then there are the "specialty exams" which are the "eyes, ears, mental, dental." If he is claiming any eye or vision condition it will require an exam by certified ophthalmologist. Any hearing/ear claim will require a certified audiologist. Any type of mental claim, even such as depression, anxiety, insomnia, or anorexia, will require a certified psychologist or psychiatrist. If he is claiming traumatic brain injury (TBI) that will require an initial diagnosis to be made by a physiatrist, psychiatrist, neurosurgeon, or neurologist. For the veteran's initial claim, he may have to report to the VA hospital on as many as 5 or 6 different days to get all these examinations done. They are done by physicians and other staff that could be helping take care of sick or injured veterans.

Now, once the veteran gets his first decision, and he's not happy with it because he didn't get 100%, he will file an increase claim the following year and he will have another one to 20 exams for the conditions he's already been granted. Again, he has to have the specialists to perform the exams for the special issues, but no matter how simple the issue, he is taking up the time of a physician or LPN (licensed practical nurse) or PA (physician's assistant). This will continue year after year as the veteran tries to increase his evaluations.

For most of the past 30 years, a claim for increase, any time, would trigger automatic scheduling of a review exam, and the regulation supports that. In recent years, some stations have implemented a policy that a review/increase exam will not be ordered if he has had one within the last 12 months, unless there is other medical evidence that the condition has increased. In other words, they can potentially have a new exam every year, just by claiming an "increase." This is a tremendous waste of resources (VA physicians time!) at the VA medical centers.

Due to the drastic increase in claims and number of issues on each claim, the VA medical centers are no longer capable of performing all the needed exams. So VA is now contracting out to private physicians (companies such as QTC, VES, and LHI) for a great number of exams, and this is a tremendous new expense, of almost $7 billion per year.

If a claim is denied, the veteran will reopen the claim by submitting additional new evidence or lay statements from family, or perhaps a statement from a private doctor. This doctor doesn't need to have ever treated the veteran for anything; he may be someone the veteran plays golf with, or lives next to, or is a family member or married to a distant relative. I have seen some statements from doctors the veterans found on-line. There are doctors who will provide an opinion for a fee when they have never seen the veteran and have never reviewed his medical history or treatment records. (Yes, I reported these, and No, nothing was done about it.)

Anyway, when a veteran provides any of this stuff to reopen the claim, he gets another exam scheduled, this time a VA medical opinion is also ordered. So the VA doctor not only has to do the DBQ, but is supposed to perform a complete review of the file, so he has to (supposed to) spend hours reviewing the veteran's medical history, including his service treatment records (which could cover 20 years and be 10 volumes thick), and any post-service medical records he has provided. Then the doctor must provide an opinion as to whether the claimed condition is at least (50/50) as likely as not to have been incurred in or caused by military service. Do you think the doctor actually reads those records? Considering the shortage of doctors at VA hospitals and the pressure on the few doctors they still have? Of course not. And do you think the doctors often give a negative opinion? Very rarely. Perhaps they're afraid there might have been something in those records they didn't have time to read.

For whatever reason, it seems that most of the physicians are scared to give a negative opinion or to write anything negative in a VA exam. They are brainwashed the same as the VA rating specialists that they must give everything possible to the veteran. These doctors have heard about the veteran in Texas who was denied and then went and killed the doctor who did his exam. They've heard of others who have come into the VA centers threatening to do harm to the doctors and their families. It is very easy for a veteran to know the name of the doctor who examined him. It's written on the appointment letter inviting him to the exam, and on the doctor's nametag, and on the exam report that is accessible online. There's no way to protect a doctor from a disgruntled veteran.

In addition to the time being wasted on exams (DBQs), the veterans are also abusing the VA healthcare system for treatment. If they've been denied because there's no post-service evidence of a condition, then they must simply make an appointment at the VA, go in and get the condition put in their records. For example, the veteran twisted his left ankle back in 1972, and now he wants to claim the ankle disability. The claim gets denied because he has never seen a doctor for any ankle condition in the past 40 years since discharge from service. So after denial, he makes an appointment at the VA to be seen for a left ankle condition. They can't refuse him. He goes to the appointment at primary care, claims he has ongoing left ankle pain. This gets put in his records. There is a claim of pain, even if there is no objective evidence of any condition, and probably no diagnosis. The veteran will typically be given an X-ray and it will show nothing abnormal. Still the complaint of left ankle pain is in the records.

Veterans are wasting billions of hours of health care services by going to the VA hospital primary care, and into the VA clinics, to claim these bogus issues, just to get it documented in their records so that then they can file another VA benefits claim or reopen an old denied claim to get compensation for the issue.

Then billions more hours and other resources (test equipment, facilities, medical assistants, facilities) are spent on bogus exams for these frivolous claims. If the service records made any mention, even one little 3-word mention of a left ankle complaint in service, and now there is this current medical record showing a complaint of left ankle pain, then this is automatic justification for getting a full VA exam (DBQ) and medical opinion regarding whether the current condition was incurred in or caused by military service. This will require tests, physical exam, records review, and report preparation and submittal. The VA examiner does a full ankle exam, generally including an X-ray or even an MRI, and usually they show no abnormality. (Other non-musculoskeletal conditions may require CT scans, EGD scopes, blood tests, etc.) The examiner measures the ankle range of motion and finds no difference between the left and right ankles. He sees no abnormality of gait, no swelling, no scar, nothing. BUT, the veteran is claiming painful motion so he has to put that in the exam report, so then since there's a symptom the VA examiner must provide a diagnosis. It's ok for a primary care physician to just list "pain" in the treatment records without any diagnosis, and that is what the VA examiners *should* also do on exams. The rule for raters is that in order to grant a condition it must have a diagnosis, so if the examiner fails to give a diagnosis it is sent back to him. He *should* simply clarify "there is no diagnosis" then

VA could deny the issue saying there is no chronic disability. But that rarely if ever happens. Lacking any objective evidence, the examiner will diagnose the condition as "strain" or "sprain." The fact that these are *acute* diagnoses is ignored, even though regulations say compensation is for only for *chronic* disabilities. Then the examiner has to provide an opinion as to whether this condition has continued since service. How is the doctor to say? The VA regulation says the answer must be Yes if it is "at least as likely as not" meaning there is at least a 50/50 probability, not greater than 50, just equal to 50 percent probability, that the pain may have continued since service. The examiner provides his opinion. The VA rating specialist must rate based on whatever opinion the examiner gives. The rater is not allowed to say that it just doesn't sound logical since there was no continuity of this problem over the past 40 years. The VA regulations *do* say that there must be *continuity* shown, and in the past such claims were automatically denied without getting these foolish medical opinions, but now the definition of continuity has been expanded to include any report opining that the condition *may have* continued since service.

Can you see how horrible it is for a VA doctor to be in this position of having to examine these liars day after day, and having to write these bogus opinions day after day, in time that should have been spent treating sick people? We are wasting billions of taxpayer dollars on these foolish exams, and clogging up all the VA hospitals and VA clinics with veterans who are not sick, just greedy.

(15) THE CLAIMS PROCESS

WHAT IS A VA DISABILITY CLAIM?

A VA disability claim is a legal claim, a "law suit" filed against the federal government, and a grant of a VA claim is a ruling in favor of the veteran, awarding him monthly compensation payments due to injuries incurred during his federal military service. It's different from a tort law suit which would be filed at the courthouse, decided by a judge/jury, and any payment awarded by the court would usually be a one-time lump sum. It's very similar to a workers' compensation claim, except the benefits keep going on forever, long after the injured person has recovered.

The veteran submits a claim for compensation when he wants to get a monthly check from the VA based on a disability, illness or injury, caused by his military service. He submits the claim by filling out a simple standard form, such as a VA Form 21-526EZ, Veterans Application for Service Connected Compensation, and mailing it to the VBA Claims In-processing Center (scanning office), or he can fill it out and upload it on-line at myBenefits.gov.

He can have a claim completed and submitted for him by a VA employee if he goes to one of the VBA regional offices or a field station, or he can have a claim prepared and submitted at any local Veterans Services Organization such as VFW or American Legion.

On the claim form he needs only to provide his name, address, dates of military service, and then list whatever disabilities he wishes to claim. He will list such issues as hearing loss, left ankle sprain, asthma, and PTSD. A typical claim will have from 2 to 20 issues, but some have more than 150 issues listed. The claimant does not have to provide any written narrative to justify how and when any of the conditions were incurred. If he has had treatment since discharge at any private or federal facility he is asked to indicate that on the claim form so that the VA can obtain those records.

The VA claim is received, processed, and decided by admin personnel (with no legal or medical training) at the Veterans Benefits Administration. If a claim is granted, payments will be issued to the veteran on a monthly basis for life, theoretically subject to decreasing or increasing if the level of disability changes.

It is the VA's responsibility to obtain and review the veteran's military personnel records and military medical records, also known as service treatment records (STRS), and to also review any treatment he may have had at a VA medical center. If the veteran has indicated treatment at a private doctor or hospital, he will be asked to provide a "release" form authorizing VA to obtain those records, and then VA will get the records and review them before deciding the claim.

Theoretically, service connection for a condition will be granted IF the condition started during service or was caused by service, AND that condition has continued after discharge from service, and is still present at the time of granting the claim. If the claimant/veteran is submitting the claim prior to discharge (within 6 months before discharge) he does not have to submit any medical evidence to show that he ever had the claimed condition. Since he's still in service when he files the claim, the claim form itself serves to indicate that the condition existed in service. Otherwise, if he's already out of service, an in-service "event" must be shown in the military records. For example, his service treatment records may show that he complained of or was treated at least once for the condition during service. Or if it's a PTSD claim, the military records may show an event that happened in service that the post-service condition could be linked to. If he's claiming an Agent Orange (herbicide) related condition such as type II diabetes or coronary artery disease, then the military records must show that he served in Vietnam.

If he's already out of service at the time of the claim, and he filed the claim within a year of discharge, the VA will order a full general medical exam, as well as specialty exams for any claimed mental, dental, vision, or audio condition. Even if the veteran has had no treatment since discharge, the VA exams will serve to prove the ongoing existence of any condition diagnosed on the exams.

If the veteran has been out of service more than a year before filing his original claim, then exams are not always automatically ordered. The veteran should provide (or tell VA to obtain) some post-service treatment records to show that he has complained of or been treated for the conditions he is claiming. There are exceptions. An audio exam can be ordered if the veteran had hearing loss in service because the condition is considered chronic, or if he served in combat or in a type of duty with high probability of hearing damage. A PTSD exam can be ordered if the veteran received a combat medal because that represents an automatic stressor for PTSD. And a big exception is made for any Gulf War veteran, which includes any serviceman or woman who went to Southeast Asia since 1990. All they have to do is claim symptoms related to Gulf War exposures, and boom, they get a full general medical exam with all the extras, regardless of how long they've been out of service, or lack of any treatment since service. But in general, the regulations say that a veteran needs to show that he has been treated after service, so often many issues on his first claim will be initially denied because there is no post-service evidence of the condition. It used to be that many claims were also denied due to no *in-service* record of the condition, and that still happens to older veterans, but these days the military well-educates the soldiers to get every symptom they can get into those service treatment records while still on active duty. If the veteran doesn't have private treatment records (after-service records), all he has to do is go to his nearest VA medical center, make a complaint about the issue, and voila! A post-service record will be established. Then all VA needs is a competent medical opinion to indicate that the current condition is as likely as not a continuance of a condition that started in service.

The rules are not unreasonable. The problem is that just because there was a single complaint at one time during the veteran's service, does not mean that a post-service occurrence of a similar condition was *caused* by military service. The decision should be made based on logic and reason, but any VA employee will tell you there is no logic in the VA world. For example, the veteran claims a "bilateral knee condition, bilateral ankle condition, and bilateral foot condition." The service records show that in basic training he complained of his feet, ankles, and knees hurting. This is extremely common because basic training is a rigorous fast-paced physically challenging program. New soldiers must march and run many miles in combat boots! Practically every one of them has some complaint or blisters or shin splints in basic training. But these minor "over-use" injuries *heal*! The soldier goes on to spend 20 years in service with never another complaint. After service he gets a job as a postman or policeman or prison guard and is on his feet 8 hours a day for another 20 years until retirement. When he's 65 his joints all ache and he seeks treatment for his aching feet, ankles, and knees. He files a VA disability claim, and the VA examiner gives a medical opinion saying that his current condition was "at least as likely as not" incurred in military service. So his claim is granted and he receives a fat monthly check for the rest of his life.

If the veteran doesn't like the rate of compensation he's receiving, he simply files a "claim for increase." He can submit increase claims over and over as often as he likes for the rest of his life. He doesn't have to show any evidence of a worsening condition. VA will order an "increase exam" and the condition will be reevaluated based on the new exam. The VA examiner or contracted examiner has never seen or treated the veteran before. He meets with the veteran for 10 or 15 minutes, does a few range-of-motion tests on which the veteran exaggerates, and then based on the veteran's responses to a few canned questions, the examiner provides a report by checking off a string of boxes on an exam template. It's multiple-choice answers, not personalized to the veteran. And the answers are not based on a review of any medical treatment records unless an opinion has been requested. And this little form of checked boxes becomes the data that VA will enter into their computer to spit out a numerical evaluation (severity level) for each condition.

If the veteran is denied service-connection for any new issue or if he's denied an increase, he can appeal the decision, and have it reconsidered based on the same evidence of record. Or he may choose to file a "reopen claim" and submit new evidence for consideration. The new evidence may be additional medical treatment records not submitted before, or lay statements from family and friends. In many cases, the evidence to reopen is simply new treatment records from the VA medical center, a wasting of VA medical resources to coddle and provide unnecessary tests and treatments for this claimant who is just trying to get an increase in compensation. Receipt of new evidence of any kind generally also leads to a new medical opinion from a VA physician or contracted physician, a further waste of resources.

It is illegal to file a fraudulent claim of any sort against the government. It is illegal to provide fraudulent testimony in the form of statements or fake medical records. The veterans who do it should not only be denied benefits but should be prosecuted with fines and jail time. I think they do not know the seriousness of their crime because they've never heard of anyone being punished for this. I personally have never in 10 years seen or heard of a case denied due to fraud or prosecuted for fraud. The worst that happens is denial of the claim when a rare physician makes a statement that the claimant is "malingering." Most physicians are afraid to note such opinions, for fear of being killed in retaliation.

A disability claim is decided by a rating specialist (rater) and the decision is not based on the rater's opinion, logic, knowledge or experience. The decision to grant or deny is based on federal law, as interpreted by VA policy makers and procedure manual writers, and provided in the working manual, MR21-MR. If granted, the evaluation for each issue is determined from a federal regulation, with assistance from a computerized "evaluation builder."

The federal laws which govern the awarding of disability compensation are published as guidance in the Code of Federal Regulations (CFR) Book 38, primarily 38 CFR Part 3, for adjudication or procedures for handling claims, and 38 CFR Part 4, the Schedule for Rating Disabilities. In the Part 4 section, Subpart A provides general rating policies, and Subpart B provides very specific detailed criteria for rating each condition, for granting and assigning an evaluation based on typical possible residuals of each injury or disease. The specific diagnosed conditions are grouped by body systems, so under The Musculoskeletal System you would find any joint, bone, or muscle problem, and under The Digestive System you would find stomach or intestinal problems. Under Mental Disorders you would find PTSD and schizophrenia, and so on for every system of the body. For each specific medical condition, possible evaluations are provided, representing different levels of disability, and criteria/symptomology or lab test or exam findings necessary to support each possible evaluation.

A disability evaluation is supposed to represent how much ability to work is lost due to that condition; for example, a 20% evaluation means that the condition reduces one's ability to work by 20%, so now he can only work at 80% of the capacity he did when fully functional. Evaluations are assigned only in increments of 10%, from 10 to 100%, and it varies for each condition. A knee condition could be 0, 10, 20, 30, or 40%, or a temporary 100% after knee replacement; coronary artery disease may be 30, 60, or 100%; and the options for irritable bowel syndrome are 0, 10, or 30%. Some conditions, even at their most severe level are not considered to be more than 30 percent disabling. Some, such as residuals after a stroke, or residuals after a knee replacement, even if there is no apparent current disability would still be granted a minimum of 10% for the stroke or 30% for the knee. The percentages assigned to each condition are then combined by a special calculation/formula, not added together, and the total compensation evaluation will determine how much the claimant will receive monthly.

The current VA compensation regulations have been in effect since 1945, and there are modifications/revisions every year which allow for granting more issues and with less objective evidence required. The payment amounts also go up every year with cost-of-living increases. Since 2010, the VA has been processing more than one million disability claims every year, including new claims, claims for increase, and reopened previously denied claims.

WHAT DISABILITIES CAN THEY CLAIM?

Veteran X claims disability compensation because he believes his "ears changed shape during service." He submitted a hand drawing (photographs would have been preferable) showing how his ears used to be round but became elongated over time in service, and he wants money for this. No disability mentioned. So that may be the only time that particular issue has ever been claimed, and there are hundreds of other one-of-a-kind silly issues received on claims every day. Veterans have been told to claim anything they can possibly identify that might have first occurred during their military service or resulted from service, and they may get paid for it! They can claim anything they want to, and no matter how obsurd, VA must devote time and manpower to fully develop the claim and provide a rating decision.

There are "extreme" claims, consisting of hundreds of pages of handwritten, mostly illegible, garbley-gook, usually received from veterans in prisons or mental institutions who have made claim-filing their hobby. These often ramble on and on about how veterans are not appreciated and how they only want what they deserve for serving the country; i.e. they want continued payment just because they once served, even if they were kicked out of service due to mental or criminal problems.

Other perfectly normal healthy veterans submit claims listing literally *hundreds* of medical issues, basically every part of their body they can think of. Why? Why not? They have nothing to lose and everything to gain. Maybe the VA will find something the veteran doesn't even know he has! If within a year before or after discharge, the VA will have to examine for every single issue regardless of any prior or current medical treatment.

If a soldier was discharged early from the military due to medical issues, those issues become the basis for his VA claim, and he can add anything else he likes. Some copy a long list of "issues" from the summary page in their military treatment file, a list of simply everything ever annotated by a medical provider, including results of routine tests, records of immunizations, vital statistics, references to medical history such as conditions the veteran's parents died from, and of course acute illnesses such as head colds, tension headaches, and minor skin abrasions.

Many claims are prepared by Veteran Service Organization representatives (VFW, American Legion, VDVS, etc.) and the veteran has no idea what was claimed, even if he signed it. These POAs (power of attorneys) are famous for listing unspecific conditions such as "undiagnosed illness due to Gulf War exposures" or "respiratory problems due to exposure to fire pits" and they also list hearing loss and tinnitus on every single claim. When the veteran goes to exam he has no idea what symptoms to report, has no idea what tinnitus is, and denies claiming such things.

An honest claim would be one that lists specific medical disabilities that resulted from a serious injury or illness incurred in the line of duty, and would explain when and where it happened in service. For example: residuals of a gunshot wound or an IED blast, residuals of an open fracture due to falling in a hole on a two mile run after which that leg was shorter than the other, respiratory residuals of tuberculosis contracted in service.

For this book, I considered contacting about 100 rating specialists and asking them to tell me the strangest or stupidest claims they'd ever rated, but I changed my mind because my point is not to show the rare unusual claims. There are certainly plenty of very strange claims submitted from veterans abusing the system and that's not likely to change. But my point is to show the "usual" "normal" claims and how they're routinely handled and granted by VA. The normal VA misappropriation of funds is what *can* and must be changed.

The examples in this book are all cases I truly personally experienced and not over the course of my career, but just over the course of a few weeks in one recent year, and they do represent the "normal claims." Although every case is a little different in the claimant's history or in the list of specific disabilities claimed, these examples are representative of cases seen over and over and over again, just with a different name.

In the latter half of this book, under the section of "Specific Medical Issues" I provide many examples of claims for specific disabilities after discussing the problems of rating that particular medical issue. But this chapter is to explain what a typical claim might look like, and the claims processing and rating procedures.

TYPICAL CLAIMED ISSUES

Sleep apnea (not service-caused, no symptoms if treated)
Little finger was cut, mashed, or got a splinter in it (chronic?)
Sprained ankle (from playing basketball)
Erectile dysfunction (male)
Inability to obtain orgasm (female)
Stubbed big toe
Ingrown toe nail
Discolored fingernail
Hair loss (common hereditary baldness)
Diabetes (acknowledging that parents and siblings have it too)
Acid reflux (after eating certain foods)
Depression due to weight gain
Obesity

Aging (claimed as "disability" because it's why he can't work)
Dry eyes
Dry skin
Acne
Asthma (had since childhood)
Sinusitis (not a chronic disability)
Rhinitis (allergies)
Hysterectomy (would have had regardless of service)
Uterine fibroids (ditto)
C-section scar, (the military provides free pre-natal care, delivery by Cesarean section surgery, and postnatal medical care, then she sues for the residual scar)
Scar from having melanomas removed during service (military provides free cancer removal, saves his life, then he sues for scars)
UTI (urinary tract infections) (not chronic)
URI (upper respiratory infection) (colds) (not chronic)
Sexually transmitted diseases (syphilis) (chlamydia)
Flat feet (present at entry to service)
Degenerative arthritis (common old-age condition)
Left shoulder dislocation (has happened throughout life, including before service)
TMJ (temporomandibular joint disorder) (opened mouth too wide when biting a big burger)
Ganglion cyst left wrist (not related to any injury)
Headaches and/or migraines (most always diagnosed as common tension headaches)
Left knee meniscal tear (from playing basketball)
ACL tear (from playing football)
Hearing loss (often first claimed 50 years after service)
Tinnitus (subjective, also claimed 50 years after service)
PTSD (for stressful situations in their current post-service life)
Psychoses (schizophrenia, bipolar disorder, often preceded service)
Anxiety or Adjustment Disorder (due to current post-service problems or inability to adjust to civilian life)

TYPES OF CLAIMS

An "original" claim is the first one the veteran ever files, doesn't matter how long he has been out of service, and he can file it prior to discharge, within 6 months of discharge. If a claim is received within a year after discharge, the veteran will be given a full general medical examination (entire body) and he will get additional specialty exams if he has claimed a mental, dental, audio, or vision problem. The exams are especially helpful to the veteran because they can establish symptoms that he has never reported before and conditions he has never been treated for.

If the original claim is filed more than a year after discharge, he will receive exams specific to the issues claimed *if* (1) the service treatment records show an injury or complaint of the symptom during service *and* (2) the post-service records show the condition has continued since leaving service. In the not too distant past, if the evidence failed to show an in-service condition and post-service treatment, or if there had been too long between the two findings (lack of chronicity) the claim was simply denied. But the policies have become increasingly relaxed. The veteran is not required to have continued treatment after service; his complaint of symptoms is enough. Gulf War general medical exams are being given to Gulf War veterans many years after discharge and regardless of whether the condition was shown in service or after service, and the exam becomes the evidence. Medical opinions are being requested for all sorts of cases whenever the evidence is not fully supporting the veteran.

After the original claim has been decided and closed, if he submits another claim for any issue not on the first claim, this will be a "new" claim. It's treated just like the original claim except that he won't get an automatic general medical exam unless the claim is received within a year after discharge. There will be full consideration of all military records, lay evidence, and medical records past and present. If the condition was shown in service and since service, an exam and medical opinion will be obtained.

Once granted, veterans will continue to ask for greater and greater compensation. Sometimes they just list the issues again on a claim form with no supporting evidence and that's ok. Often they will explain that they are asking for an increase because they need or deserve more money, without any mention of a worsening condition. If a veteran submits a claim for an issue already granted, that will be an "increase" claim. Once a veteran is granted service-connection for any issue, he is allowed and encouraged to continue requesting increases in that condition for the rest of his life. Each rating decision will tell him why he got the evaluation he did, and what the evidence must show in order to support a higher evaluation. There's no time frame for waiting between submitting another request for increase. If he has medical treatment records, the claim will be rated again, even if it was just rated last week. Until recently, another new VA exam was also ordered with every increase claim, but some stations are now requiring one year to lapse before ordering another increase examination (unless there is other medical evidence supporting a higher evaluation). Increases will be granted effective the date the increase claim was received, regardless of how long before it's rated.

You will rarely ever see "improvement" in a veteran's case file. They won't admit that a condition has resolved in any way; they just keep claiming increases. They go get the knee replacements and get their bunionectomies and have their arteries cleaned out, and then just keep on saying that every condition is worse. Furthermore, each condition, and the medicine or treatment for it, has caused new secondary conditions for them to claim. All the VA medical centers are apparently treating for naught, never healing or improving anyone's conditions. The C&P exams sometimes show improvement, but the claimant will never accept that, nor will he need to accept that. If an exam shows improvement the VA simply continues the prior evaluation and advises the claimant, "Although improvement has been shown, sustained improvement has not been shown on two consecutive VA exams within the past 5 years." If by chance improvement has been shown on two exams in 5 years, then a "proposal to reduce" decision will be sent to the veteran. He's given 60 days to contest it and he will generally be able to provide some lay statement or private medical statement to keep the evaluation going, so another rating is then done to continue the prior evaluation. If he doesn't respond, a rating will be done to make the reduction, but in order to give him plenty of notice, the reduction won't happen for another 3 months (at least 60 days due process, to the first of the 3rd month, plus time for the rating procedures). If his overall evaluation does get reduced, he can appeal or he can simply request another increase the following year and this time he must grimace, groan, and gripe a little bit harder on the exam. By the time all the due process periods expire and rating processes are completed, it'll be almost a year anyway since the last exam. His new (restored) evaluation will take place the date of the new exam no matter how long before it gets rated.

When a claim is received for an issue that has already been denied, no matter how recently or long ago, that will be a "reopen" claim. If any sort of new evidence is received, such as new medical records, or lay statements from friends, family, or coworkers, the claim will be fully reviewed and re-rated. Less than half the VA claims processing resources (people, time, materials, exams) is spent on original, first time claims. *Most* resources are spent on increase and reopen claims. Veterans never give up; they keep resubmitting the same old denied issues and more time and paper is wasted on denying them again. And the claims for increase will keep coming until the veteran is finally paid 100% disability.

So resources are wasted over and over again for the same veteran instead of just looking thoroughly at that veteran's history and condition, making a fair and final decision, and moving on to new veteran. Thousands of new soldiers turn into veterans every day, and with their current knowledge and technology *every* new veteran will file a VA claim. It's ridiculous to waste time rehashing the same old claims over and over. I've seen veterans resubmit the same issue for denial 20 or more times and each time it must go through the whole process. Other veterans choose to keep making up new issues in attempt to raise their compensation, and each issue, no matter how unrealistic must be developed and fully considered.

Of course some legitimate service-connected conditions will worsen in time and increases are warranted, and sometimes secondary medical issues develop. However, VA could handle those with scheduled review exams and simple review ratings, and this would be more fair to all veterans, rather than devoting unproportionate amounts of time and resources to those who keep coming back in with too frequent increase claims, repeating denied claims which have already been fully adjudicated, and adding new issues every year just to try to get their total evaluation raised.

EXAMPLES OF ORIGINAL CLAIMS

***

Veteran X is a 38-year-old perfectly healthy male. He entered service at age 18, served 20 years, got out and drew military retirement. On his separation exam there were no chronic/serious disabilities noted. However, throughout service he had spent plenty of time in sick call, complaining of upper respiratory symptoms, stomach aches, knee pains, and erectile dysfunction. Within a month after discharge he filed a claim for 17 conditions, all over his body, nothing serious. On VA exam there was no loss of motion shown but because he claimed painful motion, he got 10 percent disability for each of 10 different issues, and 0 percent for 5 more issues. He was only denied for hearing loss because his hearing was perfect, and for vision because refractive errors correctable to 20/20 with glasses is congenital and not subject to service-connection. His total compensation evaluation is 70 percent plus SMC-K for erectile dysfunction (not due to any disease such as diabetes or prostate cancer, just claimed dysfunction, totally subjective).

***

Veteran X served 11 months from 1976 to 1977 and was released early "under honorable conditions" so that qualifies for VA benefits. Forty years after service, in 2016, he submitted his original claim for arthritis in both hands, both knees, both elbows, and both feet, low testosterone, high cholesterol, tinnitus, and hearing loss.

***

Veteran X served a 4-year term in CONUS, never went abroad or saw any conflict, and never had any significant injury in service. Three months before discharge he started working on his VA claim. He requested a sleep apnea study and admitted himself for a psychiatric evaluation due to depression and anxiety. He listed 89 issues on his claim form, including every joint and organ in his body. He had a pre-discharge VA claim and on that exam reported numerous complaints not seen in the treatment records. These things, since annotated while still on active duty, are considered "in-service" complaints so they will be service-connected as long as he can get this doctor or any future doctor to provide a diagnosis for each one. His issues, no matter how minor and non-disabling each one is, with the help of his sleep apnea and mental disorder, will easily total 100% disability, and the payment will be effective the date after discharge.

EXAMPLES OF INCREASE CLAIMS

***

Veteran X said he had promised his niece that if she graduated high school he would help her through college, and now she was ready for college, so he needs more money! He has no concept that increases are supposed to be based on increased severity of medical conditions.

***

Veteran X had been 0 percent for his knees since 1976. Forty years later he claimed an increase and with the way the laws are now, the minimum for each knee had to be increased to 10 percent each just based on his subjective complaint of pain. There is no regard to the fact that this man had worked successfully for 30 years as a mailman, a walking door-to-door delivery mailman!

Many other similar claimants have worked 30 years as a policeman walking a beat, or a machinist squatting in the shipyard. When they retire from those jobs and their income drops, they come to the government to pick up the slack so they can continue the standard of living to which they have become accustomed.

***

Veteran X wrote on his claim, "I haven't worked in 11 years, and the money you (VA) pay me is not enough to pay my bills anymore." Nothing about being any sicker, just needing more money.

***

Veteran X put on his IU claim that he couldn't work because he had owned his own company and it had gone out of business. No physical reason, just no more demand for his services.

***

Veteran X, and hundreds of other men, received a gunshot wound in Vietnam and right after service they were each granted a 0 percent disability because there was a scar, but there was no pain, no limitation of function, or any disability from the gunshot wound. Forty years went by, during which they worked in construction, or walked the beat as a police officer, or worked as a mail carrier, or as a prison guard. At age 65 they retire and start drawing social security. The income is less than they are accustomed to. They need more money! They file a claim for increase with the VA. Now they say the scar is painful, and the limb that was injured is painful and they can't use it fully. No VA doctor will question the integrity of a Vietnam veteran. Everything that can possibly be granted to them is granted. It would seem better to me to put an end to these foolish claims, and all the cost involved with processing them. Just give every veteran who served in the Vietnam war (on land, air or sea) a "Vietnam stipend" and be done with it.

***

Veteran X was granted 20% for his back, and 10% for radiculopathy of each lower extremity secondary to the back, and tinnitus 10%, totaling 40%. The rating decision told him what he would need to show in order to get higher evaluations. Six months later he filed for an increase and got another VA exam. This time, based on his reported symptoms he qualified for 40% for the back, and 20% for each leg, so his total went up to 70%! Immediately upon receipt of that decision he submitted a claim for IU; and that's the way the game is played.

***

Veteran X retired early at age 46 because he could, although he could still work if he wanted to at that or some other job. But he doesn't need to work considering his VA supplemental income. In 1990 he filed his first claim and was granted 0% disability, but he filed increases year after year. He finally got it up to 20% in 2006, about the time VA went off the deep end and started giving away the farm. "Grant if you can, deny only if you must." He got 30% in 2008, 50% in 2010, 60% in 2012, 80% in March 2015, 90% in October 2015, and finally got his 100% in February 2016.

EXAMPLES OF REOPEN CLAIMS

***

Veteran X served 11 months from 1966 to 1967 "under honorable conditions" so he's entitled to VA benefits. Forty years after service, in 2007, he submitted his original claim for multiple issues including hearing loss. Some were granted but his audio exam showed no significant hearing loss so that issue was denied. He reopened the claim 10 years later, in 2017, when he was over 70 years old, and included a current private audiogram showing very mild hearing loss at high frequencies. The VA exam then also showed hearing loss in both ears and with a positive opinion, it was granted! Even though he had no hearing loss in service, and VA records verify he had none in 2007, he still got granted for hearing loss that first manifested in 2017 when he was over 70!

* * *

Veteran X filed a claim for "knees, feet, and stomach" (no mention of anything wrong with them) as if healthy people do not have these body parts. He filed the claim 10 years after discharge so he did not get an automatic VA exam, and he did not submit any medical evidence or any reference to any treatment he'd had in or after service. His service records did show complaints of pain in the knees, feet, and stomach, but all were noted as "acute" conditions and no chronic disabilities were shown on the military separation exam.

A VCAA (Veteran Claims Assistance Act) letter was sent to him explaining that VA needs evidence that a condition was incurred in service and has continued to the present. He did not respond to the letter. The VA rater reviewed his service treatment records and verified there had been no treatment at any VA medical centers, then denied the claim based on no evidence of a current disability. The veteran made several irate phone calls to the VA 800 number, and sent in a rude letter proclaiming that he couldn't be denied because he had never received *his* VA exam! He demanded to have a VA exam and reconsideration of the claim. There was no new evidence, but since the time frame was still one year since the last rating, the case was reviewed and a new rating done, confirming and continuing the previous denial. The notification letter explained that C&P exams are for evaluating the severity of a condition, not for diagnosing a disability, and that he should go to his local VAMC if he needs treatment for any service-incurred injury or disease.

Within a year of that second decision, he went to his local VAMC, complained of symptoms with his knees, feet, and stomach, then resubmitted his claim to VBA. Now VA has "current" evidence of symptoms, subjective though they may be, so exams and medical opinions were ordered to determine whether the conditions in service were chronic. Despite the fact that the man functioned normally and required no treatment for knees, feet, or stomach for 10 years after service, the examiner opined that it was "at least as likely as not" or 50/50 probability that the conditions had existed since service. The knee conditions were diagnosed as strains because there was no visual or x-ray evidence, and no reduced range of motion, nothing but a purely subjective report of pain, warranting 10% each. The feet condition was diagnosed as plantar fasciitis at 50% based on nothing but a complaint of extreme tenderness on bottom of the feet. The stomach condition was diagnosed as irritable bowel syndrome, granted 30% based on veteran's report of severe alternating diarrhea and constipation, despite no evidence of complaint or treatment in the past 10 years. VA says a veteran cannot be required to obtain treatment, and just because he has never sought treatment cannot be held against him. His combined evaluation is 70%, a payment of over $1600 a month based on his family size.

He then submitted another reopen claim to ask for IU, for which he meets the schedular requirements, but it was denied because he is gainfully employed. He can continue to submit "reopen" claims asking for an increase, or adding new issues to his claim.

DEPENDENTS' INDEMNITY COMPENSATION

After a serviceman or veteran dies, his or her spouse or children may continue to receive VA support, and this is through the Dependents Indemnity Compensation (DIC) program. While alive, a veteran receives disability payments in his or her name and the compensation amount includes allowances (additional amounts) for having a dependent spouse or children; they don't get separate payments. The veteran's compensation or pension payment stops when he or she dies. Then the dependent spouse files his or her own claim for DIC and if it's decided favorably the spouse will receive monthly payments in his or her own name. If dependent children are still living with the surviving spouse, the spouse receives an additional amount based on the number of children. If there is no surviving spouse, a surviving dependent child can claim DIC.

DIC is paid in cases where a serviceperson has died during service, regardless of the cause, or in cases when a veteran's death resulted from a service-connected injury or disease. The death certificate may list multiple different conditions contributing to his demise, but as long as any one of them was a service-connected condition, the dependent's claim may be granted.

In order for a surviving spouse to qualify for this benefit she (or he) must meet a few requirements. If they married before 1957, no more questions asked. If married after 1957, the marriage must have occurred during his service or within 15 years after the veteran's date of military discharge. The marriage must have lasted at least one year prior to the veteran's death or the spouse must have had a child with the veteran while cohabiting continuously with him until his death. The surviving spouse cannot be currently remarried, unless she or he is over 57 and remarried after December 16, 2003, then he or she is entitled to continue to receive DIC based on the prior spouse's (veteran's) death. (This raised many an eyebrow on Nehmer claims when hundreds of thousands of dollars of retro-active payment was paid to the surviving spouses of Vietnam veterans even though they are now remarried to someone else, and in no financial need!)

A dependent child may qualify for his or her own payment of DIC if he or she is unmarried, not included on a surviving spouse's DIC, and either under age 18, or up to age 23 if attending school. Even a child who has been adopted out of the veteran's family will qualify if the other criteria is met.

WHERE ARE CLAIMS PROCESSED?

When a soldier is seriously injured in service, he is transported to Walter Reed Army Medical Center in Bethesda Maryland. The VA claim paperwork is filled for him there at the hospital and it begins while he is still on the military payroll so there'll be no loss of pay. He'll continue to get military pay until he's ready for discharge from the hospital, at which time VA compensation will begin effective the day after discharge. The VA evaluations are done while he's in the hospital, still considered active duty, and when the rating decisions are ready, and when the veteran is stable enough to be discharged to home or to a long-term facility, then and only then is he discharged from service. His VA claim is "case-managed" by a special operations team member, and it will be finalized shortly after discharge (when he is officially a veteran). VA cannot grant a claim for someone still on active duty, but they can begin the process, and coordinate with the military, so there is no loss of pay for these seriously injured soldiers/veterans. Working these cases must be a very heart-wrenching and difficult job for the claims examiners who review these cases, just as it is difficult for the health care providers at Walter Reed hospital. These are cases of truly disabled veterans, truly deserving of every benefit we can give them. I have no complaint with what we are paying these injured veterans; I'd even be willing to pay them more. How can a price be put on loss of limbs, brain damage, or disfigurement? This book is not about those veterans. This book is written in honor of those veterans and in defence of those veterans.

All VA disability claims are developed and decided by veteran services specialists working for the Veterans Benefits Administration (VBA), not by anyone in the VCA (cemetary admin) or VHA (health admin). There are currently fifty-eight VBA regional offices, including one each in the District of Columbia (Washington DC), Puerto Rico, and the Philippines, and at least one in each of the 50 states. The more populous states have more; California has 3, New York and Texas each have 2 offices. According to the VA website, 56 of the VA regional offices are developing and deciding VA compensation claims. These are not VA medical centers and are not under the jurisdiction of the Veterans Healthcare Administration (VHA). These Veteran Benefits Administration (VBA) offices do not treat medical conditions, do not diagnose conditions, and do not give advice on medical treatment. Thousands of Veteran Service Representatives (VSRs) and Rating VSRs (RVSRs) work in these 56 offices, or work out of their homes, to process the disability claims. They request and review evidence, generate rating decisions, generate correspondence to the claimants, and generate authorization documents to DFAS for payment of benefits. Processing is now totally electronic. All claims and all evidence received in VA mail is sent first to a contracted scanning service provider who scans all hard copies into the VA's electronic claims processing system. Evidence can also be uploaded anywhere by veterans or VSOs or medical providers. A claim submitted anywhere in the world can be reviewed or decided anywhere else in the world by a VBA employee with authority and internet access to the secure system.

The VBA has a few other functions which are sometimes carried out in the same federal buildings but in separate offices with specialists trained in processing other benefits to include VA home loan guarantees, VA educational benefits (for veterans and their dependents), and VA vocational rehabilitation benefits. None of those issues are intended to be fully discussed in this book. VA pension claims are currently being handled by a single federal office in Philadelphia; however, if a veteran claims pension and compensation at the same time, one of the compensation offices will have to address both issues. As previously noted, the details and problems of VA pension are also not to be fully addressed in this book. The purpose of this book is to disclose and expound the problems of the *VA Disability Compensation* benefits program only.

THE RATING SCHEDULE

The Veterans Affairs current "Schedule for Rating Disabilities" used for assigning compensation evaluations, hereafter referred to as the "rating schedule," found in 38 CFR Part 4 and Book C, is an antiquated reference that has been in use since 1945. Annual amendments/modifications since 1946 are found in Appendix A. The schedule is occasionally modified as science and medicine evolve with better understanding of conditions, and as new disabilities are added. Based on GAO recommendations, VA has recently committed to reviewing/revising the criteria for each body system once every 10 years.

The Rating Schedule is a tool for assigning evaluations to hundreds of different disabilities, each one generally having from two to six possible evaluations. The evaluation for each condition will be from 0% up to 100% disability, in increments of 10, depending on the severity of the disability. (Other regulations declare how much money will actually be paid for 10%, 20%, and so forth, and cost of living allowances increase those amounts almost every year.) For many conditions the percentages of disability are unreasonable for certain symptoms, and the regulations haven't kept up with modern medical treatments, so they don't match up very well to current treatment or exams. But a bigger concern is whether certain conditions should be granted at all, especially once they've been treated and cured.

"Disabled" means *unable to work* and, per the law, veterans disability is supposed to be awarded commensurate to the degree of work impairment. For example, an award of 10 percent disability means that the veteran can now do only 90% of work that he might otherwise have been able to do. A 50% evaluation would mean that he can only do half as much physically or earn half as much as he might have if he didn't have the disability. A 100% evaluation for one condition means that condition in and of itself is totally preventing the veteran from obtaining and maintaining gainful employment.

Most veterans who have filed claims have filed numerous conditions. So there may be one condition 40% disabling and two more at 20% each, and two more at 10% each. This sounds like 100% disability but actually it is only 70% when put in the VA calculator, because the percentages are not added, they are combined by a special complex formula. The veteran may have 20 different service-connected issues that would add up to 150%, but it only comes up to 70 percent in the VA calculator because none of them are very serious disabilities so he should still be able to do some sort of work. The calculator starts with the most serious condition, then other lesser conditions are added in, with extra attention given to "bilateral" conditions such as when both knees are affected or both wrists.

Technically the VA calculator works as follows. If you have a 30% disability rating, that is multiplied against 100%, which is assumed to be good health. This gives you 30%. Subtract that from 100% which leaves you with 70%. Consider 70% as the new starting point for the health rating. Then subtract 70% from 100% and you are left with 30%. If that is the only disability, then the final VA Service-Connected Disability Rating is 30%. If there are multiple ratings, you continue with the process, using the final number each time as the starting point. Continuing with our example, if the next rated issue is 10%, you would multiply 10% against 70%, which is 7%. You subtract that from 70%, which leaves 63%. Subtract 63% from 100% and you get 37%. The total disability rating is 37%, which rounds up to 40% total compensation.

The rater never has to do this calculation. The VA software program does the calculations and spits out a "code sheet" for each rating decision; of course, garbage in is garbage out, so it's all dependent on the VSR entering the correct information in the computer when he is closing out a claim/rating decision. Further explanation and the actual "Combined Ratings Table" can be found in 38 CFR 4.25.

A Rating Decision, referred to as a "rating," is a decision made by a Rating Veterans Services Representative, herein referred to as a "rater" working at one of the VA's Veterans Benefits Administration's 56 Regional Offices. Decisions are not made by the military, and are not provided by any VA hospital employee. Claims are received into the VBA's electronic on-line system then assigned to a VBA Regional Office for processing. All possible evidence to support the claim is consolidated into the veteran's claim file. This includes everything sent in by the veteran or his representative, including any claims forms, statements, or private medical records he has submitted, and any medical records for which he has provided a consent for release of the records, then obtained by the VA claims processors. The claims file will also include the veteran's military service treatment records (VA obtains from the military department) and treatment records from VHA (Veterans Health Administration) for any treatment he has received at any VA Medical Centers. If the claim is for Individual Unemployabilty the processors may also request statements from prior employers, or records from the Social Security Administration. Once all reasonable efforts have been exhausted to receive all potentially helpful information in support of a claim, the claim is marked as "ready to rate" and assigned to a rater. That person reviews all evidence and, based on application of the federal law and VA policies, will make a decision as to granting or denying service-connection for a disability, and if granted, will assign a specific evaluation for that disability.

The "Schedule of Rating Disabilities" was developed to be a guide, to help the rater with an appropriate decision, while the regulations clearly explain that the evaluation is to be assigned based on the degree of functional impairment evidenced. 38 CFR 4.10 discusses functional impairment: *"The basis of disability evaluations is the ability of the body as a whole, or of the psyche, or of a system or organ of the body to function under the ordinary conditions of daily life including employment. Whether the upper or lower extremities, the back or abdominal wall, the eyes or ears, or the cardiovascular, digestive, or other system, or psyche are affected, evaluations are based upon lack of usefulness, of these parts or systems, especially in self-support."*

But VA pays little attention to functional impairment anymore. Furthermore, the Rating Schedule is rarely looked at by a rater; the Evaluation Builder (supposed to reflect the rating schedule) spits out an evaluation, and there can be no deviation from it. The rater is not allowed to use his personal judgment, common sense, or logic in rating a case. A common joke among VA employees is, "Well that would be logical, so it can't be right. It's not the VA way." A VA rater is paid anywhere from 50K to 100K a year (plus more for overtime) to make these decisions, but he is not allowed to use his brain in making any decision; he simply feeds the computer certain bits of the evidence from the file, and whatever the computer spits out is what the veteran gets. The decisions are becoming increasingly automated, deliberately, because this is supposed to provide more consistency across America. It's also supposed to save money by requiring less time from the rater, but it's actually wasting more money because so many unjustified grants are being paid.

Sometimes the schedule-based evaluation is actually not in the best interest of the veteran. For example, a claimant may have eczema, herpes simplex, and hidradenitis suppurativa, all serious skin conditions affecting different body parts, but on one veteran, he would only be granted 10 percent for all of them combined as one issue, because skin conditions have to be evaluated together. On the other hand, a veteran who has frostbite affecting one toe gets 30% and a veteran with left arm radiculopathy affecting the middle radicular group, which only occasionally affects her typing ability, gets 30% for that. Practically anyone who is granted PTSD will get 30% or greater regardless of the lack of symptoms. A scar on the head which is actually covered by hair could warrant 30%, and sleep apnea (totally asymptomatic) warrants 50%.

Even the regulations state that the rating schedule (and corresponding evaluation builders) are to be used as a tool after thorough consideration of all evidence, specifically consideration of functional impairment, but raters are required to grant whatever the evaluation builder spits out. Raters are told that if you go off your own instincts and assign an evaluation, even if you fully support it by noting medical evidence, you risk getting an "error" and that if you assign what the evaluation builder tells you then you'll never get an error for it. In this madhouse of mass production, if a rater wants to survive, his goal is to get as many claims rated as fast as possible, without error, so raters quickly learn to punch the DBQ results in, and grant whatever the tools spit out. Don't ask questions; just move on to the next one.

(16) PROBLEMS IN THE RATING PROCESS

PROBLEMS WITH VA EXAMS

All granted "diagnoses" and "evaluations" are based primarily on VA C&P (Compensation and Pension) examinations. Thousands of pages of treatment records are uploaded to many of the claim files, and the most common reason a decision is delayed is because VA is waiting to receive very old and useless medical records the claimant has mentioned. But in reality, the treatment records are rarely even reviewed, because the VA exams take precedence. They are considered more probative because they are specific to the issue being claimed, provide more objective details such as measurements and frequencies, and the date of the exam is usually more current than the dates of treatment.

Any claimant filing his initial claim within a year of discharge from service will receive a full General Medical exam, as well as specialty exams for Mental, Dental, Eyes, or Ears conditions. This exam will serve as "current" evidence of a condition, regardless of whether there has ever been a treatment record or a complaint of the condition before. Veterans who served in the Gulf War regions of Southeast Asia will be given a full Gulf War General Medical exam regardless of how many years they have been out of service, and again, the evidence on exam will serve as "current" evidence of the condition.

Many VA C&P exams are now being conducted by private examiners who don't propose to know anything about military life or circumstances, or VA claims, and certainly have not previously treated their examinees. One contractor, QTC, has been doing the exams since 2003, and in 2016, the federal government spread the wealth among five corporations including QTC, VES, LHI, VetFed, and MSLA, with a ceiling cost of $6.8 billion for a 12-month contract with four 12-month extensions.

In the past, an examiner would often be the veteran's primary care physician at the VA and he would incorporate information from the claimant's history and treatment records into the C&P exam. The examiner would actually prepare a lengthy written report of findings and comments. But now that has been replaced by "DBQs" which are Disability Benefits Questionnaires that have been created for each medical condition. They are supposed to correspond to the specific rating criteria noted in the Rating Schedule and in the automated "Evaluation Builder" used by VA, although often there are great discrepancies between the two. Many DBQs do not address all the symptoms the evaluation builder asks about, and sometimes the DBQ provides information that indicates a serious illness, but there's no place to put the information in the evaluation builder. The rater does not get to use common sense in those cases, just click it the best you can.

The DBQs came out about the same time that the VA started contracting out to have exams done by private physicians in the communities where the veteran lives. They did it to get the exams faster, and so that veterans won't have to travel too far for an exam. I have seen notes in veterans' files, and remarks in internet blogs, from many Service Organization representatives (VFW, American

Legion, etc) who do not even consider the DBQs to be real exams. They will tell the veterans, "You tell the VA you want a real C&P exam, not a DBQ done by a contractor." But DBQs have replaced "exams" and they *are* now the only C&P exams.

Whether done at the VAMC or by a private physician, the DBQ is usually filled out by an examiner/doctor who has never seen the claimant before. It's the luck of the draw for the veteran. Some veterans have had serious symptoms for years, noted in their records, but they just don't impress the examiner. Perhaps the veteran is too arrogant and comes off as exaggerating, or he's or too timid and won't describe his symptoms, so the doctor clicks off the "mild" boxes and a low evaluation is given.

I really don't know how the VA doctors and contracted examiners can stand to do these exams. No wonder the VA medical centers are short about 50,000 physicians and other providers. VA is now subcontracting thousands of private physicians to help do the VA exams/DBQs, and there is a constant turnover of those examiners too.

Everything rides on these DBQs. I know the regulations stress over and over again that "all" evidence is to be considered and "weighed in equipoise" but that is not the way raters are taught or allowed to do it. They must use the DBQ to develop the evaluation. If the claimant doesn't like it he can appeal or come back next year for an increase and new exam. If the veteran is rated too high (based on the bogus DBQ), well then we're just stuck with it. In order to reduce it there will need to be two consecutive VA exams within a 5-year period both showing improvement.

Generally, if a condition is 20% or more and is expected to possibly improve, a routine future exam (RFE) should be diaried in the VA system for approximately 3 years in the future. If an exam actually shows improvement, then the evaluation remains the same but a RFE is scheduled for 18 months in the future. If improvement is shown on two consecutive VA exams within a 5-year period then a "proposal to reduce" can be issued. That gives the veteran 60 days to present more evidence to show that the condition has not really improved, and they almost always come in with some statement, and the evaluation is continued.

A veteran may have 10 different conditions each evaluated at 10% so his total is 70% disability. Future exams are not warranted for conditions that are 10% or less disabling. Most likely the mild 10% conditions have probably totally improved after about 6 months, but we never know it, because it is not examined again! He could potentially receive 70% forever with nothing wrong with him.

Raters must rely on doctors who have no idea the consequences of their exams. They have no idea that the decision to grant, and the evaluation assigned, is based solely on what they put on that exam/DBQ. Several times early in my career as a rater, I disagreed with a VA exam or opinion and I made a decision based on my review of all records, based on my knowledge of the military, and based on the good common sense and intelligence for which I was hired to do this job, and for which I was paid over $80,000 per year (not counting overtime) to make these decisions. Those decisions (the ones they caught) were kicked back to me as "errors" with the following admonishment. "You are not a doctor. You are to go with what the doctor says, and if you are ever in doubt, you rule in favor of the veteran."

I'm sorry to say it, with all due respect to the amount of schooling a person goes through to get a medical degree, but many of these VA physicians are apparent idiots, and the VA is short on medical staff so they will take any "doctor" they can get. A large number of them are illiterate, at least for the English language, and maybe they could complete a proper report in their native language, but they don't understand the questions on these DBQs. Most of the VA doctors are from India, very nice men and women, and concede everything they can for the veterans. I bet they don't realize that if they click the little box that says "very frequent" for headaches, this will be granted as a 50% disability. I really don't know where VA gets its doctors, but a vast *majority* of them are foreigners, and that is not a bad thing, it's just a thing worth looking into. Don't you want to know why American doctors are choosing to *not* work for the VA?

The VA examiners are not the ones "treating" these veterans. The day they see a veteran for a C&P exam is the only day they ever see him. The examiner asks questions of the veteran and checks off boxes on the DBQ according to the veteran's response. It is often clear that the veteran has no idea what is being asked. For example, a true flareup of a back or knee condition would usually last for several days if not several weeks, and a significant flareup would probably prompt a visit to a doctor, perhaps a cortisone shot or a prescription for Flexeril. But practically every veteran when asked about flareups will say "Yes." If by chance he is asked to describe it he will say something like he has flareups a couple of times a month, a sharp stabbing pain lasting a minute or two. Now really, is that functional impairment? Two to four minutes a month. In any case, the doctor will check the box for flareups and an evaluation is assigned despite any objective evidence of anything.

Joint exams keep getting more complex as more veterans file appeals regarding their evaluations. Whenever one of them convinces BVA that their condition was worse than it appeared on exam day, a new rule will be established and named after the veteran. A typical back exam will go as follows. On range-of-motion testing, the examiner reports that the veteran demonstrated flexion to 60. With consideration for "Deluca," after 3 repetitions of motion, it reduces to 55. With consideration of "Mitchell," with repeated use over time, it is reduced to 50. And with consideration of "Sharp," with flareups (based solely on what the veteran says) it goes to 45. The evaluation is assigned based on the most severe finding, which is of course the flareups, not seen on exam, but reported by the veteran. Is the exam being conducted during a flareup? No. Is the veteran being examined immediately after repetitive use over time? No. But the exam report is medically consistent with the veteran's statement describing functional loss with repetitive use over time or during a flareup.

What is the point of paying a competent physician to complete these exams? Why not just let the veteran fill out his own DBQ and send it in? In fact, many have tried that. Others have falsified reports by filling it out and putting a doctor's name on it.

Amazingly, some persons in the higher ranks and echelons of the VA are actually pushing for a system whereby the veteran would go on line and fill out his own determination of symptoms and severity, essentially choosing his own evaluations. This should cut down on VA employees, but OMG how it will increase the nation's debt.

***

Veteran X submitted a DBQ, prepared by a private physician, and it was one of the best reports I'd ever read, completed properly, and included a detailed written opinion in the remarks. The examiner (I'll call her Dr. XYZ) noted herself as a PhD and gave a phone number, address, signature, and gave a license number. By internet I determined that the physician was truly a certified psychologist practicing in Ohio since 2014. The veteran did not live in Ohio, so that was a red flag, but veterans can own multiple homes, especially those veterans receiving high compensation. But the DBQ looked totally acceptable and was good enough to grant and rate this issue without requesting any further evidence.

Fortunately, the VSR who developed this case did not review all the evidence submitted so he ordered another mental exam and medical opinion from the government contractor at that time. During the contracted VA exam, the veteran told the examiner that he has never met Dr. XYZ. The doctor has a website and the veteran had two web/internet sessions with her and she recommended books for him to read. (Another veteran friend told him about her, so he's not the first to use this service.) This is atrocious. The doctor was (probably still is) filling out DBQs based on internet sessions, never meeting the person, and not seeing his records or anything! The legitimate VA examiner in this case totally debunked Dr. XYZ's diagnosis and findings (which would have been granted 50-70%). The VA examiner found no mental condition other than alcohol abuse, so the claimed issue was denied.

Even though the regulations allow us to accept DBQs from private physicians, I don't believe we should accept them unless we also have medical treatment records showing that the physician has actually treated the claimant!

***

Veteran X filed a claim and his exams were ordered to be done by one of the contracted examiners. Then someone else looked at the case and realized the exams were required to be completed at a VA medical center because a Gulf War exam was needed. So the contracted exams were cancelled and the exams were reordered to be done at the VAMC. Things got crossed and the exams were done anyway, at both places, double exams for all issues, exactly 10 days apart, and the veteran never even said a word. Following are some of the findings noted on the exams.

For the claimed issue of "anemia" the first examiner said there is no diagnosis because the condition has resolved as there has been no evidence of the condition since service. The second examiner gave a diagnosis of anemia and noted symptoms of "easy fatigability" even though hemoglobin was normal on both exams.

For the issue of PTSD, the check marks on the first exam warranted a 30% evaluation, and the checkmarks on the second DBQ warranted a 70% evaluation. Same veteran, same family, same job. He actually had no reported functional troubles, so clearly even the 30% was very generous, but I had to grant 70% because that was the greatest possible benefit based on all evidence of record, and the worst findings were on the most current exam, so maybe he went from 30% to 70% in severity in the course of 10 days.

For the issue of "migraines' the first examiner noted there were "no prostrating attacks" so that exam would warrant 0 percent. The second examiner noted 'frequent and prolonged migraine attacks" so that warrants at least 30%.

***

Veteran X has been out of service for 20 years since 1996. He has provided no post-service or current treatment records. His military retirement exam in 1996 noted there were no chronic disabilities (NCD). He has now filed a claim and provided DBQs from a private physician, a physician who has never treated him, but was simply asked to complete the forms. The examiner diagnosed six physical conditions related to joints, also a mental condition which he opined was secondary to the physical issues, and GERD which he opined was secondary to the use of NSAIDS for the physical disabilities.

* * *

Veteran X has been service connected since 2002 for several joint conditions that have been 10 percent each for 15 years, for a total of 30 percent, until he filed a claim for increase in all conditions in 2017. The veteran had served 18 months in service from 2001 to 2002. On discharge he claimed joint pain and was service connected for bilateral knee strain, left ankle sprain, and back strain, the only conditions where he had voiced a complaint at some point during service. The diagnoses of "strain" and "sprain" are given when there is nothing shown on x-ray, nothing has been broken, and there is really no objective evidence of any medical condition, but he's still claiming pain. A minimal evaluation of 10 percent is to be assigned for any joint disability, including subjective joint pain.

The veteran has worked full time continuously since service and he also serves as a referee for football and basketball (running up and down the sideline and court). He has to get a review exam each year for the sports program to allow him to continue refereeing, and he gets that from his local VA medical center. Each year the report says he's physically fit. Now he claims increases in his service-connected conditions.

On the VA C&P exam there is no objective evidence of anything wrong, not even degenerative arthritis. The doctor says that the range of motion for his back is 90 degrees, reduced to 85 after 3 repetitions, reduced to 80 after repeated use, and reduced to 75 degrees with flareups. The ankle shows 25 degrees flexion on range of motion testing, reduced to 22 after 3 repetitions (Deluca), reduced to 20 after repeated use and reduced to 15 with flareups (Mitchell). If the veteran were presently having a flareup at time of exam, then 15 would be the present beginning finding, rather than 25. So how can the doctor say what the reduction will be with flareup? Most doctors will make a statement that since they are not examining during flareup, to fill in that box would be pure speculation. But plenty of doctors will fill it in and go on. And the increases are granted, despite the preponderance of evidence showing no true functional impairment.

***

Veteran X spent 3 months and 2 days in service, training only, and at the end of her training in 1981 she was discharged from active duty with an honorable discharge and put on Ready Reserves due to her "marginal, non-productive performance." She had spent numerous days on sick call each day claiming some different petty complaint to include: stomachache, abdomen pain, kidney infection, pregnancy test, mucous/congestion, trouble breathing, boots too big rubbed blisters, she hit her finger when driving a tent peg, and shin splints from running. Everyone gets shin splints in basic unless they are an accomplished runner prior to service. Basic training is rough physically, but the aches and pain heal, leaving one a little more muscular, a lot healthier, and without permanent residuals. Twenty-five years later she files a VA claim for bilateral feet, bilateral knees, and bilateral ankles all due to the shin splints in service, and she claims respiratory problems that have never been treated since service. She should not have been awarded a VA exam because there was no current medical evidence, not a stitch of medical treatment in all those years from 1981 to 2017. But somebody did order exams, so *now* there is current evidence of current complaints. So then, it all had to go back to an examiner for medical opinions regarding whether anything was caused by service. The examiner said "Y*es*, at least as likely as not," the same as saying "Maybe, maybe not" so VA rules in favor of the veteran. The examiner also diagnosed asthma per the current pulmonary function test reports and clearly stated that he believes it is due to her heavy smoking. But then he turned around and gave a positive opinion linking it to service, saying it was at least as likely as not *started* in service since she reported difficulty breathing during service.

PROBLEMS WITH MEDICAL OPINIONS

Granting service-connection based on medical opinions (MO's) has gone totally out of control. There is a time and proper application for medical opinions. For example, the claimant had a joint surgery in service or fractured a bone in service and now he has degenerative joint disease (DJD) in that same area. The examiner should opine as to whether the current arthritic condition likely resulted from the in-service injury.

The MO's are being grossly overused for cases that are clearly not service-related conditions. For example, the service records show one single incident of a complaint of back pain. X-ray was negative and the condition was never mentioned again in service, including not on the separation exam. Everybody has a back pain at some point in time, and usually it is only the slackers that go to sick call and report pain, when there has been no injury, and it gets documented in the records. Now 30 or 40 years later, after working all these years, and never having been treated again during or after service for back pain, he goes to the VAMC and reports back pain. X-rays are still negative. The rater must request a medical opinion in this case, and in about 98 percent of the cases the examiner will say, "Yes, it is at least as likely as not that the current condition was incurred in service." The only way it will likely ever be denied is when there is an "intercurrent cause" such as medical evidence showing the veteran was in a recent vehicle accident after which he was treated for a back injury.

Service connection cannot be granted for "pain." There has to be a diagnosis, so if there is nothing on X-ray, the doctor has to call it either "lumbago" which is still nothing but low back pain, or he will call it "lumbar strain." "Strain" or "sprain" means there was no objective evidence of a chronic disability. These are acute conditions, and service connection should only be granted for chronic conditions. Still strains and sprains are granted to thousands of veterans every day of the week!

So suppose there is really a current chronic condition shown on X-ray, such as degenerative arthritis, or a bulging disc in the back, or a meniscal tear of the knee. These conditions have not existed all these years since service or they would have either been treated, or by now they would have worsened to the point of needing back surgery or a knee replacement. It's common sense that these current conditions have *not* existed all the years since service, and yet they are granted over and over and over, because there is a positive medical opinion.

Many of the medical opinions are provided by physicians at the VA medical centers, and an increasing number are being obtained from private contracted physicians because the VAMC can't handle the exponentially-increasing workload. But in all cases, these examiners have been told to give positive opinions in all cases unless there is an intermittent cause for the current condition. They are told the same as the raters to concede whenever whatever as much as possible.

On rare occasion, the examiner will provide a ridiculous negative opinion, and that's even worse than the positive opinions. In either case, the rater has no authority to dispute a physician.

***

Veteran X in service in 1993 had shortness of breath with exertion and was diagnosed with sarcoidosis. He probably didn't really have sarcoidosis or it would have spread to the rest of his body by the time of this claim. He now has a current diagnosis of asthma and COPD (chronic obstructive pulmonary disease). He filed a claim for "respiratory condition." The VA examiner opined, "No, it is less likely as not that the current respiratory condition is what he had in service because what he has now is restrictive and the type he had in service is obstructive." This is a serious disservice to the veteran. If he truly had "sarcoidosis" in service, that is a very serious condition, often manifested as respiratory symptoms, and it deserves to be service connected (as much as any respiratory condition for anyone). Just because it has a different diagnosis now should not matter. He clearly had serious respiratory complaints in service.

Things were often not correctly diagnosed in service. Tests were often not done. Furthermore, medical literature shows that obstructive lung disease and restrictive lung disease both cause shortness of breath, and in the early stages of obstructive or restrictive lung disease, shortness of breath occurs only with exertion. If he had a respiratory problem in service, and now he has a respiratory problem, the opinion should have been positive and the case should have been granted; but based on the official medical opinion, service connection had to be denied, and raters must not dispute physicians.

PROBLEMS WITH EVALUATION BUILDERS

Evaluation builders are computerized check-sheets created for each medical condition, supposedly reflecting the Rating Schedule from the code of federal regulations (38 CFR 4). Instead of looking at the rating schedule in the regulation to determine what degree of severity should be assigned for any condition, the rater simply punches in the information provided on the DBQ (exam report), and the "proper" evaluation for that issue is generated into the rating decision and the code sheet. (Later all the separate evaluations are combined by another process to create the overall compensation evaluation.)

In order for this system to work, the Evaluation Builder must accurately reflect every possible entry found on the DBQ, and the DBQ must accurately assess every possible symptom noted in the Rating Schedule. This is not the case. Sometimes a serious condition gets rated as minor because there was no question about (and no place to input) the serious symptom. More often, a condition is made to appear much worse than it really is because of the way the Evaluation Builder options are worded. While the Rating Schedule may say that a whole series of symptoms together will warrant 50%, the Evaluation Builder will generate 50% when only one of the symptoms is entered.

I give for example the schedule for rating bilateral pes planus (flat foot). This issue should not even be considered disabling at all unless it was not congenital and was clearly incurred during service. Yet thousands are granted for flat feet they had all their lives and never caused them any problem, including did not prevent them from entering service. Bilateral plantar fasciitis is commonly diagnosed for complaints of foot pain when the feet are not flat, and this is evaluated using the same Evaluation Builder as for flat feet, because no separate schedule has been devised, despite it being a common military diagnosis.

So the Rating Schedule gives an option of evaluating the bilateral foot condition as Mild (0%), Moderate (10%), Severe (30%), or Pronounced (50%), with "Pronounced" being the most serious the condition can be. For a 50% evaluation the regulation states: "Pronounced" followed by a semi-colon and then a list of symptoms. A semi-colon means "and" or it means the words on both sides of the semi-colon are just different ways to say the same thing. So the regulation provides "Pronounced" then semi-colon, then describes symptoms of what represents "pronounced." The symptoms are "marked pronation, extreme tenderness of plantar surfaces of the feet, marked inward displacement and severe spasm of the tendo achillis on manipulation, not improved by orthopedic shoes or appliances." There is no "or" written after "pronounced" nor is there an "or" between the symptoms.

The regulation is written as a guide to help evaluate severity, but some common sense should be applied. The highest level of severity is not warranted unless most all of the "pronounced" symptoms are evident or at the very least the condition must appear to be "pronounced" or "*very* severe" because even the "severe" condition warranting only 30% requires "objective evidence" of marked deformity, accentuated pain, swelling, callosities. I believe that to warrant the 50%, most all of the symptoms listed under Mild, Moderate, and Severe should also be present along with at least some of the Pronounced symptoms.

The rating schedule is better understood if one reads from the bottom up, first reviewing the symptoms of a mild condition, then up to what might represent a moderate condition, then up more to what would be the most serious symptoms. In the Rating Schedule each higher evaluation builds on the lower ones, but the Evaluation Builders have not been created to reflect this. So when evaluating bilateral plantar fasciitis, an evaluation of 50% is generated simply because the veteran expresses a subjective complaint of tenderness on the bottom of his feet, when there is not another single bit of evidence of any disability.

Also grossly over-evaluated by the Evaluation Builders are most mental issues including PTSD. The "General Rating Formula for Mental Disorders" (38 CFR 4.130, DC 9400) clearly explains that the mental evaluation should be based on the degree of "occupational and social impairment." Specifically, 0% is warranted for a diagnosis but no impairment, 10% is for mild or transient symptoms, 30% is for occasional decrease in work efficiency and intermittent periods of impairment, 50% is for reduced reliability and productivity (not occasional or intermittent), 70% is for deficiencies in most areas occupationally and socially, and 100% is for total occupational and social impairment (such as a patient in a mental ward). Under each of these categories a list of symptoms is given but those are only for example. The rating is supposed to be based on the "degree of occupational and social impairment." Instead, the Evaluation Builder is written so that even one serious symptom (even a subjective complaint not verifiable by any test) is enough to trigger a 50% or 70% disability, resulting in gross over-evaluation of mental issues. If the veteran reports a "history" of suicidal thoughts, even though it was on one occasion when he was going through financial stress 30 years ago, that one symptom will cause the evaluation builder to generate 70% or even 100%. The undefined symptom of "disturbances of motivation and mood" has caused many fully functioning veterans to be evaluated as 50% disabled. What does a veteran or an examiner mean when he chooses the symptom "disturbances of motivation or mood?" It sounds pretty general and mild to me, and I believe I've had that plenty of times myself. In any case, I do not believe an examiner realizes that by clicking that one box he has justified a 50% evaluation.

A correct evaluation could be derived by starting at the bottom of the Rating Schedule, reviewing what symptoms would warrant 0% or 10%. Then move up. Are those present and then also some of the symptoms that represent 30% disability? If so, the regulation says we should assign the higher of two possible evaluations. Look at the symptoms listed for 50% and make a logical decision as to whether this veteran has a multitude of symptoms including some that would be mild, some moderate, but even some that would show a serious condition warranting 50%. But more importantly, look at the history and current status of the veteran's employment and social life, and make a logical "supported" decision on the evaluation based on the degree of occupational and social impairment shown by the evidence. Unfortunately, the Evaluation Builder, as currently created is not able to make a logical decision, and yet it has more authority than humans who were hired and trained to do the job.

***

Veteran X is vice president of a company. He travels all over the world giving sales/marketing presentations. He has only two claimed symptoms: (1) sleep impairment claimed as "dreams" (but psychology literature will tell you dreams are a good and necessary part of sleep!) and (2) memory loss (what person over 50 doesn't report some perceived decrease in memory). On exam he reported that "sometimes I lose my train of thought during a presentation." Who doesn't? He has been happily married to the same wife for 25 years and has one grown daughter; he gets along great with both of them. He has friends, loves fishing, goes to church regularly, goes to town for errands, and goes out to eat with friends and family. He hopes to travel more with his wife. The examiner diagnoses PTSD and the Evaluation Builder gives him 30%. According to the actual regulation/law, 38 CFR 4.130, he should get only 10% (or 0%) but the rater must ignore the law and assign what the Evaluation Builder spits out and grant this totally healthy unimpaired man 30% disability. It's a disgrace.

***

The Evaluation Builder will almost always generate 10% for any knee problem. Sometimes the person has stories of how he is in almost constant severe pain causing and missing a lot of work but the knee will still only be granted 10% for the pain, the same as if he just had mild subjective pain on flareups once or twice a month. Often the records will indicate the claimant has been scheduled for total knee replacement, so it must be pretty severe, but based on the DBQ and Evaluation Builder he will only get 10% until the surgery. Then he will get 100% for the next 13 months, even if he goes back to work after 3 months, and that is followed by 30% forever even if he's asymptomatic. If symptomatic it will be 60%.

***

The cardiologist notes on DBQ that Veteran X's estimated METS are between 1 to 3, so this warrants 100%. But the records show per claimant's report that he is still running marathons, real full marathons, and he spends his days taking care of grandchildren while their parents work. Doesn't sound like a true heart disability to me. Sometimes I think the physicians don't even understand the scale, that 10 is the least severe, and that 1-3 is the most severe, warranting 100%. But a rater cannot be logical and cannot question this doctor. The "estimation" of METS should not be allowed unless a claimant is so severely sick that to do a stress test would be dangerous for him. If such severity is shown, generally the ejection fraction, hypertrophy, or general limitation of function will be sufficient to support the evaluation.

***

Veteran X is service connected for his back at 40%, and that's a lot for a back condition. It indicates severe limitation of motion and the only way he can get higher is if his entire back is ankylosed (like the discs have been fused to prevent motion). He makes out to be that disabled during his back exam, but his PTSD exam, with another specialist, gives the clues to his actual physical condition.

He reportedly rides a motorcycle and works out at the gym 3 times a week. His treatment records also show he picked up his refill for Viagra the same day as the back exam. But if the Evaluation Builder says 40, it's 40.

PROBLEMS WITH INTENT TO FILE

"Intent to File" (ITF) is the stupidest thing that ever happened to the VA. Many veterans submit dozens of them so some of them expire, and many are submitted within a few days after receiving a rating decision. Besides just being a nightmare of extra work for the rater when it comes to deciding which of the many ITF's is the one that should be used for assigning the effective date, the only thing these really accomplish is more fraud.

The veteran simply submits a form (VA Form 21-0966) with a box checked saying he *plans to file* for compensation, and the date that is received by VA is preserved as his effective date for payment, when he is later granted. The Intent to File does not specify what conditions he will be claiming and this gives him a *year* to decide what to claim and to develop the claim. First he obtains copies of his service records and looks for any little issue he was treated for in service, things he probably doesn't even remember. Then he gets some current medical records created by going to doctors and documenting complaints. Whichever complaints pan out into some sort of diagnoses are the ones he will later list on his claim. For issues granted he'll be given retroactive payment back to the date of the ITF.

Veterans already service-connected use the ITF to help them get a jump on their increase claims. Perhaps there hasn't been enough time since their last exam (1 year) to justify having a new exam ordered. But they can submit an ITF immediately after receiving the decision they don't like. Then as soon as they are one year past their most recent exam, they file the formal claim and a new increase exam will be ordered. Whatever evaluation comes from the new exam, will be granted effective back to the date of the ITF, which is just a few days after their last decision, and just a month or two subsequent to their last effective date! For example, an exam in February 2016 shows his back condition warrants a 10% evaluation and the rating decision of early March 2016 grants 10%. As soon as the veteran sees this he submits another ITF, received late March 2016. If he sent the formal claim in now it would just be "reconsidered" based on the same evidence of record. He can't have another exam until February 2017 so he waits and submits his formal claim in January 2017.   An increase exam is ordered and completed in February 2017. Per information provided in his last rating decision he now knows what symptoms he must report in order to get a higher evaluation, so he reports those symptoms, or demonstrates those limitations on his new exam, and the new exam findings warrant a 40% evaluation! The increase is granted effective March 2016, the date of ITF. So although only a 10% disability was shown on exam in February 2016, he is granted 40% effective March 2016, only 1 month later. Do you think it really increased that much in one month when there is not a single *treatment* record during that whole period?

(17) SPECIFIC MEDICAL ISSUES

This section of the book addresses specific claimed issues, particular diseases or body systems or exposures, and what the problems are with rating that issue, specifically why far too much compensation is being paid based on that claimed issue. Following each section there are examples of related claims.

This is by no means a comprehensive list of veterans' claimed issues. The VA receives claims for every imaginable medical or mental condition there has ever been documented, as well as symptoms that haven't been diagnosed. Every day of the week VA receives claims for hyperhidrosis (sweaty hands), alopecia (baldness), onychomycosis (discolored toenails), and bradycardia (slow heart beat) from veterans who find these non-debilitating conditions in their medical records and have no idea what they mean, but they sound like something that should be claimed. Veterans also claim morbid obesity, personality disorder, ADHD, drug dependence, vitamin deficiency, and dozens of other things obviously not caused by service. Sometimes even the silliest claims are granted but most of these trivial non-debilitating conditions are correctly denied, and this book is not about those.

The issues I've selected to expound on here are some of the most commonly *granted* conditions that are most often abused or most often over-evaluated or perhaps shouldn't be granted at all.

AUDOLOGY PROBLEMS

Hearing loss and tinnitus are both audiological conditions, claimed together, examined together, and rated at the same time, but they are two separate issues with separate grants (one may be granted while the other is denied) with separate evaluations that will be added in the total evaluation. But tinnitus is a *symptom* of hearing loss and a claim for tinnitus can be "sympathetically construed" even if only hearing loss was claimed.

Hearing loss is probably the most non-subjective condition of all when it comes to granting or assigning an evaluation. It requires an audiogram and Maryland speech recognition test to be done by a certified audiologist. Then the regulation is very detailed with charts and formulas for diagnosing hearing loss and determining the specific level of severity and the applicable evaluation. But that doesn't prevent the fraudulence because many veterans fake hearing loss during the audiogram. Sometimes the examiner will note how interesting it is that as he stood several yards behind the veteran, the veteran could respond to his whispered questions, and yet showed significant deficits on the audiogram. When hearing loss is diagnosed and granted, the evaluation is often minimal because at most levels hearing loss is treatable by a hearing aid, therefore not occupationally or socially impairing. But while hearing loss is the strictest issue (tight requirements for granting, and minimal compensation), tinnitus is the loosest, as it is purely subjective, requires no test, and can be granted as a symptom of hearing loss even if it didn't start in service.

HEARING LOSS

Hearing loss is one of the most abused medical issues in the VA due to the nature of military training and war. The regulations say service connection for any condition should require evidence that the condition started in service, but hearing loss is treated special. It would be so much better for all servicemen and taxpayers if the VA would just manage this issue through the VA Medical Centers, not through claims administration, and would issue hearing aids to any veteran who needs them, no questions asked. Instead, millions of claims are processed every year, requiring audiograms and medical opinions. VA hasn't been able to keep up with the demand in recent years and has had to subcontract to thousands of private audiologists, not cheap. It takes pretty significant hearing loss to warrant more than 0%, so that results in millions of appeals, more exams and wasted work.

Prior to 2000, most hearing claims were denied unless there was evidence that hearing loss started in service, but now it's all about medical opinions, and hearing loss is granted to anyone who pursues it hard enough to show excessive noise exposure in service. In recent years the policies have changed such that VA will concede in-service excessive noise exposure to anyone whose MOS (military occupation) is on "the MOS list," a list of jobs such as airplane and engine room mechanics and hundreds of others that might have subjected a worker to excessive noise. Not a bad idea, but it didn't work; many with all types of MOS's have appealed that they were subjected to noises just by being near planes or ships or Army trucks, and they've won. Even though the use of hearing protection (earplugs or headsets) in the military is mandatory and enforced, many veterans, including some who never made it beyond basic training, have been granted hearing loss simply because they had to train and qualify with a weapon, and every serviceman or woman has to do that!

The older veterans' records rarely show audiograms. Their records may show they had WV 15/15 (whispered voice) or SV

15/15 (spoken voice) test on entry and again on exit and with a 15/15, there was no need for a more detailed test (audiogram). But since those cases don't have "audiograms," it's like no test at all had been done in service. Since veterans are usually 70 or 80 before they file the claim for hearing loss, VA medical opinions say it's impossible to know whether the hearing loss started during service or not. So practically everyone with one of those 15/15s in their records will be granted, giving them the benefit of the doubt. It's just as well because the military audiograms that do exist are extremely unreliable and inconsistent. In many military jobs that have high noise exposure, annual audiograms are required, and they will often show poor hearing one year followed by excellent hearing the next year.

So the bottom line is that if VA gets a claim for hearing loss, and hearing loss is shown on a current audiogram, the medical opinions are almost always positive, and service-connection will be granted because hearing loss was as likely as not incurred in service. It doesn't matter that, according to the National Institute of Health's National Institute on Deafness and Other Communication Disorders (NIDCD), one in eight Americans age 12 or older has bilateral hearing loss based on standard hearing exams, and 50% of people over 75 have disabling hearing loss.

As the number of claims was dramatically increasing, VA requested a study to be done by the Institute of Medicine to specifically address whether hearing loss could develop long after exposure. The IOM 2006 study found that there was no scientific basis to conclude that permanent hearing loss that manifested many years after a noise exposure could be directly attributed to that noise exposure if the hearing was normal immediately after the exposure. The IOM panel concluded that, based on their current understanding of auditory physiology, a prolonged delay in the onset of noise-induced hearing loss was "unlikely." Typically BVA decisions (appeals) will deny hearing loss based on that IOM report, but few hearing loss cases ever get to them. Very rarely, a brave audiologist will quote the IOM study and give a negative opinion, so hearing loss will be denied. But all the veteran has to do is reopen the claim.

He will get a new exam, a new medical opinion, and chances are very good that on the second go round the different examiner will say "Yes, it is at least as likely as not that the condition was caused by noise in service."

Ignoring the IOM studies, most examiners say that any hearing loss they find is indeed as likely as not caused by noise exposure in service. The literature they often use to support this is a paper written by S.G Kujawa and M.C. Liberman, "Adding Insult to Injury: Cochlear Nerve Degeneration after 'Temporary' Noise-Induced Hearing Loss, *J. Neurosci*, 11, 29(45) 14077-14085 (2009)" The examiner will say that although there was no hearing loss shown on audiograms done at separation from service, the current hearing loss many years later is the result of an active cochlear process that began while the claimant was in military service and continued after separation from service. But look at the title of the article they are quoting. "*After* Temporary Noise-Induced Hearing Loss" indicates that there was a *prior* temporary hearing loss, such as the temporary hearing loss after being close to an explosion, that gets better later. But the cases being supported by this opinion are mostly cases in which there was *never* any indication of any temporary or other hearing loss shown during service.

The VA needs to rewrite the regulations for this issue because currently there is great inconsistency in the medical opinions. It's not fair to grant for some and not for others. One easy solution would be to say that hearing loss not started in service is considered a developmental disorder (age-related) and will not be granted, the same way myopia (vision loss age-related) is not granted. Old age vision loss is one of the few conditions not subject to service connection, and yet old age hearing loss is granted all day long.

Ironically, the VA regulations have a strict interpretation of "hearing loss." It's one of the few conditions that can actually be measured, and there is very specific criteria that must be met in order for a diagnosis of hearing loss. The testing must be done by a state-licensed audiologist and must include a puretone audiometry test and a speech discrimination test (Maryland CNC). Hearing loss will be diagnosed if the speech discrimination score is 94 or lower for either ear, or if the puretone test shows 26 dB loss or more in at least 3 frequencies, measured at 500 Hz, 1000 Hz, 2000 Hz, 3000 Hz, and 4000 Hz, for either ear. Once that criteria is met, and the opinion is positive for service-connection, the evaluation is determined by use of a combination of several tables/charts in the regulation, tedious to interpret manually, but the evaluation builder includes a computer program that easily calculates this for the rater. The evaluation is usually 0% unless there is pretty severe hearing loss.

Hearing loss shown in service will be granted as a chronic disease regardless of whether improvement has been shown. For example, if an in-service test showed 60 dB loss at the 4000 Hz, then a subsequent test showed 10 dB at 4000 Hz, or normal at all Hz, it doesn't matter; hearing loss was still shown in service. There's no consideration for the fact that sometimes hearing loss does improve/resolve if it had resulted from infection or illness, or that some audiograms do contain errors. Medical literature shows that hearing loss resulting from a loud noise incident (such as explosion, bomb, or mortar) will generally manifest at the lower Hz levels, 500 or 1000 Hz. Oddly, most VA claims are granted based on mild deficiencies at the 4000 Hz level. Many people have hearing loss at higher levels (6000 Hz and above) but that does not meet the VA definition of hearing loss (and is not disabling).

Once a person meets the VA criteria, he almost always gets only a 0% evaluation. Even though he has hearing loss, it is not severe enough to impair or reduce his ability to work. And hearing loss can be treated by hearing aids, especially if the hearing aids are issued early enough.

Many of the older veterans who do really have hearing loss, as a common development of old age, only wish to have hearing aids and they don't have insurance to pay for them. Theoretically, if they can get service-connected for hearing loss, the VA will provide the free hearing aids. But I have known many cases where the VA issued hearing aids to old veterans who have never filed a claim, so I don't really understand how the VA hospitals work in that regard, as I never worked for VHA. But from my first week of work at the VBA, I have felt that there is such unfairness in granting this condition that hearing loss should be removed from the list of compensable conditions, and if any veteran needs hearing aids, just give them to him! The cost of the hearing aids is less than the cost of paying VA claims developers, raters, and medical examiners.

Why in the world would we not just issue hearing aids to any veteran who really needs them? Every veteran was exposed to some military noise if he served at least 90 days. Basic training does require the firing and qualifying with various weapons! Navy and Coast Guard ship engines are noisy! Army artillery, tanks and trucks are noisy! Air Force planes, flight decks, and runway areas are noisy! Even though a veteran didn't notice hearing loss until 50 years after service and he is 70 years old, all the VA will do is ask a VA examiner to opine as to whether it was likely caused by service, and 98% of the time the examiner will say YES! The other 2% of claimants are the unfortunate ones who by luck of the draw got an examiner who has brains, nerves, or morals, and who will state on his opinion, "Hearing loss occurs at the time of exposure and does not develop many years after the exposure event."

The reason I would give every veteran hearing aids, if needed, is because we are wasting millions of dollars on audiology exams, many contracted out to private audiologists. We waste millions of VA claims processors manhours, reading and develop these foolish claims, many of which are for no issues other than hearing loss and tinnitus, from older veterans who have a chance of being granted this and nothing else (because nothing is in their service records). Many of the older veterans know and accept that their others ailments did not start in service and were not caused by service, but they can be convinced by their POAs (VFW, American Legion) that their hearing loss was caused by military noise 50 years prior. And it's only fair that if one old man deserves the benefit, they all do, especially all war veterans.

All hearing loss claims should go directly to the VA medical centers. Any veteran with a DD 214 (military discharge) should be examined and if he qualifies for hearing aids, give them to him, as a benefit for serving our country. It could even be used as a recruitment promise. Stop wasting the time and money put into development and rating of these claims, when they often don't result in a *compensable* evaluation anyway.

On the rare occasion that there was a specific verifiable injury in service, some blast or explosion, where hearing loss was reported on the spot, either temporary or permanent, and hearing loss was diagnosed in service, then of course we should process and grant those cases. I actually never saw a case of a veteran being deaf due to a military event, and that surprises me, as it seems explosions could cause this condition. The only cases of severe hearing loss I ever saw were cases where the hearing loss started mid-life and by the time the veteran was 80 or 90 it had become severe.

I worked at the VA for many years before I decided to tell one of my elderly relatives that he should file a claim for hearing loss. Early in my career I had explained the VA benefits to him and asked him if he had any residuals of his service in the Korean War (1951-1953). He said no, he had no injuries in war, and nothing to claim. After many years of witnessing the types of claims being granted, and actually granting them myself against my better judgment but in accordance with VA policies, I finally encouraged him to file a hearing loss claim. I explained to him that if he currently has hearing loss and he served in a war, service-connection would most likely be granted. We both acknowledged that any 87-year-old man is *expected* to have hearing loss, but I told him the VA cannot discriminate regarding age. If the doctor says it was as likely as not incurred in service then it must be granted. Almost every VA or contracted audiologist doing the VA exams will say yes, it was at least as likely as not, because the claimant was exposed to noise in warfare and there is no proof that the hearing loss was caused by anything else. A man could've worked 40 years as a jackhammer operator building roads, or as a race car driver, or airplane engine mechanic, and it won't matter a bit, and the doctor doesn't even have to ask about that. Hearing loss is the most claimed issue, is listed on practically every claim, and if there is any hearing loss found, it is almost always granted, as it was to my 87-year-old relative.

The biggest atrocity of the hearing loss claims isn't actually the hearing loss, but the associated claim for tinnitus (ringing in the ears). Current day veterans have learned through the grapevine that all they have to do is say they have had tinnitus since service and they will be granted 10 percent disability. There is no current VA test for tinnitus. It's totally subjective. The evaluation will never be reduced. It's just one of dozens of conditions that the veteran can be granted compensation for without any proof that he has ever had the condition or that he now has it.

TINNITUS

Tinnitus is a stand-alone condition for the VA, evaluated separate from hearing loss and in addition to hearing loss, even though the audiologists consider it as a *symptom* of hearing loss. Tinnitus is described by veterans as a ringing sound, a buzzing sound, a high-pitched whistle, or numerous other sounds in their head or ears. Many claims list "tinnitus" but when questioned on the audiology exam the claimants don't even know what they claimed, or what their POAs claimed for them, and they often tell the audiologist they never had or claimed that condition. Still, claims for service-connection for tinnitus are increasing at an extreme rate, not because there is more frequent ear damage now in service, but because it's an easy way to make an extra 136 bucks a month.

According to the Nov/Dec 2008 issue of *VA Guard*, about 850,000 veterans were receiving compensation for service connected hearing disabilities, including about 444,600 receiving compensation for hearing loss, the #1 disability, and about 400,000 were receiving compensation for tinnitus, #2 of all disabilities. Notice the number for tinnitus was smaller and tinnitus was practically never claimed or granted without first a hearing loss disability. But since 2008, all audio claims have drastically increased and tinnitus has quickly risen to the #1 position; there is no need to have hearing loss to be granted tinnitus.

According to a VA website, *https://www.research.va.gov/topics/hearing/cfm*, "As of the close of fiscal year 2014, more than

933,000 Veterans were receiving disability compensation for hearing loss, and nearly 1.3 million received compensation for tinnitus. Tinnitus is now the number-one disability among Veterans." While the condition affects about 1 in 10 American adults, about 9.5 out of 10 veterans are now claiming it.

It is obvious that over a period of 6 years, the word got out about tinnitus and every veteran was encouraged to claim this automatic grant. Every grant for tinnitus is 10%, regardless of severity, and regardless of how frequently it may occur. In the past it was only granted for continuous symptoms, but that got loosened in order to grant any claim for "intermittent" or "recurrent" tinnitus, even if it recurs only once a year or less often.

A grant for this bogus issue pays $136 a month, more than $1,600 per year, so over the remaining life of your average 22-year-old veteran with cost-of-living increases, we'll pay *each one* more than $100,000 just for this issue. So for every 10 of these we'll pay over a million dollars, and in fact we have about 1.3 million veterans already receiving compensation for this. I'm not exaggerating to say that practically every single new veteran will claim tinnitus, and more of our 22 million current veterans are coming on board with it every day.

The VA website also reports, "About 80 percent of people with tinnitus are not bothered by it, because it does not affect their sleep or their ability to concentrate. Those who struggle with the noise in their head can be more prone to other mental health problems, such as depression and anxiety." Great, so soon will come the claims secondary to tinnitus!

More surprises from the VA website, *"Tinnitus is common in Veterans, but there are no objective tests to diagnose the problem. In 2013, NCRAR researchers and researchers from Oregon Health and Science University conducted three phases of testing to try to distinguish Veterans with tinnitus from those who do not have it. They found some differences between the groups, but also that no single test or series of tests could reliably diagnose the condition. The team concluded additional work is needed to develop a specific battery of tests for detecting the presence or absence of tinnitus with a high degree of confidence."* So why is it being granted?!

Very rarely the following statement will be found on a VA audiology exam, obviously before that examiner gets reprimanded. *"Tinnitus is a subjective complaint and no objective measure exists to verify the presence of or absence of tinnitus. The etiology of tinnitus cannot be determined using current clinical technology."* That audiologist will be set straight or lose his examining contract with the VA. The veteran will reopen the claim and will be given the diagnosis of tinnitus whether or not it can be linked to service. The link is almost always granted because benefit of the doubt must always be given to the veteran. If a decision is 50/50, on the fence, it must be granted in favor of the veteran.

More than half of the veterans service-connected for tinnitus do not have any significant hearing loss at all and are not service-connected for hearing loss. These cases should not be granted tinnitus but they are! One doctor was very logical and supported his negative opinion as follows. *"In the absence of hearing loss, tinnitus is usually a normal phenomenon. According to a study by Dauman and Tyler (1992) cited in the Tinnitus Handbook (Tyler), normal tinnitus is experienced by most people without hearing loss, lasting for less than five minutes less than once a week. Because the veteran's current tinnitus fits this criterion, it is considered normally occurring and therefore is less likely as not related to military noise exposure."* But that's one case denied and one doctor's logical comment out of a million claims granted. Over and over again the VA audiologist will say, "Yes, the tinnitus was most likely incurred in service because the claimant said the tinnitus started while in the military, and it was likely caused by exposure to loud noises in the military."

In summary, tinnitus is a purely subjective condition and in most cases should not be granted. VA has no and requires no test for verification/diagnosis and the veteran can have perfect hearing and still get granted tinnitus. If he reports that it started in service, then claims it, it's an automatic grant. If he claims it started any time after service, even 50 years after service, VA asks for an examiner's opinion and the examiner will say, "Yes, it is a symptom of their hearing loss caused by military noise, so it is also linked to military noise exposure." If the veteran does not have hearing loss, then the examiner may opine that it is likely due directly to noise exposure in service due to his MOS (military occupational specialty).

VA grants 10% for this condition, which is supposed to mean that the condition reduces his ability to work by 10%! I dare say I never saw a case where the veteran appeared to have tinnitus severe enough to slow him down or prevent him from doing anything. At the worst, they say it is an annoyance and it occurs no more than once a week. Some of them say it occurs once a month for a minute or two. These claimants are not going to die from this or be work-impaired by it.

Sadly, tinnitus is a real condition that some people do really suffer from, including likely some veterans, and this over-granting is a gross disservice to those who really are impaired by tinnitus. Imagine what a veteran must think about all this abuse if his life, his ability to work and socialize, is truly impaired by tinnitus. In order to be granted for this condition, I feel the veteran should be required to show proof that he has suffered from tinnitus, i.e. evidence of an event that caused it showing when it actually started, medical evidence that he has reported this complaint and sought treatment for this condition, or perhaps statements from family or employers who have experienced the veteran suffering from tinnitus symptoms, none of which is now required by VA. In any case, a compensable evaluation should only be granted to someone who has seen an audiologist multiple times due to ringing in the ears that is preventing him from sleeping or hearing or working.

INCREASE CLAIMS FOR AUDIO CONDITIONS

An additional huge waste of VA resources is spent on claims for "increase" in hearing loss and tinnitus. These issues are the most common claims for increase because the evaluations are so low, usually 0% for hearing loss and 10% for tinnitus, and the veteran wants more money.

First of all, the maximum allowed by law for tinnitus is 10% and that's what everyone gets on their initial grant. So any request for increase should simply be answered by the VA as "You are already receiving the maximum benefit allowed by law for tinnitus." And money should not be wasted on more exams or ratings.

As for hearing loss, the exams are also almost always a waste. It is true that hearing loss, when it does exist, generally gets worse over time; however, veterans don't understand that it takes a pretty significant increase to bump the 0% up to 10%, or 10% up to 20%. This is the one condition for which there are charts in the regulations for calculating the evaluation warranted for each level of hearing disability. Unless it is pretty significant hearing loss, the evaluation is 0%, because after all, early-found and mild hearing loss can be corrected by hearing aids.

But still the veterans keep coming in again year after year asking for an increase in their hearing loss. In many cases, especially the older veterans who got out 30 to 50 years ago when military files weren't packed with fraud, it's the only condition they've been granted, so they have to ask for an increase in whatever they have. The new VA exam is not likely to show that the condition has worsened, as it takes about 10 years for any significant change to be shown on testing.

The exams and the claims processing (developing for unnecessary records) is a total waste of time and money. If a veteran is granted hearing loss, he is entitled to receive free hearing aids at the VAMC. After that, no claims for increase should be accepted for that issue. The VA computers should be diaried to automatically schedule the claimant for a review hearing test, routine future exam, every 8 or 10 years at which time he will get an increase if warranted.

***

Veteran X filed his original claim at age 67. He served one and a half years in Vietnam from 1969 to 1970 and reported no particular explosion or ear damage in service. Forty-five years after service he filed a claim for hearing loss. His service records showed normal hearing on entrance and discharge exams. Still the VA examiner opined that his current hearing loss was as likely as not incurred in service due to the circumstances he served in (Vietnam War). On exam the examiner asked him whether he has tinnitus (ringing in the ears) and he said, "Yes, sometimes." She asked him when it had started and he said it started about 7 or 8 years ago, after no particular event. He had not listed tinnitus on his claim. Still, because the claim for hearing loss is a sympathetically construed claim for tinnitus, the VA had to go back to the examiner for an opinion as to whether his tinnitus was likely due to service. She said that even though the onset of tinnitus was 45 years after service, it is at least as likely as not caused by his in-service exposure to military noise.

***

Veteran X has been out of service since 1969, and his discharge exam showed normal hearing. He claimed hearing loss in 2002 (31 years after service) but was denied because the VA exam showed his hearing was still normal for VA purposes. In 2007 he reopened the claim with some private audiogram showing slight hearing loss, but no link to service, so it was denied again. In 2016, he reopened the claim again. By this time, the VA had loosened the policies on developing hearing loss claims, such that now the VA is getting a medical opinion on every VA audio exam. So his case had a medical opinion and voile! Yes! The hearing loss is at least as likely as not caused by military service 47 years ago. It does not matter that this hearing loss first manifested at age 70. Too bad the hearing loss is minor so he will only get a 0% evaluation after all this struggle. Too bad he did not claim tinnitus, for which he would have easily been granted 10% as a symptom of his service-connected hearing loss. In his case, the examiner did not address tinnitus since it wasn't claimed. In most cases, the examiner will address it anyway, and it will be granted as a "sympathetically construed claim."

***

Veteran X has submitted 14 claims (each with multiple issues) over the past 50 years and in them all he has never claimed hearing loss. He has been treated at the VAMC all these years and those records have never shown a problem with hearing loss. Now 50 years after service he submits a claim for hearing loss, the VA exam shows hearing loss, the examiner provides a positive opinion that it is "at least as likely as not" caused by military service, and so service connected compensation is granted.

***

Veteran X has been out of service for 25 years, and he was never in combat. He only served 6 months of active duty but during that time he drove a heavy vehicle and trained as an infantryman, so based on his MOS (military occupational specialty) the examiner gave a positive opinion that his current hearing loss was at least as likely as not incurred in service.

MENTAL DISORDERS

POSTTRAUMATIC STRESS DISORDER (PTSD)

First I have to take this opportunity to explain what is *not* PTSD. The most irritating thing I read over and over again in PTSD lay statements was something like this, "Johnny was so great, fun and outgoing, before service but he came back from service a changed person." Thus a claim for PTSD. Let me tell you poor parents and siblings what happened to Johnny. *He grew up.* When he left he was 18 years old. He had never been away from momma, had never been broken by boot camp, had never lived on his own, never managed his own paycheck, never laid a foreign national, and never held a gun or grenade. He learned life is more than football and video games, and that a job well done or mission accomplished can be rewarding. He experienced physical and mental exertion, as well as exhilaration, freedom, confinement, and fear of the unknown. He learned humiliation, camaraderie, and respect for authority. He no longer has much in common with his old highschool buddies. When he returned he was quieter, more introspecting, and began to sit with his back to the wall. And that's a soldier who never saw battle; the ones who saw battle learned much more and grew up even faster. But being a changed person does not necessarily mean he has PTSD.

Posttraumatic stress disorder (PTSD) is defined as "a psychiatric disorder that can occur following the experience or witnessing of a life-threatening event such as military combat, natural disaster, terrorist incident, serious accident, or physical or sexual assault in adult or childhood." VA considers the sexual assault cases as a special kind of PTSD, called Military Sexual Trauma (MST), and that issue is addressed in the next chapter. In any kind of PTSD, the patient has experienced something so horrific that he feared for his life and/or for the lives of others with him during this frightening event, and he was so scared and shocked that he has never been able to get over the event. Certain sounds or things he sees will trigger a remembrance of that event and he'll temporarily re-experience the fear. He may also have dreams/nightmares about the event, hallucinate about the event, or even black-out to avoid the re-experience.

People of all ages, in all cultures and every social status, have experienced PTSD after being in an earthquake, tornado, fire, or combat situation, but rarely does the experience cause permanent social or functional impairment. A Coast Guardsman may have symptoms after trying to save people from a sinking boat just as a city fireman may have symptoms after saving people from a burning building. Military medics may have symptoms after trying to save lives on the battlefield or in the emergency room, just as state troopers and firemen and emergency room nurses do every day.

It's interesting that a corpsman can claim and be compensated for PTSD, considering he signed up for the job, trained for the job, and practiced for the job, and he has not experienced anything greater than doctors and nurses in emergency rooms all over the world do all day long every day. Of course they all will remember and dream about certain people they treat, including many whom they are not able to save, but these non-military medical professionals are not getting any free benefit for their PTSD. Why should military medics who chose that profession? The same goes for morticians and their assistants (graves registrants). For some reason VA is willing to automatically grant PTSD to these people just because their job involved looking at dead people. Wouldn't it be something if the federal government had to give a supplemental income to every American mortician or funeral director?

Many VA claims for PTSD don't list any stressor events at all but simply provide a list of names of people who died in Iraq or Afghanistan. Sometimes they'll say something like "my friend's unit was out in the desert screening for IUDs" or "a fellow from my unit, I don't remember his name, was in a plane that got shot down." Even if these deceased soldiers were serving in the same unit with you, this does not qualify as a proper PTSD stressor if you did not witness their horrific death and you did not fear for your own life at the time they were dying. Suppose everyone could be paid by the federal government every time they witnessed or heard about a death, of family members or of people they don't even know, but just read about in the obituaries! And not just one payment, monthly payments forever.

Practically every person alive has at one time or another experienced an event that caused at least a mild case of PTSD. We've all seen car accidents and we may have seen people drowning or choking or badly injured in a fight. We have been in situations where we thought we or some of the people with us at the moment were surely going to die. Imagine people who have been in plane crashes, or hurricanes, or got trampled by a mob. Horrible things happen all the time and to everybody on earth. Yes, we may re-experience this again when we see something similar on TV. And yes, sometimes we even have nightmares about it. But do we run to the hospital afterwards and claim PTSD? Do we go through months of group therapy while continuing to raise our families and work our jobs? Usually we do not claim to be disabled by PTSD for the rest of our lives. Only a very few people who experience such a stressful event do actually have symptoms that linger and need treatment. Generally a person is not so affected by a fearful event that it prevents him from living a normal life. Even people who have chronic nightmares go on to work and function normally. After all, what is normal? Who doesn't have abnormalities?

Veterans claiming PTSD are generally relating it to war time experiences. If they received a combat action ribbon or badge, the VA will automatically concede that they were in a war situation and experienced a fear-for-life situation. But many veterans also claim PTSD related to thousands of other things that happened during service such as car accidents, witnessing others getting injured, working on a burial detail, or helping with relief efforts after a hurricane.

Some of the most ridiculous and fraudulent of all claims are those related to PTSD. Some claim they have PTSD because their drill sergeant yelled at them during boot camp, and some claim they got PTSD from watching war movies in military training. Some claim they got it because they were black and suffered discrimination in service. One guy said he got it because another soldier had lost a leg, and he had to help that soldier to use the bathroom. Many say they got it from carrying body bags or caskets of dead soldiers.

VA ratings are getting laxer every year. You once had to prove you were exposed to some traumatic event in order to get service-connected for PTSD, now all you have to do is serve during a war *period* (not actually there in the war zone) and have a doctor say you felt fearful. *Everybody* felt fearful. Most were still 18- and 19-year-old kids. They were fearful of getting on a plane and flying overseas, whether it would be going on vacation or to war. They were fearful of leaving their mommas and daddies and having to keep up with their own socks and underwear. They were fearful of living with a bunch of guys who would be seeing the size of their cocks, and noticing they had one testicle undescended. Who would not be fearful going in to a warzone??

PTSD is granted to everyone who asks for it, every single soldier who goes to Iraq or Afghanistan, and also the ones who don't go anywhere. If they didn't travel to another country they will make up some story about seeing an accident or getting beat up by someone. The white guys will claim they were beat up, attacked, robbed, or gangraped by a mob of black guys. The black guys will claim they suffered abuse and discrimination, they were taunted and given the dirty jobs and put at the back of the chow line. Multitudes are now coming forward saying they were abused as gays or transgenders.

PTSD is the most abused and easiest way to make big bucks from the VA. Some other things like tinnitus are easier to claim and get granted on the first try but that's only 10%. PTSD, even if at first denied, will eventually pay off at either 30, 50, 70 or 100 percent disability. Most PTSD claims, if worthy of granting at all, should be assigned a 10% evaluation per the regulation which says that "mild and transient symptoms" warrant 10%. But you can pull a hundred cases of granted PTSD and never see one at 10%. I have received errors for assigning 10% and was told that our "in-house policy" was to never give less than 30% for PTSD. If you read the veteran's report (on exam) of how he's doing on the job and at home, in most cases there is little to no impairment of his social or occupational functioning. Perhaps an occasional dream, or if he sees a war movie (which he could avoid) he has bad memories, or if he hears a loud explosion (how often does that happen?) then he relives the bad experience. Then everything is ok again. This is "mild and transient" and warrants only 10%. But just a little more lying and fabricating of records will pay off big.

With only one more checked box on the PTSD exam such as "flattened affect" or "disturbances of motivation and mood" it can jump to 50%. A higher evaluation will be generated by the evaluation builder because on exam the claimant said yes to "impaired impulse control," not that he's ever been arrested or in a fight or anything. The examiner often checks "disturbances of motivation and mood" when there's no real evident or claimed symptoms, and that probably sounds real mild and general to the examiner, as it does to me, but that checked box can bump the evaluation up to 50%. A lower 30% is allowed only if the rater is willing to go the extra mile and justify why the lower evaluation is being assigned. I chose to assign and justify the lower evaluation frequently but I never knew another rater who would do it. My co-workers all just awarded whatever the evaluation builder spit out. They were more concerned about making their production quotas and getting those big bonuses for producing a ridiculous high number of ratings. It was clear to me that many of them never read a word of the evidence, only looked at the DBQ checked boxes.

An evaluation for PTSD will almost never be reduced once it is granted. VA may "threaten" to reduce it when an exam shows symptoms have improved. However, mental conditions cannot be reduced based on one VA exam because the symptoms may "wax and wane" so another exam is required after several years. That's right, even though the current exam shows NO disability, the evaluation cannot be reduced and another exam cannot be ordered until at least 18 more months go by. At one point between 2012 and 2016, the VA claims were so backlogged that such a follow-up exam (to verify non-disability) would be scheduled for *5 years* in the future. So when the 5 year exam came around, considering the time it took VA to order and receive the exam, it would be actually about 5 years and 2 months after the first exam. Even if this exam also showed no disability, the evaluation could not be reduced because improvement had not been shown on two consecutive VA exams "within 5 years." Finally, they got around to fixing that faux pas and the follow-up exams are now typically scheduled 3 years off rather than 5. So the veteran can keep his current evaluation for 3 or 4 more years and then he'll be sent to another exam at which time he'd better whine louder or else he'll be reduced. Once threatened, they will never let down their guard again. Before that next exam they will let their facial hair grow out for about 3 days, drink a shot of whiskey right before entering the exam, and wear stinky wrinkled clothes into the exam. If you're shooting for the 70 or 100 percent evaluation, simply state that you have suicidal thoughts, and a higher evaluation will be assured. Before DBQs came to be, the PTSD examiners gave lenghthy useful assessments in the exam reports. They'd note the veteran had a disheveled appearance and poor eye contact, and yet reported being fully employed, often as a policeman, security guard, medical worker, or post office clerk.

Many full-time employees from all federal agencies have been granted PTSD, and Veterans Affairs (VA) is the agency with the most. Numerous VA employees are in receipt of disability compensation for PTSD; many of them are receiving 100% disability for PTSD, because they know exactly how to play the game. Double dipping our federal tax dollars. Eighty thousand per year federal salary, and another forty thousand a year for "disability" supposedly impairing their ability to work.

I did meet one veteran once who actually had PTSD and if it hadn't been for that one man, I wouldn't even believe any of it is for real. But it is real; it was so clear and obvious that anyone who knew him would have vouched for his PTSD condition. He was like a zombie. He was still in shell shock and he had been for more than 40 years, ever since he returned from the Vietnam War. He was a pleasant looking man, clean cut, skinny, very calm, very shy, without a wrinkle on his face although he was at least 60 years old. He looked like he had never undergone anything stressful in his life, when really it was just the opposite. He had been oblivious to life. According to the testimony I heard from his mother and sister, he was perfectly normal when he was drafted in 1968, but ever since he returned from the war he'd been in a daze, had never been able to converse normally or take any interest in anything. He had spent his life working on the family farm, never dating, never traveling, never wanting to marry or have kids or become anything on his own. He didn't want to talk about Vietnam and refused to even file a claim for himself. His family and VSO had pushed it through. But his claim had been denied since the beginning because there was no specific verified incident of anything horrible he had experienced in Vietnam. He was never able to talk about it and tell anyone any specifics. He did not have any shrapnel wounds or combat medals to verify combat. After several reopens and denials of the claim, his family and VSO had filed an appeal, also denied by the Board of Veterans Appeals due to lack of evidence. Then they went to the State Department in D.C. in attempt to research military records in effort to find any evidence to support that the man had served in combat. (That's not where his military records were, but they traveled there.) They requested a personal hearing with a BVA travel board judge. On the day of the hearing, the VSO told the judge, "Forget it, they didn't bring any additional evidence with them. They have nothing." But the judge said, "They traveled 4 hours to get here. Let me at least hear what they have to say. And the story put forth by the mother and sister, as I stated above, was a tearjerker. Not only that, but the veteran sat there in a daze, never offering a word of agreement, never pleading for himself, just lip-locked and looking like he was mentally deranged and didn't even understand what the conversation was about. The judge asked him several questions about Vietnam and the veteran just had a terrible scared look on his face, and stuttered a little bit but said nothing that made any sense. It was very real and very sad. It goes to show that the ones who are truly experiencing PTSD from war may not really even be capable of expressing their claim. Those who are showing no functional, social or occupational impairment probably do not have PTSD.

In 2010, the VA implemented a new "fear and easing" standard such that for any veteran who served in a "hostile military environment" such as Vietnam, Iraq, or Afghanistan, the VA will concede that he was likely to have feared for his life. Even if he was in base camp and never heard an explosion, never saw a fire, never had to pick up a weapon, the PTSD stressor can be conceded based on the fear and easing standard. It was a good thing for those like the man I described above because he no longer had to prove he had witnessed any particular thing in Vietnam, the fact he served there during wartime was enough. So it was a good thing; however, it is now grossly abused. Practically every single veteran who has ever been to Iraq or Afghanistan has now filed a claim for PTSD, and practically every single one of them has been granted.

A grant for PTSD requires three things. First, a "verified stressor" which is the stressful event triggering the PTSD (or fear for his life due to the fear and easing standard). Second, there must be a diagnosis of PTSD by a psychiatric specialist. And third, there must be a simple medical statement linking the diagnosis to the stressor. If the person goes to a VA medical center and claims the symptoms, he will be given the diagnosis. If he has the diagnosis, then the medical nexus statement is a sure thing. Very few will be denied PTSD if they will simply go in and report some symptoms. Totally subjective symptoms. Yes, there are batteries of psychiatric tests the examiners can do, but they're rarely done, and they're easy to lie on. Occasionally a suspicious examiner will give a validity test that indicates the person may be lying, then he will say the claimant does not have PTSD but is malingering (making up symptoms). In that case the condition may be denied. But no worries; the claimant will reopen the claim and the next examiner will give the diagnosis. Even if it takes 3 or 4 tries, he will eventually convince an examiner that he has PTSD, and VA will grant it.

The first thing one needs to do if he has been denied, or wants to assure he'll be granted, is to go to a VA medical center and request treatment. Tens to hundreds of hours of screening, and testing, and group and individual therapy are provided to any veterans who want to claim PTSD, or depression, anxiety, bipolar disorder, schizophrenia and anything else they can think of.

The DSM-IV, psychiatric diagnostic manual used for many years, was very lax on what could be diagnosed as PTSD. With the new DSM-V, the diagnosis of PTSD became much more difficult to support. Most doctors just fudge the answers, check the boxes to make it work. But under DSM-V more and more often the doctors are saying, "The symptoms do not meet the criteria for a diagnosis of PTSD; however, a diagnosis of 'other trauma- and stress-related disorder' is given." Then another medical opinion is needed for the doctor to say that the made-up condition is at least as likely as not related to an event that occurred in military service. Many thousands of hours are spent on processing these claims, and millions spent on providing more and more psychiatric exams and medical opinions, which have to be done by a licensed psychiatrist or psychologist.

Now here's a remarkable fact about PTSD. The claimant *never* gets better. The VHA has all these new elaborate treatment programs for PTSD, and the VHA counselors report remarkable success, but the veterans never report any improvement to VBA. The doctors' reports may indicate improvement, but the claimants will never acknowledge it; to do so would mean a reduction in their disability income! In fact they report the opposite; they say that discussing their stressors in counseling has caused more memories, more nightmares, and more anxiety. So they come back in year after year asking for an *increase* in their PTSD evaluation. And it is very easy to get. Most start out with an evaluation of 30 or 50 percent disability. Then they are told exactly what symptoms would need to be reported in order to qualify for a higher level. So they come back in and report those symptoms they were told to report! Then they're up to 70 percent (and can get IU granted based on that) or they get a schedular 100 percent for their PTSD.

A review of granted claims for PTSD will reveal shocking evidence of how many veterans are drawing 50, 70, or 100 percent disability for PTSD, and yet are living perfectly normal, productive lives. They are happily married, raising a gang of children, and they are working good jobs including federal government jobs. Many of your full time local policemen and firefighters, most all postal service workers, security guards, prison guards, and personnel developing claims at your local VA office, are drawing their fat 40-hr-a-week pay check and drawing a fat VA disability check on top of it. If most employers knew an employee was diagnosed with 100% disabling PTSD, do you think he would actually have been hired or allowed to keep the job? Well, employers never know because this is confidential information; no veteran has to disclose to anyone that he has PTSD. And as for the VA workers, yes, the VA knows in many cases, but does not care. That is the function of the VA, to help veterans and give them as much as possible, and that includes a pay check as well as a disability check whenever possible.

Many veterans, especially females, claim PTSD due to being beaten or abused by their military spouses during service. No doubt that can cause PTSD, but really, is it "military-related?" Wouldn't it have happened if one or both of them were civilians? How can the government take responsibility for this? Where is the advocate or attorney to represent the federal taxpayer in this law suit against the federal government? The government should take action to report and punish the abusive criminal (which they won't do) instead of just paying the victim as if she was injured in a military conflict.

Numerous veterans who left service at the rank of O-4, O-5, or O-6 are claiming PTSD because since they served during the Gulf War they can claim an automatic "fear and easing" stressor. Some of them did serve in combat zones and they lost people who were under their command. That's war! And that's what they signed up for and that's what they were trained for at West Point. Then they spent 30 years in service, with nary a complaint, and wore all their badges proudly! Now that they are drawing their fat military officer retirement checks they want to claim functional impairment. If they were all that impaired on returning from the Gulf War then they should have been discharged as soon as they returned to CONUS. But no, they continued to serve for 20 or even 30 years to get the maximum possible retirement, then went to work for TSA or CIA or the Railroad or as a consultant for any number of defense contractors. They are not impaired! And it is a crying shame to see these people abusing the system when many of their underlings have suffered true injuries in war, injuries that will forever affect their employment prospects, limit their social/recreational activities, and cause true symptoms of PTSD.

We all have stories of people we know who have been injured. All military jobs and most jobs in general do carry a degree of injury risk. That is not PTSD. PTSD results when something so traumatic happens to *you* that it scares you so bad that it throws you into a temporary state of shock. Later, when sights or sounds remind you of that scary moment, you may reexperience the fear again. For some people, the trauma is so severe that they may be obsessed with the memories for many days or months.

In many cases, the military events veterans claim are events that happened so long ago they don't remember much of anything about it. They don't remember the names, dates, or what ship they were on. If they had a temporary shock, they got over it, and it should not be considered a chronic disability. A chronic disability is one that continues to cause social or occupational impairment. If the incident and remembrance of the incident has never prevented the person from having normal relationships and a normal work history, then it should not be granted or paid for by my tax dollars.

***

Veteran X was happily married 32 years before his wife died from cancer. He's a little depressed about that. He has close family relations and close friends. He went to college after service and got a degree in computer science. He has had a successful progressive work history since discharge from service including working for the past 22 years for a large utility/gas company. He is a senior systems analyst and he tells the examiner that he enjoys his work very much with good pay, good people, and good benefits.

In accordance with 38 CFR 4.130, General Rating Formula for Mental Disorders, "occasional decrease in work efficiency and intermittent periods" of impairment represents a 30 percent disability. In this case (and many others), there was little if any social or occupational impairment shown by the records, but the evaluation the VA rater must assign is 50%, generated from the PTSD exam template and VA evaluation builder. The rater would love to explain in the rating, "There is little if any social or occupational impairment shown in your records, but the 50 percent disability evaluation assigned is the minimum allowed by use of the mandatory VA exam template and evaluation builder." Of course the rater can say no such thing. The rater must remain empathetic and grant the highest possible evaluation based on tools provided. The rater must assign the 50 percent, tell him what to say next time in order to up it to 70 percent, and move on.

***

Veteran X is asking for 100% for his PTSD. He is fully functioning, retired from work, has a family and good social life. He's already has an unjustified 70% for his PTSD and is therefore in receipt of IU which pays him at the 100% rate, but he wants to get out of sending in the "can't work" form every year. If he's granted 100% for PTSD it will not pay him a penny more than he's getting, but he wastes the VA employees' time with claim after claim for increase in PTSD. In my opinion, a 100% evaluation for PTSD should be reserved for someone who is so totally mentally disturbed that they should be either in a mental institution or a prison.

***

Veteran X was an airplane mechanic and served in peace-time only. One day, per his account, he had to crawl inside an airplane wing to repair a fuel leak. He felt claustrophobic. He felt panic, but he completed the job. There was no record of the incident in his personnel file or in his service treatment records. He got out of service in 1962 and the incident was not mentioned for more than 50 years! In 2016 he filed a claim for PTSD based on that claustrophobic, not-injurious incident, and he was granted service-connection for PTSD without any symptoms of phobia; he was granted "PTSD with depression, without agoraphobia." In other words, even though his stressor incident was a form of phobia (claustrophobia) and his current diagnosis is specifically not associated with phobia, the VA granted it, because they grant everything they can. There was no proof the incident ever occurred, but it was considered to be "consistent with his job duties" and a medical examiner said his current condition was as likely as not related to service.

***

Veteran X only served in the Philippines, not Vietnam, but claims he was spit on and criticized when he came back to the US and this caused him to have PTSD. He was granted PTSD and eventually IU for 100 percent compensation. No Vietnam *era* vet is likely to be denied PTSD, whether he saw war or not.

***

Veteran X is a drug addict, preferring cocaine and marijuana. A couple years after he got out of Vietnam and out of service he went into a Greek restaurant. The waiter came over from the bar and made some comment to the effect that they don't serve Negroes. The veteran pulled out a gun and shot the waiter. The veteran was sentenced to 20 years in the penitentiary for attempted murder. He was released after five years and ever since he got out he's been nothing but a drug addict. He has never worked in the now 30 years since he got out of prison. He's been reportedly homeless but he has managed to get married and have at least one child. That child has committed several crimes, has been in and out of prison, and is currently in prison. The veteran puts on his claim form that he has PTSD due to his son's problems. However, on his PTSD exam, the examiner says that's not a good enough stressor, so he tells the examiner that shortly after he arrived in Vietnam some weapons were fired, mortars were coming in, body parts were flying, and he was splattered by the remains of dead human beings (classic textbook). He didn't receive any combat medal saying that he was involved in combat so it's just his subjective report. But the VA psychologist determined that the man has PTSD and that has caused all his problems all these years. The psychologist says the man is unable to work and is unable to have social relationships. He is unable to perform any type of occupation; therefore, we have to pay him 100% disability. So we are fully supporting his drug habit while providing him all the basic comforts of life.

***

Veteran X never set boots on the ground in any war zone. However, his job was "target analysis" so he watched casualties through video feed. His job was to find the targets, then someone else would fire a missile to blow them up. I can see the stress in this; however, I cannot see how this caused the claimant to "fear for his life." He was sitting in cozy computer room thousands of miles from the action. Those who were stationed on the ground in the area where he was aiming would surely have been fearing for their lives, but not him, so I do not see a basis for PTSD here. The same goes for the drone operators. But these are treated by VA regulations the same as if they were flying a real plane dropping bombs, as if they could be shot down. The drone pilots are thousands of miles away and it's just not fair to the pilots and foot soldiers who have actually feared for their lives in a war zone.

The definition of PTSD does include "or the lives of others" but that means being in a situation where you and others are likely to be killed, such as a wreck or hurricane or combat where you might die or others experiencing the same thing with you might die. You are still fearing for *your* life, not *just* the life of others. This definition has been erroneously stretched to be applied to cases where a veteran has treated a dying patient in the hospital or operated a drone that might kill someone. I could never do these jobs, but I also wouldn't sign up for them. More importantly, if PTSD is to be granted for such stressors, then at the very least they must be evaluated based on the true degree of residual *disability*. Generally if they successfully performed the job in service, they either liked it or hardened to it, and they are not seriously disabled after service.

***

Veteran X worked during his military service in an office job in the states. He sometimes found out that the soldier whose paperwork he was processing was now dead! He says this was extremely stressful for him because his job was to help soldiers and he couldn't help them if they were dead! So that was his PTSD stressor and of course PTSD was granted simply because his stressor (job) was verified. This is ridiculous and must be changed.

***

Veteran X was granted for PTSD because he flipped his Humvee in service. He was never in combat, but he wrecked while trying to avoid hitting a deer. Wouldn't it be something if the US federal government could pay every American who has ever hit a deer or wrecked while trying to avoid it! Not just a little one-time payment but $1000 per month for the rest of their life!! If the guy was physically injured in the wreck I'm all for paying him, but PTSD, give me a break!

***

Veteran X claimed his PTSD stressor was his job as a policeman in service. He feared for his life when he had to initiate a drug bust, after which the criminal's friends may have wanted to endanger him. Policemen in our society deal with this every day of the week, fear that someone they arrest, or the family and friends of that person, will retaliate in some way. The same fear is experienced by attorneys, judges, and any person who has ever had to testify in court or serve on a jury! Of course there is the chance of retaliation, but it's just one of a million risks we take in everyday life. The chances are greater that you'll die in a car accident that you caused, or that you'll die due to obesity, your own fault. What irks me most is that this soldier signed up to be a policeman. The military gave him the job he wanted but he's not happy that they paid him to do the job he wanted for the years he served. He could have stayed in and continued to work it and to get paid for it. But he wants to be out of service and paid for the rest of his life for doing nothing. This is not true PTSD. It should not have been diagnosed and should not have been granted. But practically all PTSD claims are granted.

***

Veteran X was a military policeman, never in a combat situation. He attended to a vehicle accident on the autobahn in Germany, and as a result claims PTSD. This was his job! This incident did not threaten his life!

***

Veteran X was a black man preparing for a parachute jump. A "white" man teased him that someone had tweaked his parachute, so the claimant was afraid to jump. They pushed him out and he peed himself. The chute worked perfectly but he was so ashamed and he thought about it every time he had to make another jump. He still thinks about it sometimes lying in bed. It is an example of classic victimization. He hates white people, but he is not suffering from PTSD.

Numerous PTSD claims come from blacks who say they were mistreated because they were black, but they never have any evidence. Their records show normal progression through ranks and normal physical exams. Meanwhile many white veterans also report they experienced an unfairness in that white men had to live up to extreme expectations while blacks were allowed by their supervisors to get away with misconduct and poor job performance, untouchable, for fear of discrimination charges. And there's no evidence of that either.

***

Veteran X is a 67-year-old Caucasian male. The examiner completed a DBQ but also provided the old type of narrative report (probably felt like I do that DBQ's don't explain anything). According to the examiner's remarks, "the veteran arrived early for his scheduled appointment, was casually but appropriately dressed in jeans and a long-sleeved t-shirt with a baseball cap. He was neat and clean in appearance with no obvious impairment in personal care tasks, was average in height with an average build and looked his stated age. He displayed a euthymic mood with congruent affect. He ambulated without assistance. The veteran was calm and relaxed in his demeanor throughout the examination. His insight and judgment appeared intact. He displayed good eye contact and was easily engaged with the examiner. His speech was clear, logical, goal directed, and relevant. There was no evidence of any psychotic processes. He denied current suicidal or homicidal ideation. He was oriented to time, person, place, and situation. He was able to successfully count backward by sevens, starting at 100, with one error. He was able to recall two of three objects after five minutes of distraction. He was able to manage five digits forward and three digits backwards. He successfully completed simple and complex arithmetic problems and was able to display good social judgment and abstraction skills. Based upon his vocabulary, grammar and general fund of knowledge, he appeared to be of average intelligence. He scored a 28/30 on the MMSE; scores below 23 are indicative of a possible cognitive problem and would need to be evaluated further."

The veteran reported that he and his fifth wife divorced after almost two years together because they were "incompatible." Then approximately six months later, he married his sixth wife and they have been together for almost 3 weeks. They enjoy spending time together and doing things together despite "some trust issues." He also feels some discord with children, but enjoys spending time with friends and engaging in hobbies/interests. No problems with ADLs (activities of daily living). The veteran remains retired and noted no occupational or educational pursuits. He says he keeps busy doing "whatever he wants to do" such as spending time visiting friends, going to the VFW, shopping, and taking care of stuff around the house.

Despite practically no impairment or problems discussed by the examiner (only a tiny bit of memory loss which is normal for age 67) the examiner checked off several boxes on the DBQ such as "difficulty establishing and maintaining relationships" and "disturbances of motivation and mood;" therefore, he had to be granted 50 percent disability.

***

Veteran X has been out of service for 30 years. Suddenly at age 62 he gets granted PTSD, 70% disabling. He sent in a statement from a private psychiatrist he saw twice. The VA examiner says he cannot work due to PTSD because he has nightmares and is suicidal. The man has been married to the same woman for 35 years. He has grown children, and several grandchildren. He attends church every Sunday. He was earning $133,000 per year as a logistician, but he quit work immediately after he was granted 70% for PTSD. Then submitted a claim for IU. He needs more money to continue the standard of living to which he has become accustomed.

***

Veteran X is a Vietnam veteran but he had no "shell-shock" experience. He received a combat action ribbon (automatic conceded stressor) because he participated in a defensive firing event. Later his sergeant told him there were five confirmed dead of those they fired upon. He never saw the people, and he never came close to dying, per his own comments of the incident. However, he did see a scary poisonous snake once in service, so he feels he came close to dying at that time.

***

Veteran X is a Vietnam vet who got out in 1976. His first claim for PTSD was in 2016, about 40 years later. He had already been service connected for other conditions since 2000, for 16 years, and he had been receiving treatment at VA medical centers for all those years. In 2016 he filed another claim for increase in those conditions but was denied because after several successful claims for increase over the past 16 years he is now at the max he can get for each of those particular service-connected conditions. Now the only way to get a higher total evaluation is to add a new condition. His POA adds PTSD to the claim, and tah dah, yes that gets him up to the

100%. All Vietnam veterans will be granted PTSD simply for the asking.

***

Veteran X, at age 70, claimed PTSD and IU. He had served 2 years in 1966-1968. After service he got a degree in Biology Wildlife and he obtained a good job in the Forestry Department where he stayed a few years. After that he worked for 25 years in Nuclear Energy as a consultant and manager. Then he started his own pest control company which he has run successfully for the past 20 years, while at the same time managing a 25-acre walnut farm. Does this sound like this man has been disabled from PTSD? Where is the impairment? But as a Vietnam vet, his stressor is automatic, and the examiners either don't want to deny these Vietnam vets, or maybe they've been warned (like VA warns the raters).

***

Veteran X served 27 years, then after service filed a claim for PTSD. It's amazing how a person can continue working in the military, especially to continue for seven years beyond the date he could have retired, if indeed he were suffering from any sort of military-induced symptoms. Anyway, this veteran says that his stressor is that about 10 to 12 of his soldiers (serving under him) or their family members have died from various non-combat injuries. One was a car accident. One was a boating accident. One was a bar-fight shooting incident. One was a single aircraft accident. One teenage soldier committed suicide, and one died from alcohol poisoning. So what! He did not cause these deaths. He did not witness these deaths. He did not fear for his own life while these incidents occurred or at any time afterwards. He was never blamed for the deaths. These are just people he knew in the course of 27 years who died for one reason or another. He never even served in a combat zone. If so, he may have seen many more deaths. He has no reason to feel responsible for any of the deaths of people who served in his unit. And even if he did or even if he *was* responsible, it would not meet the criteria for the definition of PTSD! PTSD results when you experience something so horrific that you fear for your life, and you go into a sort of shock that you never forget, and you'll dream about it, and you'll relive it whenever you are in similar conditions in the future. He has none of this. But the VA was able to verify at least one of those deaths occurred. Then the examiner linked current depression to the in-service event and called it PTSD, so it was granted.

***

Veteran X is service-connected at 70% for PTSD. He has recently married and has a one-year-old child; these relationships were established after the alleged disabling PTSD incident. He maintains contact with his parents and siblings in other states, something many "well" people don't do. What a great life he has; he reportedly sleeps in every morning, then gets up and plays with the toddler. He and the wife build furniture (because he has no physical disabilities whatsoever) and they hope to open their own furniture business soon (because he also has no trouble managing finances or dealing with employees or the public).

***

Veteran X served two years although much of it was in AWOL status. He was discharged in 1978 under honorable conditions due to misconduct and drug abuse. In 2011, more than 32 years later, he filed for PTSD. He said his grandfather had physically and sexually abused him when he was a child, and that two officers sexually assaulted him during service and threatened him not to tell. There was no evidence in the military records of such an event, except that he did go AWOL.

The VA examiner in 2011 found no diagnosis of PTSD but diagnosed anxiety due to the childhood abuse and alcohol/drug abuse the veteran had experienced all his life. He appealed the decision and BVA granted service-connection based on a letter from the VA Medical Center treatment program. Just because he is now attending a PTSD program (which anyone can join), they conceded his diagnosis and granted PTSD.

BVA does not have to justify their decisions. Sometimes they grant a case, and grant 100%, just to get a case out of the system whenever the claimant has continued to submit appeals over and over. In this case BVA granted 70% for the condition and retroactive pay from 2015 (time appeal was settled) back to 2011 (date of claim), so he received a fat retro check of over $100,000.

In 2016 the veteran filed an increase claim, asking for IU. The VA examiner wrote a 5-page review of the file, noting there was no evidence of an in-service event. The in-service markers (AWOL) were long after the date of the claimed sexual assault, and the claimant was discharged for misconduct and drug abuse, not because he went AWOL after an assault. The doctor conceded that the claimant *may* have PTSD related to his childhood abuse and not related to anything in service, but that primarily he has an antisocial personality and drug/alcohol abuse problems.

He reported to the doctor that he has friends. He has skills and experience as a carpenter and painter. He is in healthy physical condition. He now works in construction with a friend "just to have something to do" and reportedly does not take any payment from his friend. Therefore, since he's not accepting payment, he says *that* work should not prevent him from receiving IU.

He says he hasn't worked since 2011, but numerous medical records show that he failed to make medical appointments "due to working." Also, he had been in a VAMC "work program" but he got out of that because he had a "new job" that would prevent him from participating in the aftercare part of the program. His reports are basically all lies. He changes his story regularly about what happened when he worked or not. He also said his SSDI was stopped because he was getting 70% compensation from the VA, and that just doesn't happen. Receipt of compensation is not counted by the IRS, or the SSA, or by anyone! It just free money, paid by the taxpayer, to some of the most dishonest lowlifes of society.

***

Veteran X worked in a supply room stocking and loading ammunition into clips. He stated that he became stressed due to thinking about who may have been killed with the bullets he loaded. Stressor was conceded, as it was consistent with his job description, and service connection was granted. It shouldn't have been because this is not truly PTSD; he did not fear for his life. Fearing "for the lives of others" is misinterpreted. The definition of PTSD says it happens after being in a situation where one fears for the lives of himself and/or others, meaning this explosion or this earthquake could kill me and/or many of those around me. It should not apply when one is looking in on a situation where others have been in danger or killed, but the individual himself was in no danger. Although one may see or hear about horrendous things, that does not create the intense shellshock one experiences when he fears he himself is about to die.

***

Veteran X worked in an aircraft maintenance shop. An airplane crashed. The veteran claimed he was stressed because he had once met the pilot who died, and his shop had once done work on that aircraft. The maintenance logs showed that the airplane was in perfect condition prior to takeoff, and the crash was blamed on pilot error. Still the claimant's records verified that he was an aircraft mechanic, so it was reasonable to assume the plane could have been in this man's shop, so the stressor was conceded, and service connection granted. This should not have been considered PTSD as the claimant had no fear for his life, and had no involvement in the accident! So many veterans grasp at straws to find some excuse for PTSD, and fabricate totally subjective symptoms, and the VA is a sucker for it. The more veterans granted and treated for PTSD, the better the VA looks!

***

Veteran X had submitted no stressor statement with his PTSD claim, but he'd been out of service for less than a year so he was given a general medical and PTSD exam. At the PTSD exam, the examiner asked him for a stressor so he was pressed to think up something/anything stressful that happened in service. He said that while serving on a ship, a fellow soldier got tangled in a line and he had to go help him get untangled. On another occasion, while the ship was being re-fueled, a line snapped and one sailor was hit by the line and knocked unconscious. The claimant admits that he was not even on the ship deck at the time of the incident, he just heard about it afterwards. It was a seaman he knew and worked with. PTSD was diagnosed and compensation was granted. It shouldn't have been, because there was no actual verification of those events anyway, but they were conceded as "consistent with his job duties."

***

Veteran X is a woman who can't even explain why she's claiming PTSD. She puts nothing on the 0781 (stressor statement) except that she was in Saudi Arabia for a few months doing admin work. VA sent her a letter requesting stressor details and received no answer. She was in service for 20 years from 1981 to 2001. On VA exam she told the examiner she feared that she might be hit by scud missiles but that she never actually heard or experienced one. She got married during her first year of service and she has been married now for 40 years at the time of her claim. Their children are grown.   She still works in an admin job which she enjoys. She has no drug or legal problems.   She takes no medication for anything.   The examiner diagnosed PTSD and checked a few boxes on the DBQ. She was granted 30% disability despite the fact the woman has lived 40 perfect years since the claimed event that never actually even happened. How angry this must make a veteran whose life was ruined because he was blown up by a scud missile!

***

Veteran X was granted PTSD because he served in Vietnam. The exam was questionable/doubtful, but benefit of the doubt is always given to the veteran, so he was granted, and a routine future exam was scheduled for three years later just to be sure. It's a technique raters use to relieve their guilt of granting something they don't believe in, all the while knowing that once granted this decision will never be reversed.

On the review exam the veteran told the doctor he is depressed because his dog died. He kisses the dog's collar every day and "almost cries." He says he would kill himself if not for his wife. He has 6 grandchildren and is planning an out-of-state trip to visit them next month, so he requests a refill of Xanax to help him deal with that visit. (The examiner is not his treating physician so he cannot provide it.) The claimant makes no mention of Vietnam or of having any nightmares or remembrances of Vietnam.

Based on the exam checkmarks indicating depression, anxiety, and difficulty adjusting to work and social life, his VA disability is increased from 30% to 50%. How infuriating this must be to some other veteran who stepped on a punji stick in Vietnam or who wakes up sweating with nightmares of war!

***

Veteran X filed numerous claims for joint conditions which he does have now in old age, but the claims were always denied because he had never gone to sick call for anything while in service. After 18 years of denials he decided to try a new approach and filed for PTSD, based on the fact that he had been to Iraq. Of course PTSD was diagnosed and service connection was granted, even though there was no obvious functional impairment due to this or any condition.

***

Veteran X claims PTSD was caused while he was serving in the Reserves. His CSM was harassing him and his wife (both Reservists in the same unit). The CSM said he would split them up just to break them up. He ordered the man to Ft Lewis (in the states) and the wife was never sent anywhere, so she could have transferred to Ft Lewis area but didn't. The claimant spent one year in Ft Lewis on active duty alone, and he claims he developed PTSD "due to being lonely for his wife." Others in his unit were mobilized to Iraq and

Afghanistan *war zones* while he hung out at Ft Lewis. He says that when he got back with his wife one year later, his wife had become accustomed to doing everything for herself so she didn't need him anymore. No, they did not separate or divorce, but he claims he still has PTSD as result of that separation from his wife. Are we really going to grant PTSD to every serviceman who has to be apart from his wife for a year?

***

Veteran X served 18 months from 1960 to 1962 during peacetime. He says he got discharged early because he couldn't deal with drill sergeants. (Well he only had to deal with a drill sergeant for 8 weeks, or 16 if he got recycled, so obviously that wasn't really the problem.) At age 72 he filed a claim for PTSD and was granted! At age 73 he filed for IU, reporting that he could not work due to PTSD. The mental exam made no mention of the military at all. He discussed being depressed due to being overweight and having physical limitations. He says he's in a wheelchair and has two teenage grandchildren living with him who take up all the space! He likes to paint but has no room to paint due to these kids living with him, so he feels he deserves an increase! Are we going to pay every grandparent who helps support his grandkids? If so, I deserve some too.

***

Veteran X has been married to the same wife for 10 years, has several children and stepchildren, and gets along great with his siblings. He was discharged in 2010 and since then he has worked as a civilian policeman (carrying a gun), despite having PTSD 50% disabling. He is still in the Reserves and plans stay in until he can retire from the Reserves in a few years. He gets along great with his family, coworkers, and Reserve unit buddies. The examiner noted that he has "disturbances of motivation and mood" so that raised his PTSD evaluation to 70%. There was no mention of any violence, suicidal thoughts, panic attacks or obsessional rituals.

How can a person 70% mentally disabled (a level VA often accepts as total disability for purposes of IU) be allowed to carry a gun and serve as a policeman?   How can he continue fully functioning in the Reserves and presumably be ready for deployment any day if needed?   Why can't a VA rater ask for written reports from his police supervisor and his Reserves commander as to how much this man is occupationally impaired by this mental condition? (The answer is that mental health is confidential and cannot be leaked in ways that could jeopardize the veteran's employment.) He clearly denies any social impairment, so what is it?   It's a wrong evaluation, that's what, and it's ridiculous. The rater must rate based on the VA exam boxes checked. The rater is never allowed to "develop to deny" which is to request evidence that might be not in the veteran's best interest, that might result in denial, severance or reduction.

***

Veteran X is service connected for PTSD. He's filed a claim for increase because while beating his wife he hurt his hand. He thinks the beating represents that his PTSD has worsened, warranting an increase, and he is also asking for service-connection for the hand injury, secondary to PTSD.

***

Veteran X was in service in 2003 when her non-military husband was murdered. She wasn't there, didn't witness it, but only heard about it from the police as they showed her photos of his dead body.   She continued in service for a few years with normal progression through the ranks and had three children while still in service. When her second tour ended she got out and had no trouble obtaining and maintaining an admin job.   In 2014 she was pregnant again and married the father of the child.

In 2017, 14 years after her first husband's death, she is happily married and now has 5 kids. She explains on exam, "It's a lot of work raising five children." So she quit her job and filed a VA claim for a mental condition caused by the event in service, her first

212

husband's death. It's a stressor that can be verified because it happened while she was in service. But does she have a disabling condition related to that stressor? She self-reports that she is very friendly and she gets along with everyone, has no problem with sleeping, going out in public, or taking the children around to all their sports activities. She says she has panic attacks once a week, although there is absolutely no evidence of it and she has never seen a doctor for treatment or medication for this or any mental problem.

"Panic attack" is simply a subjective symptom which means different things to different people and the exam report gives no details of it. Does her heart just race a little, unnoticed by others, or does she fall into a state of shock/comatose for hours? In any case, because she *said* she has panic attacks, the doctor checked the box, and that symptom leads to a high evaluation. The VA examiner diagnosed PTSD linked to the in-service event, so the rater has no choice but to grant it, and based on the boxes checked on exam, the condition warrants no less than 50% disability.

Wouldn't it be something if the government (we taxpayers) had to pay 50% disability to every person whose spouse ever died for any reason! Although this case was murder, the woman did not experience the event and never feared for her own life. Yes, she will always remember the police photos, just like any person will remember their dead spouse lying in the hospital bed or coffin, but that event has not affected her social or occupational functioning. It does not warrant more than 10% disability in any case, and based on a true definition of PTSD and straightforward interpretation of the VA regulations, this should not be granted at all.

***

Veteran X spent 3 months in service, all in basic training, never went to AIT (advanced training). He says that his drill sergeant pulled him off the top bunk at 8:00 AM and threw him to the ground (wow, are recruits working banker's hours now?) When he got up his back was hurting but he got dressed and went to formation. They had to run up a hill and his back was hurting so he asked if he could go to sick call. The drill instructor said "there's nothing wrong with you" and made him keep going. So there was no injury ever documented. Later, on the rifle range, he was scared from the sounds of all the gunfire. He says he was just a teenager and had never been around guns.   He went to see the Chaplain and told him he could not adjust to military life and needed to go back home. He was released from service on a "non-characterized" discharge due to "inability to adjust to military life." He reports that now whenever he hears a car backfire (how often is that?) or fireworks (once a year?) it causes him to feel bad anxiety and his ears start ringing. So of course he has been granted PTSD and tinnitus. A kid who couldn't even make it through basic due to his personal frailties, not any documented injury, who the military was kind enough to let "out" without penalty, we the taxpayers support for the rest of his life. What an insult to war-injured veterans.

***

Veteran X's wife had a C-section to remove a still-born son while he was on active duty. The veteran claims he has nightmares about seeing the dead baby in the hospital. He is granted PTSD for this, because documents show the event did happen in service and he claims subjective symptoms.   He receives 50% disability compensation for PTSD.

This is so wrong because there is no evidence anywhere to indicate that this condition has functionally impaired this veteran in any way. Must taxpayers really pay disability to every veteran who fathers a still-born child, or who experiences any death in their family? If not, then it's not fair or right to give it to this one.

***

Veteran X has been granted service connection for anxiety neurosis since 1966. After one year of service he could not stand being away from his wife any longer and he wanted to go home. He said this was making him nervous and anxious. Releasing this man from service was the best thing for everyone; the military does not need wimpy slackers. But paying him for this behavior is sending the wrong message to all the other troops and veterans. *And if*

214

indeed it was military service and being away from his wife that was causing all his problems, then why didn't he get better as soon as he got back home? Why have we continued to increase his evaluation over the years. By the way, he subsequently divorced the wife, but he didn't give up the VA compensation.

***

Veteran X had no problems in service and worked for 40 years after service with no problems. He has been happily married and now has three grandchildren which he says "make his day!" He retired at age 65, and at age 70 he filed his first VA claim, claiming PTSD. The examiner diagnosed PTSD and noted that the claimant "has difficulty establishing and maintaining effective work and social relationships." Really? There's never been a better adjusted individual in history. A person with real true PTSD, having trouble with work and social relationships, is one who does not work at all or at least does not have employment gainful and steady enough to retire from, and he generally does not marry or last long in a marriage or relationship, and generally does not have good relationships with children, period.

***

Veteran X was the executive officer (XO) of a military company when several soldiers in his unit were in a vehicle accident and one of them was killed. When the accident happened, one of the passengers called the XO and he raced out to the scene. He was not in the accident and did not witness it happen. There was nothing mentioned about this incident in his personnel or medical records. The records all just said what a great officer he was. There was no disability or mental symptom noted on his military discharge exams. Five years after service he solicited a private physician to complete a DBQ for him, providing a diagnosis of PTSD and linking it to that accident in service. This event does not meet the definition of a PTSD stressor, but because the death of a soldier was verified, his claim was granted like they all are.

***

Veteran X was in Afghanistan for a few months so VA concedes that he may have feared for his life based on the relaxed "fear and easing standards." The examiner found no symptoms to support a diagnosis of PTSD, so he diagnosed "Unspecified Depressive Disorder" and linked it to back pain that had started in service. The veteran has been married for 16 years and has three young children. He coaches his son's soccer team, works as a DJ part-time in clubs and bars, and sees several friends daily. He has 2 bachelor degrees, one in Criminal Justice and one in Business, and he has a Master's degree in Public Administration. He works full time as an Inventory Management Officer for Department of Defense. He admits on exam that his job "is great" with "no problems in terms of responsibilities or interpersonal relationships." He gets 30% disability for his depression, the same as if PTSD had been diagnosed. It doesn't matter that the DSM-V tightened up their criteria for a diagnosis of PTSD (over DSM-IV criteria which was loose). Now the doctors simply diagnose any other thing they can find in the DSM, and it gets granted anyway.

***

Veteran X claims he has PTSD due to "financial stress." He listed no stressors that would qualify for a PTSD diagnosis so the examiner diagnosed "Persistent Depressive Disorder." His family consists of a wife, one child aged 13, and a mother-in-law who provides child care and does the housework while he and his wife both work. He earns $60,000 per year working at the shipyard in Norfolk. He finished his AA degree last fall and is now working on his BA. He is already in receipt of 90% disability from the VA, which is over $2000 per month, and this 30% for his mental depression due to financial stress will take him over the 100% mark, for more than $3000 a month. So when his "financial stress" is relieved by the 100% disability rating, won't his evaluation then warrant reduction?

***

Veteran X spent less than two years on active duty in Vietnam from 1965 to 1966, then spent 28 years in the Reserves and retired as a Command Sergeant Major (CSM-E9). He then worked 35 years as a police officer at a psychiatric hospital. His wife also worked at the same hospital. He retired from the police force at age 67, and promptly submitted a claim for PTSD. He has never had a substance abuse or legal problem. He was married 50 years to the same woman and has grown children. He receives military retirement, and he and his wife both receive SSA. But to keep his income up there to where it was while he was employed, he needs this VA disability compensation. He believes it is his *right* because he went to Vietnam, although he was never injured there, and he spent less than two years of active duty with no injury or illness incurred during service. Any Vietnam veteran who claims PTSD is granted PTSD. The doctors and the VA do not have the guts to deny it.

This is totally wrong. If you want to pay a man just because he went to Vietnam or any combat zone, then pass a law that pays anyone who went to Vietnam or a combat zone, but stop these disability lies. It's a disgrace and a disservice to the truly war-injured disabled veterans.

MILITARY SEXUAL TRAUMA (MST)

Military sexual trauma (MST) is a special kind of posttraumatic stress disorder (PTSD). More and more veterans, both women and men are claiming this each year. The following definition of MST comes from a VA fact sheet.

"Military sexual trauma, or MST, is the term used by VA to refer to experiences of sexual assault or repeated, threatening sexual harassment that a Veteran experienced during his or her military service. The definition used by the VA comes from Federal law (Title 38 U.S. Code 1720D) and is 'psychological trauma, which in the judgment of a VA mental health professional, resulted from a physical assault of a sexual nature, battery of a sexual nature, or

sexual harassment which occurred while the Veteran was serving on active duty, active duty for training, or inactive duty training.' Sexual harassment is further defined as 'repeated, unsolicited verbal or physical contact of a sexual nature which is threatening in character'... It includes any sexual activity in which one is involved against one's will – he or she may have been pressured into sexual activities (for example, with threats of negative consequences for refusing to be sexually cooperative or with implied faster promotions or better treatment in exchange for sex), may have been unable to consent to sexual activities (for example, when intoxicated), or may have been physically forced into sexual activities. Other experiences that fall into the category of MST include unwanted sexual touching or grabbing; threatening, offensive remarks about a person's body or sexual activities; and/or threatening or unwelcome sexual advances."

So, based on the above definition, MST can be diagnosed and service-connection granted for someone who has endured offensive sexual remarks or unwelcome sexual advances, and that is what most of the cases are about.

The VA Health Administration literature shows that about 1 in 4 women veterans, and about 1 in 100 male veterans, state they suffered sexual harassment or trauma in service. The literature stresses that MST is an "experience," *not* a diagnosis, and treatment needs will vary. Some people are not sick as a result of the experience, but the VA medical centers will still care for them as needed. And yet the VA Benefits Administration continues to grant disability compensation using the PTSD rating schedule whenever an examiner indicates MST, as if it *was* a disorder. In other words, VBA *does* accept any "MST" as a diagnosis of illness and then it's just a matter of deciding the connection to service and how much the claimant can be paid based on the DBQ boxes checked.

The most current and popular way to get PTSD granted is to claim MST. That's because a MST grant does not require any proof of a rape, assault, harassment, or other stressful event in service. It only requires that something must look a little out of the ordinary in the military personnel file. For example, the person asked for a transfer, or got pregnant, or got treated for a sexually transmitted disease, or got demoted due to bad behavior of any sort, right around the time of the alleged assault. Since the assault is not documented, it is easy enough for one to place the alleged date of assault within a few days or months prior to that "stressor." I'm not saying there's no rapes and assaults in service. There are plenty, the same as there are plenty in every city in America, especially for people of military age indulging in a lot of drinking and partying and cohabitation. Life in military barracks is similar to college dorms. What if every college kid filed a charge of rape every time they got drunk and had sex, or every time someone they didn't like gave him or her a sexual compliment or bedroom eyes?

I'm not saying unwanted sexual advances and comments are right or acceptable. I'm saying it happens in all walks of life, not just the military. And victims continue to live, to go about their business, without receiving compensation from the government (us taxpayers). Rarely does true disability result from sexual harassment. In most of these cases wherein MST has been granted, and the veteran is receiving 50 or 70 or 100 percent disability, the evidence shows that the veteran went on to become happily married, raise a number of children, graduate from college, and maintain significant employment, often federal government employment. So the "PTSD" or "MST" is clearly not "disabling" but that compensation benefit will never be reduced or ended. It will simply continue to be increased until the day they die.

In the majority of cases there is no verification or indication of any harassment, rape, or any type of sexual trauma shown in the military personnel records or the service treatment records. Often the veteran reports that he didn't want to hurt his career or suffer the embarrassment by reporting the incident. Sometimes they say they reported it but were just told to suck it up, and it was never documented in the records. The veterans are coming in now 20, 30, or 40 years after discharge from service and claiming they were abused in service. The charges against basic training drill instructors are stacking up as fast as altar boys claims against priests. Apparently, according to unsupported claims, it's just normal practice for drill instructors to verbally harass the recruits with sexual comments, both males and females, and this is defined as MST, payable after service.

It is the rater's job to review all the service personnel and treatment records and see if there was any "marker" to indicate that something odd was going on in service. For example, did the soldier ask for a transfer, did she become pregnant out of wedlock, was he or she treated for venereal disease, did his or her performance appraisals suddenly drop, did she have sudden weight gain or loss? Any of these things can and are used to support the grant of MST even though they likely as not had nothing to do with an MST event. In the VA, if a rater is ever on the fence about any decision, he must fall to the side of the veteran.

Despite the regulations putting this MST decision squarely on the shoulders of the rater, I have seen hundreds of MST cases sent erroneously to a psychologist/psychiatrist for a medical opinion. The examiners do not have time to read all these service personnel files and treatment records, and no markers have been pointed out to them. Almost inevitably the psychologist will diagnose MST and opine that it is at least as likely as not incurred in service because the claimant's story sounds logical and the psychologist personally believes the story to be true.

For no other condition would it matter whether the examiner believes a story to be true, such as a knee injury. In those cases, the service records must show at least one complaint of knee injury or pain, or it would never land on the physician's desk for opinion. But MST is granted all the time based on an examiner's opinion when there is nothing else in the world to support it. I'm sorry to be so crude, but many people are just excellent liars and they will take advantage of every opportunity to increase their income.

Everyone at VA believes the MST claims; they have to! They are not allowed to say "the alleged incident" or "the story." They must address it *as if* it is in a documented police report.

In fact, there *are* some documented harassments and rapes. Some perpetrators have actually been kicked out of service, or at the least demoted and punished. In many cases, both documented and undocumented, no doubt the claimed events *did* happen. But when something this bad, rape or assault happens, a grown adult should have enough sense and nerve to report it to a doctor or the police. There is plenty of military training telling them to report any sexual harassment. If they haven't reported it, then unfortunately they should void their opportunity to collect on it later.

Furthermore, they shouldn't collect unless they have been actually *affected* by the incident. Per VA regulations, compensation is payable for conditions causing functional, occupational or social, impairment, not just exposure to an incident. A soldier may suffer a severe disease during service requiring hospitalization for weeks, but if he recovers with no residuals, it should not be service-connected for life-long compensation. Bad things happen in everyone's life. If no permanent chronic disability resulted from the event, it does not warrant "service-connected disability compensation."

I propose that all sexual harassment and worse incidents should be reported and the perpetrators should be punished appropriately. Courts should award the claimant general damages (pain and suffering) for what they went through and/or punitive damages to the defendant. But I do not agree with paying monthly disability compensation to a claimant who is showing no disability and has shown no loss of income or any other negative affect on his/her life as a result of the incident. If subsequent to the claimed event, the claimant has married, reared children, graduated from college, and worked successfully for 20 years in the job of her dreams, where is the disability?

***

Veteran X is a man who filed a claim for MST because while in service another man sat next to him on the bed and placed his hand on the claimant's thigh. It was a one-time incident. Nothing else happened. He never reported it until now, 40 years later. But allegedly this has caused every subsequent problem that the claimant has ever had in his life.

***

Veteran X is another man who claimed PTSD/MST, reporting that a higher ranking soldier (man) put his hands on his shoulders and kissed him. He cursed at the offender and as a result received an Article 15 and was transferred to another unit. There was no mention of this incident in the Article 15 or reassignment records. But it is clear that an Article 15 was issued and reassignment did occur, and these are accepted as "markers" by the VA, so the claim is granted, even though the MST incident is not verified. The evidence should include punishment of the offender and there was none. The claimant doesn't remember the offender's name or else it could be researched. Don't you think that one name might would have stuck with him? Do we want to believe that the military is turning a blind eye to aggressors, even those in supervisory/ leadership roles and only the victims are the ones being punished?

***

Veteran X claimed PTSD and reported on his VA Form 21-0781 (details of PTSD stressor) that he was kicked out of service after 18 years because *he* was charged with rape, assault, and lying to the courts. He is claiming compensation for PTSD based on the fact that the military incident has affected his ability to get jobs and to have personal relationships. No doubt such a thing in your records would influence prospective employers and girlfriends (as well as family members and neighbors). He'd be best to keep the details to himself. The incident certainly did not cause PTSD, and yet the examiner is able to diagnose PTSD, and the VA is willing to pay this man forever so he never has to work again, simply because there is a documented *in-service incident.* He should have been given a dishonorable discharge and it should not be reversed to "honorable for VA purposes."

***

Veteran X was a 40-year-old Army Captain female who was married with 4 children when the alleged MST event occurred. She went to training out-of-state, socialized that evening with two men from the training class who were also Army officers. They went to bars and all got drunk, then they all went back to her room and both men had sex with her. She later said it was non-consensual, but there was no violence and no struggle; she was just drunk. The day after the incident she went for medical care and reported the incident as rape. The examiner saw no evidence of force or injury, but confirmed there was evidence of recent sexual intercourse based on body fluids. The woman's husband subsequently found out about the incident and became very angry. Now every time he gets drunk, which is a lot because he is an alcoholic, he berates her about the incident again. So now she has to seek counseling to help with her marital problems, and she is granted service-connection for MST.

What is wrong with this story? For one thing, the VA regulations clearly prohibit granting of conditions that result from alcohol misuse, considered willful misconduct. What's different about this? It happened due to willful misconduct. If she has an injury or illness it was not caused in battle or in the course of completing any assigned military duty. Secondly, the condition did not result in any chronic physical or mental disability. It affected her husband. It did not affect her continued success in the military through retirement, or the continued rearing of her four children, and she continued to function normally occupationally and socially after service. Are we going to pay every veteran who ever got drunk and screwed someone he wasn't married to? Are we going to pay every veteran who has an alcoholic spouse?

***

Veteran X claims he has PTSD because in basic training his drill sergeant pushed him up against a wall, grabbed him in the groin, and said, "I can do anything to you I want to." He did not have his pants down and he was not sexually molested. It was just like a slap in the face or a kick in the butt; both are totally wrong but sometimes happen in basic training and nobody goes crying about it and filing a claim for MST (military sexual trauma).

Every woman in the world has at some point in time had her breast or ass grabbed, but does she suffer from MST for the rest of her life? I don't think so. Still, in today's society, a lot of attention is being put on sexual harassment and I agree there should be no uninvited touching.

The military authorities should line up every new group of trainees and say to them, "If anyone on this base touches you or sexually harasses you physically or verbally, to include your co-soldiers or your military superiors, *you report it! Immediately,* not 20 years later! Do not fear that you will demoted or discharged on grounds of reporting this crime, any more than if you had witnessed a murder."

Yes, they already have sexual harassment training in the military and in all branches and all offices of the US federal government! It is repeated every six months. Everybody jokes that they're being taught how to do it. But these soldiers need to be assured that their chain of command *wants* to hear about harassment or assault, and that there will be no repercussions for reporting. This would save the government millions of dollars every year, currently paid out to veterans claiming sexual trauma or harassment in service.

OTHER MENTAL CONDITIONS

According to the Social Security Administration's (SSA) disability guidelines, in order for a mental condition to be disabling, it must result in at least two of these findings: -- marked restriction of activities of daily living, --marked difficulties in maintaining social functioning, -- marked difficulties in maintaining concentration, persistence or pace. Otherwise, the condition must be manifested by repeated episodes of decompensation, each of extended duration. This sounds fair and reasonable. But that's the SSA.

So what does VA require to make such a determination that a mental condition is disabling? Nothing. If the veteran claims it, and the examiner checks enough boxes on the DBQ, he will be granted up to 100% disability. Doesn't matter if he's fully active, working, and partying with friends every night. And you better believe he is partying, because VA is amply providing funds for the drugs and alcohol.

As proof of this extreme over-evaluation for mental conditions, there are many VA employees who are in receipt of 100% compensation for "mental issues" such as PTSD, while earning anywhere from $50K to $100K per year. They are working amongst the other 400 admin employees at their office, getting the job done, socializing, and if you walked into the room you wouldn't be able to figure out which ones of them were the mentally disturbed! Because they're not disturbed; they're just milking the system.

The VA psychiatric exams (especially prior to DBQs) are most interesting to read because the examiner often asks about their entire history, from childhood through the military, and through the present.   It is herein that the liars are revealed. Many times they will report things on the mental exam totally contrary to what is shown in the military records, and/or totally contrary to what they have reported on a back or knee exam because this is a different doctor. It also may be years later, and they don't realize that when a rater looks at his file, he or she can see his entire medical history, thousands of medical documents from the time he served in the military to the present. Stories they told 20 years ago about how injuries came to be, they have now forgotten, and they make up new ones.

On one psychiatric exam the veteran reported that his parents were not married and his mother was a drug addict so he had never known either of them but he had been in various foster homes all his life. He reportedly suffered "horrible" physical, mental, and sexual abuse at the hands of his foster parents and finally got away from that by joining the service. On his ankle exam, the same week, but in a different medical office, he reported that during service he was at home on leave helping his mother when he twisted his ankle and that's why there's no record of it in his military file.

Practically every new claim received since 2015 will include the issues of "anxiety" and/or "depression." The military leaders and the veteran service reps advise the soldiers to claim this. These issues are subjective so who can dispute it? And in fact, who among us has never had a single day of either depression or anxiety or both? Not just in the military, but in all realms of employment these days, employees are encouraged to go to in-house counselors to discuss their problems and partake of these totally confidential free services provided by the employer.

So while in service, the soldier goes to counseling and talks about his marriage problems, infidelity of his wife, financial stresses, and problems with teenage kids. After service he can now be granted for depression or anxiety. It started in service! Had nothing to do with military service, but that doesn't matter, it started during service. The stress, depression or anxiety after service still has nothing to do with the military service, but it is a continuation of the diagnosis he had in service. In fact, the after-service stressors are usually different. He can't find a job, or his mother died, or his dog died. It doesn't matter. He's depressed about something so he has depression, and depression was first diagnosed in service, so VA grants him disability compensation. It's wrong. Episodes of "acute depression" should not be granted; it's not a *chronic* disability.

Drug and alcohol addictions are classified and treated as mental disorders, but the regulations say that VA will not grant compensation for drug and alcohol abuse because it is now considered willful misconduct. However, thousands of veterans are service-connected for drug and alcohol abuse anyway because they got in under the old law (before any law addressed it) or because it's now ok to grant it if the condition is piggybacked on top of PTSD or any other service-connected mental diagnosis. Most of the symptoms are actually due to the drugs and alcohol, and yet all symptoms are considered when raising the evaluation of the total mental condition. They keep coming back in for more increases, and with every increase VA is giving them more money for drugs and alcohol. Their dependency problems become increasingly worse and they continue the cycle of asking for more increases until they reach 100%, and sometimes they come back for more than that.

If they are not yet at the 100% level, they quickly learn the trick to get themselves admitted to a VA or any 30-day drug/alcohol treatment program because they will be paid 100% for any period of time when they are hospitalized for more than 21 days for a service-connected condition, and this includes living in the DOM to attend daily group drug counseling. As long as their primary mental condition such as PTSD or depression is also mentioned in the therapy sessions, the temporary 100% is paid. This regulation (38 CFR 4.29) is greatly abused, some veterans readmitting themselves to the VA several times a year every year, and it should be changed so that it does not apply for drug and alcohol treatment programs. The VA should require medical or other *evidence* of impairment, to show that the mental condition *required* at least 21 days of hospitalization, not just that the claimant admitted himself for another program to get the temporary monetary increase.

***

Veteran X beat his wife in service. He threatened to kill her with a butcher knife. He was sent to mental health counseling and was diagnosed with adjustment disorder, alcohol and drug abuse. He refused treatment in the military. They kicked him out and he was barred from reenlistment, but he was given an honorable discharge. The mental problems and drug abuse continued after service, so when he filed for service-connection he was granted. There is no indication that anything in service *in-the-line-of-duty* caused his problems, but VA will pay him for the rest of his life.

***

Veteran X served in the military for more than 20 years and attained the rank of Colonel. During service he was prescribed psychotropic medications for a diagnosis of ADHD (attention deficit hyperactivity disorder). After service he immediately went to work for a defense contractor where he continues to work. He has been in a great marriage for the past 11 years. Where is his impairment?

He filed a claim for service-connection for ADHD. On the VA mental exam, he reported that he had been diagnosed with ADHD at age 8 and treated with Ritalin. He said the condition resolved with age and did not impact him in adolescence or early adulthood but then it started again during service. He gets granted because

227

he took psychotropic medicine in service and he still takes it now after service. Although VA now knows this man had the condition since childhood, if he indeed has anything, it must be conceded that the condition was incurred in service because his military entrance exams showed him as "whole" and did not mention any problem. Later in service he sought medication. He is abusing the system. There is no indication that any event or illness in service caused or aggravated this man's ADHD.

Medical literature shows ADHD is a "developmental" disorder, either genetic or caused by other circumstances of birth such as premature birth/low birth weight, mother's malnutrition or use of drugs/alcohol during pregnancy. The federal law, as provided in 38 CFR 4.9 regarding congenital or developmental defects, states *"Mere congenital or developmental defects, absent, displaced or supernumerary parts, refractive error of the eye, personality disorder and mental deficiency are not diseases or injuries in the meaning of applicable legislation for disability compensation purposes."* This clearly means that VA should *not* grant service connection for developmental disorders and yet they are granted every day. Sometimes when a soldier is having lots of problems in basic training the military will discharge him honorably but on the grounds of "personality disorder" and service-connection has been erroneously granted for that developmental issue many times over.

***

Veteran X is a female who had mental problems throughout her childhood; she was abused by family members physically, sexually and mentally. She tried to commit suicide at age 16, was removed from her home, and she joined the military at age 18. She had problems throughout her five years of service. During the five years she was married three times and gave birth to a child with mental and physical defects, which led to the claimant's depression. The child was designated as terminally ill so the claimant got out on a hardship discharge to care for the child. The child died a year after discharge then the veteran tried to commit suicide again. She has been in and out of mental treatment since discharge.

During service she was never in a combat situation, never traveled to a foreign country, and there is no evidence in the record of any stress due to service. Her stress was all family-related and the military did its best to provide for her in every way, including treatment in service and a hardship early discharge.

The VA examiner opined that her mental condition which existed prior to service was exacerbated by events in service; therefore, her mental condition was granted on a secondary basis. It should have been direct if anything because he she was accepted as whole into service, and then was treated during service for depression due to her relationships and child problems. It doesn't matter, the evaluation is the same.

My point is that this woman's mental condition was not *caused* by military service. This does not fall into President Lincoln's promise to provide for those who have borne the battle. She did nothing in service to deserve being supported for the rest of her life. She is being supported simply because she is one of "our great veterans." If this grant is appropriate then why wouldn't it be appropriate to grant for everything that ever happens to a veteran after service, as well as what happens to her in service? It's all the same if it was not incurred in the line of duty.

***

Veteran X has schizophrenia. He served only nine months in 1973-1974, and the Vietnam fighting was over by this time. One night during service he became drunk and high on marijuana and PCP or other unknown drug (per the records). He became violent and was taken to the hospital. The mental report showed he was *not* hearing voices, but he was "remembering voices." So, for whatever reason, he was diagnosed with schizophrenia and subsequently discharged from service.

He was initially granted 30% disability from the VA. Every couple of years since then he has submitted a claim for increase, or had a routine future exam (due to improvement shown), so the VA has generated 20 rating decisions for this man, each one requiring many manhours of development besides the cost of VA exams. His evaluations have gone from 30% to 70% to 50% to 100%, back down to 50% then up to 70% then back down to 30%.

His most current exam shows he has been working as a gas station attendant (dealing with people and money) and as a city trash collector (they are paid well). He is thinking about taking some college courses. He has a girlfriend and enjoys going to movies and building model airplanes. He has several friends he enjoys spending time with. He has a good appetite and no trouble sleeping. There is no indication of "schizophrenia" and yet the VA examiners continue the diagnosis because it is in the VA records. Once a diagnosis is established, the examiner doesn't have to clarify or support the diagnosis anymore; he just notes the symptoms and severity of the condition.

So VA will continue to pay this man for life. Service-connection cannot be severed if it has been in effect for more than 10 years and no one bothered to try to sever it when they should have years ago. An evaluation cannot be reduced if it has been in effect more than 20 years, so his evaluation can never be reduced below 30%.

***

Veteran X is a female who by habit always missed one day of work on the first day that her menstrual period started. Her military co-workers took a sanitary pad, soaked it with red ink, and hung it over her desk while she was on her day out. She claims this caused her to have "depression" in service and the VA has paid her disability compensation ever since discharge. She went on to have a perfectly normal life with successful work and relationships, but that doesn't matter. VA's worst rating practice is that they do not abide by the regulation that says compensation for mental issues is to be based on the "degree of social and occupational impairment."

***

Veteran X has per his own report been a chronic alcoholic since age 14, but since that was not noted on his military entrance exam the VA accepts that he was "whole" until he developed this condition in service. He was charged with "drunk and disorderly" several times while on duty and was noted in his service medical records to be an "antabuse failure" so he was discharged early from service with an honorable discharge. He now drinks 6 to 9 beers and a fifth of rum daily. The VA supports his condition by paying him IU, service-connected compensation of 100%, because he cannot work due to alcoholism. They put another name on it in service, "depression," and they continue to diagnose it as depression, but it is alcoholism of the purest degree.

***

Veteran X is a 28-year-old female with 2 kids. She has been diagnosed with "primary cerebellar degeneration," a condition characterized by "less brain matter than a normal person" based on a brain MRI in service, which was done as a last resort when they could find nothing wrong with her. Five years after the diagnosis, a new MRI showed no changes, and she still has no symptoms other than subjective complaints of weakness. VA grants her IU, because the condition (weakness) is claimed to affect all her upper and lower extremities, and it is rated analogous to Parkinson's disease, with separate evaluations for each limb. Her husband is also a veteran receiving compensation. Neither of them work. Per her remarks on exam, they both sit home all day with their 5- and 7-year-olds watching movies and playing video games, and go out to restaurants almost every night. Must be nice.

***

Veteran X served from 1991 to 1994 during which time he went on sick call almost every day, so he was finally forced out of service with a PEB (Physical Evaluation Board) discharge. His complaint was that he had right flank pain all the time. He had multiple tests, X-rays, CT scans, and full work up of his gastrointestinal system, all with no problems found. A diagnosis of "somatoform pain disorder" was given in service and continued on the post service VA exam so that's what he was granted for, at 30% disability. It's a mental condition diagnosis given when one complains constantly

231

about pain, usually in multiple locations in the body, but in this case it was just his right flank. There's a fine line between a lie and a mental disease, but VA must rule in favor of the veteran. And we (you and me) have to pay him more than $400 a month for the rest of his life, or if he has a wife and 2 kids, more than $500 a month. He can work all he wants to in any sort of laborious job he wants to and no one will question this disability compensation.

***

Veteran X served only 6 months and had an enviable MOS of "illustrator." He was discharged with severance pay for a left shoulder condition. When he got out in 2012 there was no complaint or diagnosis of any mental problem on his separation exam or his VA general medical exam. Three years later he claimed depression and anxiety and PTSD all secondary to his shoulder condition. He says the drill sergeant made him do shoulder lifts, and everyone called him "weak" in basic training. He was a no-show for two VA exams and opinions. He finally went to a VA exam and the examiner stated he was clearly depressed due to the following reasons: his mother died, his girlfriend broke up with him, and his dog died. He requested a service dog from the VAMC to help him with depression.

***

Veteran X had served less than 2 years when he was released from the military due to a bi-polar disorder. The military decided it was pre-existing so they gave him no severance pay. VA then promptly granted him 70% for bipolar disorder. This is wrong because pre-existing conditions should not be granted, but since the military *entrance* exam didn't mention it (even though later military records did), the entrance exam is all the VA cares about. It doesn't matter that the doctor and even the claimant himself says it existed before service and that he was hospitalized for it before service. The claimant also had a few other minor complaints, and the examiner for those actually stated on exam that the claimant was "exaggerating" his symptoms, but that doesn't matter either, so his

232

total came up to 100% disability compensation. He is 25 years old, lives with a girlfriend, and is attending college at Georgetown University. He reported on the mental exam that he is sexually active with no problem, but he was granted erectile dysfunction and special monthly compensation for loss of use of a creative organ anyway because on the male reproductive system exam (different examiner) he told a different story, claiming sexual dysfunction.

***

Veteran X is a 26-year-old female who has a reportedly successful relationship with her parents, siblings, and boyfriend. She completed her Bachelor's degree during service and now attends college for her Master's degree. She has no drug or legal problems. She sought treatment once during service for anxiety and was prescribed Zoloft. She filed a claim for anxiety and on VA exam the same month of discharge she was diagnosed with adjustment disorder, anxiety, depression and obsessive-compulsive disorder. The diagnosis was not based on any medical treatment records, it came from the DBQ because she reported that she has "obsessional rituals." She did not describe them, so it could have been nothing more than that she always double checks to be sure she locked the door. Many of us do that, but because the doctor checked the box for "obsessional rituals" on the DBQ, the evaluation builder generates 70% disability. A perfectly functioning 26-year-old working on a Master's degree, has a boyfriend, and has her whole life ahead of her, and the VA is granting her 70% disability, which is enough to get IU (100%) total disability.

***

Veteran X fell in service in 1989, landed on his hand and broke his wrist, and service-connection was granted on discharge from service (all fractures in service will be service-connected). For almost 30 years he lived a normal life, worked in various jobs, and was happy with his 10% payment for residuals of a broken wrist.

In 2016 he filed a claim for PTSD and depression secondary to his service-connected wrist. The VA examiner diagnosed PTSD with a symptom of depression and linked this condition to the fall in service in 1989.   So that got him up to 70%.   Since he met the schedular criteria, he claimed IU, and was given another increase exam in 2017.

The new VA examiner says the claimant is "malingering" and that there is no evidence to justify a diagnosis of PTSD. He says a proper diagnosis would be "phobia: fear of heights/falling."   But VA cannot sever the previous diagnosis and cannot reduce his rate based on a changed diagnosis.   They also cannot reduce based on one exam. All they can do is add the new mental diagnosis, diary a new future exam for at least 18 months from now, and then incur the expense of re-examination and processing and rating another claim. It's such a mess that they will likely just grant the IU in order to get the case closed.

VIETNAM WAR AND AGENT ORANGE CLAIMS

One of the most frustrating issues of VA disability is the granting of Agent Orange related claims. As you read this, VA is working ardently to add more and more conditions to the list of already more than 20 diseases attributed to exposure to the Agent Orange herbicide in Vietnam. Is there truly any medical basis for this? Or was one brave VA physician correct when he completed his medical opinion with, *"Agent Orange was not a medical decision, it was a political decision."*

AGENT ORANGE – WHAT IS IT?

Agent Orange was a defoliant, chemical herbicide, used to destroy the forests of Vietnam during the Vietnam War so that our soldiers could more easily see the approaching enemy forces. This product was sprayed by small crop-duster planes or spread by hand-sprayers in some cases and it did a great job of destroying vegetation. The composition of Agent Orange included a *trace* of a dioxin, not an intentional ingredient, but a hazardous byproduct of the production of Agent Orange. Many years later, laboratory studies showed that applying *pure dioxin* to mice can cause certain cancers to develop. There is no formal record of any individual soldier being personally sprayed, but if one was, he probably died many years ago. It has been more than 45 years since the last spraying of Agent Orange. Pure dioxin was never dumped on anything or anyone in Vietnam and the trace amounts in Agent Orange have yet to be scientifically or medically proven sufficient to cause any particular disease in humans. Various herbicides were used in Vietnam from 1961 to 1971, but Agent Orange was used only from 1965 to 1970, and was used along the DMZ in Korea from 1968 to 1969.

For any servicemen or women who served during those dates and in those places, their exposure to Agent Orange is conceded, and if they are diagnosed with any herbicide-presumptive diseases, at any time after service, at any age, they will be granted disability compensation benefits. The biggest problem with this is that there are millions of veterans of the same age-group who did not serve in these places but who still suffer from the same diseases. There are also millions of non-veterans of the same age group who also have these diseases and they have never been exposed to Agent Orange.

Although many veterans have filed and will continue to file claims for "exposure to herbicides/Agent Orange," service-connection cannot be granted for "exposure." One must claim a specific medical condition in order to have a valid disability claim. Their exposure claim will get them referred over to a VA medical center for a "Agent Orange Registry Exam" and on that exam they will be able to express any symptoms they can think of that might be diagnosed and used on a formal claim.

In character with VA's liberal policies, veterans may be granted service-connection for any conditions that VA has decided are associated with Agent Orange exposure, *if* they served in the country of Vietnam or inland waterways of Vietnam from January 9, 1962 to May 7, 1975, or on the Korean DMZ from April 1, 1968 to August 31, 1971. Strangely, the dates don't actually match up to the dates Agent Orange was sprayed, but that's a minor issue in the grand scheme. Recent changes have also allowed service-connection for veterans who served on the perimeters of military bases in Thailand during the Vietnam War, or on C-123 aircrafts from 1969 to 1986. Ongoing conferences are considering expanding benefits to Navy veterans who never set foot in Vietnam.

Non-Hodgkin's lymphoma is the only current exception, as it may now be granted to any veteran who served in Vietnam or in the blue waters off the coast of Vietnam, and that includes a lot of Navy sailors and Marines. Perhaps that decision was in part due to a study done in 1987, printed in *Journal of Occupational Medicine, May 1988*, that compared the causes of death among approximately 25,000 Vietnam veterans and 25,000 non-Vietnam veterans. The study showed that the US Marines in the group had a higher percentage of death due to non-Hodgkin's lymphoma but it was not true for Army veterans, even though 80% of ground troops in Vietnam were Army. Interestingly, the main causes of death among

Army Vietnam veterans was vehicle accidents, non-vehicle accidents, and accidental poisoning (drugs).

In addition to that study, there have been hundreds of studies over the past 50 years in effort to find patterns of illness and death among Vietnam veterans, and for the most part they have come up short in finding any true medical evidence of Agent Orange causing any illness. Many of these studies are synopsized in an ongoing VA newsletter, *Agent Orange Review*, that has been provided for veterans since 1982, currently 29 Volumes as of summer 2017.

Another set of interesting studies were those done on the Air Force veterans who handled Agent Orange and did the spraying over Vietnam, a mission known as Operation Ranch Hand. Studies in 1983, 1984, 1985, 1986, and 1989 all showed no differences between the actual and expected number of Ranch Hand deaths from all causes.

More than 800 scientists from around the world brought their knowledge and study-findings to a symposium in North Carolina in 1991, and none of them had strong evidence to show for dioxin-related illnesses other than chloracne. In fact, studies show that every human has dioxin in their tissues. The Italian scientists reported that the highest dioxin levels ever measured in humans were those who were exposed due to an accident in Seveso, Italy, and no adverse health effects have been observed in the residents there other than transient chloracne (not chronic).

Numerous studies have been done on each particular disease that VA has associated with Agent Orange and occasionally the statistics "suggest" a "possible" correlation, but for the most part they show *no* indication of higher incidences of *any* disease due to Agent Orange exposure other than chloracne. I encourage anyone who wants to know more about the studies, to read the archives of the *Agent Orange Review,* published by the VA. Despite lack of any strong scientific medical evidence, the VA keeps adding more and more conditions to the long list of diseases they deem to be associated with Agent Orange exposure.

What a waste of time. Just give every Vietnam veteran a million dollars and be done with it! Some people tell me, "Forget it, the Vietnam war veterans won't be around much longer." Actually, some of them are barely 60 now and may live another 40 years, and as for those who are dead or will die soon, many spouses and children will continue to receive benefits.

Meanwhile, for every Vietnam vet who passes, there are about four Gulf War veterans to take his place on the VA payroll, as the Gulf War includes anyone who served there from 1990 to the present and future, and the number of conditions being attributed to Gulf War exposures will soon surpass the number that have been attributed to Agent Orange. It's like, well we did something for Vietnam veterans, now we better do something for Gulf War veterans. I say all this exposure crap needs to be done away with.

AGENT ORANGE LITIGATION AND LEGISLATION

A class action law suit, the Agent Orange Product Liability Litigation, was filed by Vietnam veterans in 1979, not against VA, but against the manufacturers of Agent Orange. There were no particular illnesses specified in the suit or subsequently in the awarding of payments. There were never any studies to show that Agent Orange itself had caused any serious disabilities. Nevertheless, to avoid individual claims from a million veterans, the suit was settled out-of-court in 1984 for an initial $180 million dollars (later increased to $250 million) as the Agent Orange Settlement Fund. Monies were distributed in two ways from 1988 through 1994. A total of $197 million was made in cash payments to veterans or survivors, each receiving about $3,800. An additional $74 million was distributed to 83 social services organizations through the U.S. to provide special services for Vietnam veterans. The Fund was closed in 1997 as all funds had been distributed.

Meanwhile, VA began working on policies to grant service-connection on a presumptive basis (not manifested in service) for diseases based on herbicide exposure in Vietnam.

In October 1984, the "Veterans' Dioxin and Radiation Exposure Compensation Standards Act" was signed into law establishing service-connection for chloracne, porphyria cutanea tarda (a liver and skin disease) and soft-tissue sarcoma.

In 1985 the scientific research done for the VA determined that there was no evidence of any disease resulting from Agent Orange exposure other than chloracne (skin condition), and only if that condition had developed within a within a year of exposure. A chloracne relationship is common sense, as exposure to many irritants and chemicals we use for cleaning and manufacturing or for treating our lawns and gardens will certainly cause a skin reaction in most normal people.

A "final rule" under the *Veterans' Dioxin and Radiation Exposure Compensation Standards Act (Dioxin Act),* issued in August 1985, became law on September 25, 1985. The VA regulation stipulated that only chloracne was connected with dioxin exposure, and that there was not enough scientific or medical evident to support cause-and-effect relationship between phyria cutanea tarda (PCT) and soft-tissue sarcomas. Due to the law change, interim benefits could be granted for PCT or chloracne manifested within one year after the last departure from Vietnam, but could not be paid for any period prior to Oct 1, 1984, nor for any period after September 30, 1986. Also, the VA would continue to address claims for any disease if there was evidence supporting that the condition was related to in-service exposure.

A subsequent study released by the National Cancer Institute in 1987 confirmed the finding that veterans who served in Vietnam did *not* have an increased risk of soft tissue sarcoma compared to those men who had never been in Vietnam, while other studies showed no clear evidence of dioxin causing porphyria cutanea tarda. Regardless, both of those conditions would later be added back to the list of herbicide-presumptives.

The main significance of the *Dioxin Act* was that the VA would no longer have to determine the herbicide relationship of each individual claim, but VA would establish certain conditions as *herbicide-presumptive* and any veteran with those conditions (and with the required service in Vietnam) would be automatically granted service-connection for the conditions. At the time, the writers of that act probably never imagined that so many conditions such as lung disease, diabetes, and heart disease, all of which have significant other risk factors, would someday be granted based on herbicide exposure, without regard to any other factors in the person's life such as diet, obesity, smoking, or genetics.

The VA regulation implementing the *Dioxin Act* provided that any veteran who served in Vietnam would be presumed to have had herbicide exposure, but it also stated that chloracne was the only disease that could be granted on this basis because there was no cause-and-effect relationship between dioxin and any other condition at that time.

In 1987, a class action lawsuit filed on behalf of all Vietnam veterans against VA, *Nehmer vs. VA,* challenged the decision that chloracne was the only disease associated with Agent Orange. In 1989, the U.S. District Court invalidated the portion of the VA regulation that says chloracne is the only condition associated with herbicide exposure and that others require proof of a causal relationship. The Court ruled that rather than using a cause-and-effect standard, Congress had intended VA to grant service-connection for any disease for which evidence showed a "significant statistical association" between dioxin exposure and that disease, and the VA regulation as written was erroneously requiring proof that a causal relationship existed. The court voided all VA decisions that had denied claims based on the invalid regulation. The Court also ruled that VA should give "reasonable doubt" to the veteran when weighing evidence in each claim. That is, whenever the evidence is 50/50, on the line, benefit of doubt goes to the veteran.

The Secretary of VA at that time decided that an appeal would not be in the best interest of the VA or veterans, due to media blasting that would surely ensue. In 1989 VA amended its regulations regarding how VA would determine when a significant statistical association exists between dioxin and specific diseases.

In 1991, an agreement between *Nehmer* and VA was negotiated, requiring that whenever new scientific evidence shows a positive relationship between Agent Orange exposure and a new disease, that VA must identify all claims previously denied for that condition and pay disability benefits to those claimants retroactive to the initial date of claim. As a result of the *Nehmer* consent decree, over the past two decades, VA has paid more than $4.5 billion in retroactive disability and death benefits related to Agent Orange exposure.

Meanwhile, study after study continued to show no relationship between dioxin and various claimed diseases, and studies of Vietnam veterans versus non-Vietnam veterans (American and other countries) showed no increased illness or mortality of the Vietnam veterans.

A study released by the National Cancer Institute in 1987 reported that veterans who served in Vietnam did not have an increased risk of soft tissue sarcoma compared to those men who had never been in Vietnam. Other studies showed no clear evidence of dioxin causing porphyria cutanea tarda.

A Center for Disease Control (CDC) study in 1988 studied mortality rates comparing Vietnam veterans to non-Vietnam veterans of the same era (served in CONUS, Europe, or Korea), all discharged between 1965 and 1971. They found that during the first 5 years after discharge, the Vietnam veterans did suffer a higher mortality rate, but that was due to external causes such as motor vehicle injuries, suicide, homicide and unintentional poisonings (mostly by drugs). There was no difference in the number who died from diseases, and after the first 5 years, there was no difference in the mortality rates.

Nevertheless, after the District Court invalidated the VA regulation, Congress enacted the *Agent Orange Act of 1991*. The Agent Orange Act established that presumptive service-connection could be granted for any condition that VA determined to be related to Agent Orange exposure. The statute established a "presumption of exposure" if the veteran was actually in country, that freed the veteran from having to prove that he was actually exposed to herbicides. The act initially specified non-Hodgins lymphoma, soft tissue sarcoma, and chloracne as conditions that VA on its own authority had decided to be related to the exposure. However, the Act also directed VA to contract with the National Academy of Sciences (NAS), Institute of Medicine, to conduct comprehensive and independent reviews of all scientific and medical literature on the health effects of exposure to Agent Orange, and this was to be updated every two years. Interestingly, the first reviews found that evidence did not support a connection for non-Hodgkin's lymphoma or soft tissue sarcoma, but VA kept them anyway. So as of 1991, the herbicide related conditions were non-Hodgkin's lymphoma, soft tissue sarcoma, and chloracne (but only chloracne that was diagnosed within a year after service).

The NAS, Institute of Medicine, initial report in 1994 established the template for all future reports. The findings are published as *Veterans and Agent Orange Committee to Review the Health Effects in Vietnam Veterans and Exposure to Herbicides,* which is still updated biennially. Most of the studies reviewed have been done on civilians who were exposed during industrial accidents or who were exposed occupationally in the workplace. Very few studies have been done of Vietnam veterans themselves and no long-term studies have been done. After reviewing the studies, the NAS determines whether there is "sufficient evidence of an association" between exposure and a particular illness. They may also determine that evidence of association is "limited or suggested," or "inadequate or insufficient," or "limited or suggestive evidence of NO association." VA then takes the NAS opinion to an internal task force of scientists, medical doctors, attorneys and compensation experts, who come up with a recommended veteran compensation policy for the VA Secretary. The Agent Orange law requires that if "credible evidence for the association is equal to or outweighs the credible evidence against the association" then there must be a positive association for VA purposes. All of the conditions categorized by NAS as having "sufficient evidence of an association" and most of those with the weakest positive level of evidence "limited/suggestive evidence of an association" have been recognized by VA for service-connection.

After the initial NAS report of 1994, VA decided to recognize or continue recognizing the following conditions as presumptive to herbicide exposure: soft tissue sarcoma, non-Hodgkin's lymphoma, Hodgkin's disease, chloracne, porphyria cutanea tarda, multiple myeloma and respiratory cancers (lung, larynx, trachea and bronchus).

After the second NAS report, dated 1996, the VA added prostate cancer and peripheral neuropathy (manifested within one year of exposure) to the list of presumptives, as well as spina bifida in children born to exposed veterans.

After an occupational study released in 1998 from the National Institute of Occupational Safety and Health, a NAS special report of 2000 found "limited/suggestive evidence" of an association between exposure and type II diabetes, so VA added diabetes mellitus type II in 2001.

After the NAS 2002 report, chronic lymphocytic leukemia (CLL) was added in 2003.

After a 2006 report and a lengthy delay for more evidence, AL amyloidosis was added in 2009.

In 2010, ischemic heart disease (coronary artery disease, myocardial infarction), Parkinson's disease, and all B-cell/hairy cell leukemias were added.

VA is currently considering whether to add bladder cancer, hypertension, stroke and various neurological ailments similar to Parkinson's Disease.

VA is also finally considering whether to grant benefits to Navy veterans who only served on ships in the waters near Vietnam but never went ashore. To date, the only ones granted are those who set "boots-on-the-ground" in Vietnam or went on small boats up into the inland waterways.

Also not granted are those who flew over Vietnam dropping bombs, or landed on ships or planes just long enough to pick up or drop off soldiers. It's totally unfair; some Vietnam vets are getting $3,000 a month while other Vietnam vets with the same diseases are getting nothing. And other Vietnam vets have other diseases that have not yet been correlated to Agent Orange so they get nothing, although their widows probably will.

THE AGENT ORANGE DEBACLE

Rarely if ever did an individual actually get "sprayed" by Agent Orange although veterans often report it, but being "sprayed on" is not a requirement. It seems to me that if exposure was simply due to touching things that Agent Orange had landed on, such as foliage or dirt in Vietnam, that those people on the ships and airplanes were all also exposed to things that Agent Orange had landed on. All the soldiers who trudged through the contaminated jungles eventually were loaded onto those ships and planes, along with all their weapons, gear, tents, blankets, clothes and boots that had been dragged through the jungles. None of that stuff was ever washed.

Many soldiers who were actually in country never walked through the jungle or treated areas, and the periods of spraying were intermittent anyway, so it is simply not fair to grant to only those who stepped into Vietnam. For example, there are many claims from veterans who were cooks or admin specialists who never went out of the tents in base camp. There are many claims from Air Force veterans who were aircraft mechanics stationed in the Philippines and only on one occasion did they have to fly over to Vietnam where they spent about 2 hours repairing an airplane on a runway in Vietnam, then flew back out. They never even ate a meal or used a latrine in that country, but they can now be granted service-connection for their diabetes and prostate cancer, no matter how old they are, and no matter how the disease runs in the family.

But the veteran whose job on an airplane or ship was to pick up, load up, and transport those Agent Orange contaminated foot soldiers, or to handle that contaminated equipment back in the states, or who had to sit in those same seats on the planes and ships where the contaminated soldiers sat, he gets no respect. And there's no consideration for the Navy veterans who stayed on their ship, even though Agent Orange could have blown through the wind onto their ship as it was docked in harbor.

Am I arguing that we should grant to more veterans? No, I don't think it's warranted for any of them unless they have had one of the dioxin-related diseases since 1980 or maybe earlier. The last Agent Orange spraying was in 1970 and the last troops left Vietnam in 1975.

It is not logical to me that any of these conditions manifesting 50 years after exposure could possibly be related to the in-service event. It is apparent that the federal government simply wants to award those who served in Vietnam. But it would be less costly, especially considering the time and resources to rate these cases, to just issue a check to these veterans and call it "Vietnam compensation."

Many veterans claim "Agent Orange exposure" without listing any condition associated with that exposure, and on review, indeed they don't have any applicable disease. Many others say, "I've got Agent Orange." Internet blogs are full of "My husband has Agent Orange. He's acted weird ever since Vietnam. What can we do?" I've heard veterans in the VAMC waiting rooms discussing their conditions. "I've got Agent Orange; I was there in 1968, but the VA won't pay me!"

Do we really believe that a person exposed to Agent Orange in the air, or on foliage, in 1968, would live a full healthy life, and then 50 years later, at age 70, would suddenly develop diabetes or any condition that was caused by that exposure 50 years ago? Do we believe that? Then we see that the person's father or mother and several siblings have also developed the disease and they never went to Vietnam. And we see hundreds of claims from veterans aged 55 to 80 who never went to Vietnam and they now also have all these diseases, at the same rate as the Vietnam veterans do. Distribution of funds for these 20-plus odd conditions VA relates to Agent Orange is totally unfair, therefore causes a lot of anger and resentment for many Vietnam Era veterans. Some are getting rich while others are devoting their lives to appealing for service-connection.

DIABETES MELLITUS TYPE II

The most granted herbicide-presumptive disease is diabetes mellitus type II. Type I diabetes is "juvenile diabetes" and anyone with that should never have been admitted into service. But I have actually seen it several times, because for some reason (lack of pre-service medical care) it was not diagnosed until a few weeks into service. Of course that issue gets granted too because it was first diagnosed in service, even though it had nothing to do with battle or service duties, and we will wrongly pay that veteran for the rest of his life for all the complications of juvenile diabetes. But in this chapter "diabetes" refers to type II diabetes mellitus which is "adult-onset diabetes."

Since 1950, the incidence of type II diabetes has increased by 800% in the general populace; so of course there is higher incidence in veterans too. Most all Americans in the 21st century are ever-wary of developing diabetes because we see it all around us, and we all know diabetes is more likely to occur in people who are inactive, overweight and who are not following a healthy diet. The American lifestyle has changed over the years. Fewer of us now have physically laborious jobs because machinery does the work for us. The availability and convenience of pre-packaged food and junk food restaurants have corrupted our diets. So of course diabetes is being diagnosed more every year, but it has nothing to do with the Vietnam War of 50 years ago.

Although diabetes is not directly caused by sugar consumption, I find it notable that Americans who are now in their 60's, 70's, and 80's, were the first who began to consume tons of soft drinks and candy. Coke had been around since the late 1800's in the downtown soda fountains, but in the 1940's and 50's suddenly we had country corner stores and coin-operated machines full of bottles for only 5 cents, and consuming a few pieces of hard penny candies gave way to large individually wrapped chocolate bars! Ask anyone who was a young adult in the 50's or 60's. They were grabbing Cokes all day long although the price eventually went to 10 cents in the 60's, still very affordable. Drive-ins with hotdogs, burgers and fries became a national pastime. Earlier generations ate home-grown vegetables and breads with no preservatives, and did not have these junk food diets of starch and sugar, so the human body has had to evolve its function to process glucose, but that's a slow evolution. Younger generations are now more health conscious, more likely to work out in a gym, and there are now many healthy alternative products for consumption in stores and on restaurant menus, so the tide should turn. My point is, the people who are now developing diabetes (usually aged 60 to 70) are those who bore the brunt of that transition, less physical activity, more junk food, not to mention the other bad habits (wild life, psychedelic drugs, free sex) of the 60's and 70's. It does not surprise me that that generation of people are now more prone to developing diabetes or other systemic diseases. Coincidentally that is also the generation that went to Vietnam, so a correlation is totally reasonable, without regard to Agent Orange.

Regardless of the specific cause, thousands of Americans in their 60's and 70's are being diagnosed with type II diabetes, veteran or not veteran. So yes, there is some "correlation" between being a Vietnam veteran and developing diabetes, since most Vietnam veterans are in their 60's and 70's and most people are in their 60's or 70's when they develop type II diabetes. But *correlation* does not reflect *causation.* And the fact that just as many non-Vietnam veterans get diabetes is proof enough to me of intercurrent causes.

Diabetes alone would not break the bank because it only warrants 10% if controlled by diet, or 20% if it is managed by insulin or other medication (usually Metformin). But diabetes leads to multiple complications including peripheral neuropathy of all extremities, kidney disease, diabetic retinopathy, erectile dysfunction, and anything else a doctor opines has been worsened by the diabetes. Kidney disease with no symptoms at all (just lab tests) warrants 60% disability, and it is not uncommon for a veteran to be granted 100% disability based only on diabetic complications even though he may appear to be functioning as well as anyone his age.

PROSTATE CANCER

Another Agent Orange presumptive condition that does not seem justified is prostate cancer. Medical literature I've read says every man will eventually get prostate cancer if he lives long enough, and a man can live with prostate cancer for 20 years or more without having any severe symptoms. Treatment for prostate cancer usually results in residual symptoms worse than the active condition symptoms. That's why so often the diagnosis is just met with "watchful waiting" which means that although prostate cancer was indicated on biopsy, there'll be no treatment unless things worsen. All active cancer is rated by VA as 100% disability (even with no symptoms), and after treatment it's rated based on residuals, so it's in the claimant's best financial interest never to be treated. The veteran has to choose whether he'd rather keep the money or risk dying, and sometimes he chooses the money.

The prostate cancer screening starts with a routine PSA test and if PSA is over 4 ng/mL it's considered as a "risk" for prostate cancer, even though some have had prostate cancer with lower PSAs, or not had cancer with much higher PSAs. According to the American Cancer Society (www.cancer.org), of men with PSA of 4 to 10, only 1 in 4 will actually have cancer. With higher than 10 PSA the chance is still 50/50. It is not uncommon for a man's PSA to continue to rise the older he gets and it is can be due to other conditions.

Again, Vietnam veterans are in a position to obtain free health care at their local VA medical center or clinic, so they go for routine tests and exams all the time, while non-veteran men in the general public do not. And again, the VA goes over and above, tries to catch the disease early and start the treatment, diagnose early and start paying the veteran. The VA jumps on any PSA of 4.0 or higher to perform biopsy after biopsy. Some men go through 4 or 5 biopsies over a period of 20 years before it finally comes up positive for prostate cancer and I can't help but wonder if all the tampering is what caused it! I have seen several VA cases where prostate cancer was found on biopsy, and with no treatment, just watchful waiting, the follow-up biopsy was actually normal. Errors or miraculous healing, I don't know, but VA won't take it back once it's been diagnosed and granted, so a perfectly healthy man gets to keep his 100% disability. I do know that many older veterans suffering with prostate cancer never went to Vietnam, and it's unfair that some veterans get granted while some don't.

The only correlation to Vietnam I ever noticed from reviewing veterans' records was that many men with prostate cancer later in life had been treated for venereal diseases (VD) in service. VD was more often treated in Vietnam than it was for stateside soldiers, but I don't know if any formal studies have been done on that correlation. If VD causes any subsequent disease I would not consider that as "incurred in the line of duty" (but VA would).

Current cancer research has revealed that we probably all have or will develop one or more cancers in our body but if we live a healthy lifestyle and keep our immune system strong that cancer may never manifest into symptoms. The severity of prostate cancer is measured by Gleason scores which are made up based on findings from usually 12 core samples taken from the prostate, then a Grade Group is assigned based on the combination of Gleason scores. New research shows that a Gleason Score of 6 or below (Grade I) should not even be considered as "cancer," but as far as I can tell VA is still diagnosing and treating (at the veteran's option) anyone with cancer showing in even 1 of the 12 core samples. It's actually a disservice to veterans, health-wise, because there is a chance they can live out their life symptom-free, whereas after a prostatectomy (removal of prostate) or radiation therapy the veteran most often then does have symptoms including frequency and leakage of urination, and of course erectile dysfunction.

VA pays people with any active prostate cancer diagnosis (even symptom free) at the 100% disabled level. They'll continue to get the 100% until it has been resolved by treatment, or forever if they choose not to have it treated. If treated, by surgery, radiation, or chemotherapy, the 100% will continue through the treatment period and until 6 months after the last treatment. Six months after treatment ends, the veteran has an exam to show residuals of the disease or treatment, and this is when he will generally report symptoms of voiding dysfunction. It's all subjective, and the veterans all quickly learn what answers they must give to get a 40% or 60% permanent evaluation. If you report that you need to urinate once every 2 to 3 hours per day, or twice during the night, that will only warrant 10%. If you urinate every 1 to 2 hours per day, or 3 to 4 times per night, that's worth 20%. If you report that you urinate more than once per hour by day, or you have to get up to urinate 5 or more times per night, or you have to wear absorbent materials (pads, Depends, or a wad of toilet paper) and change those pads 2 to 4 times a day, you'll get 40%. If you report that you have to wear and change pads more than 4 times per day you'll get 60%. And nobody will check you on these answers, even though the American Cancer Society says such symptoms are very rare.

If you review a hundred files of veterans who have had a prostatectomy, about 90% of them will say they are changing pads more than 4 times a day, whether it has been 6 months or 10 years since surgery. Meanwhile, medical literature shows that while 30 to 50% of men will have some initial urinary symptoms or urgency after prostatectomy, the symptoms will gradually improve. The Prostate Cancer Foundation states that 25% of men may still have frequent leakage or no control at 6 months after treatment, but by the end of 3 years after surgery, less than 10% of the men report using any pads at all. A veteran who undergoes a prostatectomy is granted 100% disability for 6 months after the surgery, and that's plenty of time for the voiding symptoms to resolve. That's why the regulation was written to give them 6 months of 100% after the end of treatment! But oddly enough, veterans never report improvement, only worsening.

When the first evaluation is given, the rating decision explains what criteria would have to be met to get a higher evaluation, so if he reported low the first time, he simply files a claim for increase and reports the higher frequencies. Who can dispute him? No one is out there counting how many times he will get up to pee or change a pad, and there is no requirement for him to keep a log, or for his doctor to confirm this problem.

But 60% is the max a veteran will get for this condition unless the cancer recurs, so it really disturbs a veteran who has been getting 100% for a year or more, to suddenly have that reduced to 20% or 40% or even 60% because he had surgery and the cancer was cured! Most would rather have the money than their health; it is evident from the letters they write the VA. They write angry letters, they file for reconsideration, then they appeal, then they finally realize they just need to find another herbicide-related disease to claim and work their way back up to the 100%.

PARKINSON'S DISEASE

Another problematic herbicide-related condition is Parkinson's disease. There is no easy way to diagnose this disease and most medical literature states that it takes about two years to develop an accurate diagnosis because the symptoms are extremely varied for different individuals and there is no specific list of symptoms which can be used for a firm diagnosis. The most common symptom is tremors/trembling of the hands; however, not all tremors are Parkinson's. "Familial tremors" is common and is hereditary. But time and again I have seen VA physicians diagnose Parkinson's when there was nothing more than mild tremors and unsteady gait in a person 90 years old. Then other worse-off veterans are given a diagnosis of "parkinsonism" which is not a true diagnosis so it cannot be granted; it simply means that the person has some symptoms similar to Parkinson's but there's no firm diagnosis. Ironically, once a diagnosis is finally given, the condition will be evaluated based on those symptoms that were not adequate before the diagnosis.

So the granting and denial of this condition is quite unfair and luck of the draw. VA needs to revise their regulations to state what specific symptoms will be accepted as evidence of Parkinson's, and then clarify how to evaluate the symptoms. Currently 40% is granted if there's a diagnosis with few/mild symptoms, and some raters take the easy route by granting that and moving on. But separate evaluations are supposed to be given for every part of the body affected, for example 10% or 20% granted for each affected extremity being rated analogous to having peripheral neuropathy, and maybe 10% for slurred speech, and 10% for twitching of the face, and 10% for constipation. But there's no good analogy for weakness of the core and unsteadiness of gait and difficulty rising from a chair. The result is that many are over-rated (by pyramiding) and many are under-rated for this condition because it's just hard to rate.

All the while there's no study showing a causative relationship to herbicide exposure, but the law says cause-and-effect is not needed, only a correlation is needed. Of course more veterans have a diagnosis of Parkinson's than do non-veterans, because veterans go to the free VA, complain of the right symptoms, and it is an opportunity for the VA to reward Vietnam service. If you show me Parkinson's developing within 30 years of Vietnam service I will reconsider, but I've never seen that.

ISCHEMIC HEART DISEASE

Ischemic heart disease, another herbicide-presumptive, is rampant in current American society among those of Vietnam-War-Era-age. Everybody knows it's due to lifestyle, diet, and lack of exercise. The primary symptom is shortness of breath with exertion such as going up stairs. Coronary artery disease (CAD) is the most common diagnosis and this should not be diagnosed unless there has been an angiogram, heart catheterization, to prove the clogged arteries. But many times physicians will put "CAD" in the records just based on short-of-breath symptoms or based on an EKG or echocardiogram showing enlarged heart or hardened heart muscle. This "CAD" is accepted by VA as a "diagnosis" so then the claimant is sent for a heart DBQ (exam check-sheet) which can be completed by any kind of doctor, not just a cardiologist. If a diagnosis has already been given, another catheterization is not required by VA, the rating is based on the DBQ answers with as little as an EKG for testing. When symptoms are subjective and the EKG and chest X-ray are normal, no further testing is warranted. He still gets granted and if the doctor (usually a non-cardiologist) decides his *estimated* METS is 1 to 3, he will get 100%!

Another condition considered as ischemic heart disease is myocardial infarction, commonly called "heart attack." Evidence of diagnosis and treatment for a heart attack is all that's needed to grant this condition 100% for 6 months, then afterwards the condition is reviewed and re-evaluated based on residuals, a minimum of 30%. The fact is that not all heart attacks are caused by ischemic heart disease, so the policies are erroneous. The regs say that heart conditions related to hypertension and/or arrhythmias cannot be granted because no correlation to Agent Orange has been shown for those; and yet heart attacks caused by those conditions are granted every day. Another error is that congestive heart failure is often granted as ischemic heart disease when there's no evidence of ischemia in the vessels; the swollen heart condition is more commonly caused by alcoholism. Another funny thing is how true ischemia of the aortic valve, even so bad that it requires aortic surgery (a very serious condition), cannot be granted because the VA does not consider the aortic valve to be part of the "heart" even though we all learned in 3rd grade that it is.

SUMMARY OF HERBICIDE-PRESUMPTIVES

I have problems with rating any of the conditions VA has related to Agent Orange except for chloracne diagnosed within a year of exposure. I am not a physician or scientist but I'm just saying these regulations are a mess. They were apparently thrown together so fast after Congress granted each new issue that they just haven't been thought through and perfected. The bottom line is grant, grant, grant. If you can find a diagnosis for any one of these conditions and the veteran was in Vietnam, just grant it, evaluate as high as you can, and move on! There are a million more claims to rate this year!

The herbicide-presumptive conditions as of early 2018 are AL Amyloidosis, chronic B-cell leukemias (multiple types), chloracne (and similar acneform diseases, but must have manifested within one year of exposure), diabetes mellitus type II, Hodgkin's disease, ischemic heart disease (coronary artery disease, myocardial infarction, angina), multiple myeloma, non-Hodgkin's lymphoma, Parkinson's disease, early-onset peripheral neuropathy (within one year after exposure), porphyria cutanea tarda, prostate cancer, respiratory cancers (lung, pharynx, trachea, and bronchus), and soft tissue sarcomas (multiple types other than osteosarcoma, chondrosarcoma, Kaposi's sarcoma, or mesothelioma). The list continues to grow longer, simply because the Vietnam veterans are now age 60 to 80, so they're coming down with lots of medical conditions (like all the non-veterans their age).

I read a VA exam once on which the physician had been asked to link some other disease to Agent Orange exposure. He clearly believed *none* of the diseases were truly due to Agent Orange. He was so fed up (like me) and had had about all he could take of these ridiculous claims. He made a remark on the exam that I have no doubt got him fired as soon as his management found he was putting this on exams. His comment gave me the strength to fight this cause. After providing the negative opinion, he noted, "Linking diseases to Agent Orange was a political decision, not a medical decision, not based on scientific medical evidence."

Correlation is not causation, and I demand causation! I challenge Congress to show evidence that these conditions being diagnosed today were caused by herbicide exposure 50 years ago. I challenge Congress to change the law that says cause-and-effect is *irrelevant*, that only a correlation is needed. The correlation is there simply because Vietnam veterans want to be paid for Vietnam service. They get free health care, free testing, free treatment, so they will complain more and louder, and many things will appear in their medical records that you will not find for their non-veteran counterparts.

Non-veterans have to work to support themselves and their families and most can't afford health care or health insurance. They certainly can't be running off to the doctor for minor symptoms, or paying for tests just to find out if they *might* have something. But that's what the Vietnam vets do. Just take a stroll through any VA medical center and you'll see.

Furthermore, their claims tell the truth if anyone will take the time to read the volumes they send in. Their letters repeated say, "I just want what's due to me as a Vietnam vet!" and often the letters are filled with rude or vulgar remarks about how Vietnam vets were called "baby-killers" and got no respect when they came home from war, and these letters never even mention any disability or symptoms. They just say, "Pay me what I'm due!"

Often the VFW or American Legion POA fills out the claims for them, listing as many of the herbicide-related conditions they can recall, for a veteran who has no medical problem at all. Vietnam vets are encouraged to apply for everything and to keep on resubmitting and resubmitting. Yes, maybe someday they will come down with some of those conditions if they live long enough. Numerous claims are received and denied for "pre-diabetes" which is not diabetes, and for "heart attacks" which were nothing but undiagnosed atypical chest pain resolved, and for "Parkinson's" due to normal old-age symptoms.

If the Agent Orange concession was indeed a political decision and not a medical one, then it has truly cheated many veterans. Many did not step foot in Vietnam but served in "battle" just the same because they were on ships being fired upon, with no place to escape short of jumping in the ocean! They were involved in plenty of combat, firing and being fired upon, while some on the soil of Vietnam were never actually in a battle.

EFFECT ON DEFICIT DUE TO AGENT ORANGE

In 2000, only 38,000 veterans from any war era were receiving compensation for diabetes. By 2014, more than 320,000 Vietnam era veterans were receiving compensation for diabetes. That's just diabetes; the VA currently recognizes 14 primary conditions and some of those include several different specific diseases and some have many secondary diseases/complications that will also be granted. And VA is continuously adding more conditions to the list. When I discuss the number of cases being granted each year, keep in mind not just the payments added to the VA obligation, but the tremendous number of VA employees being paid just to process these claims.

In 2010 an additional $14.3 billion was added to the initial budget request for that single year after laws added service-connection for Parkinson's disease, ischemic heart disease (IHD), and hairy cell/other B cell leukemias for veterans who served in Vietnam. The extra funds were for compensation payments and to hire new VA employees. Entire teams of employees were assigned to develop and rate nothing but *Nehmer* cases. VA began reviewing and granting previously denied cases without any request from the veterans. Due to these three new conditions alone (heart disease, Parkinson's, and B-cell leukemias), about 28,000 veterans already receiving compensation reopened their claims to receive a higher combined disability rating that year, plus there were about 29,000 new claims from veterans and 10,000 new claims from survivors based on these new conditions. About 86,000 Vietnam beneficiaries became eligible that year to receive *retroactive* payments for the newly presumptive conditions.

From 2010 through 2012, VA adjudicated approximately 150,000 cases that had been previously denied for the issues of ischemic heart disease, Parkinson's disease, and leukemia. About 65% of those were granted service-connection and retroactive benefits of $2.7 billion were awarded.

By June 2013, due to the *Nehmer* consent decree, VA had paid an aggregate of more than *$4.5 billion* in *retroactive* disability and death benefits to hundreds of thousands of Vietnam veterans and surviving family members. Some veterans received retroactive payments of $300,000 or more *in a one-time payment*, and then continued to get thousands per month thereafter forever. Whenever a big chunk (like a $300,000 check) was sent out to a veteran, a VA employee had to call and warn him by phone so he wouldn't think it was an error or have a heart attack when he opened his mail. Then the office would post them on bulletin boards and in their newsletters as if it was some kind of game to see who could grant and issue the biggest retro check. I found it disgusting. Just think of all the good uses that money could have been put to. A whole community of poor folks could be given some medical care instead of giving $300,000 to one man who doesn't need it and who is already drawing $3,000 per month from the VA.

The following excerpt is from the VA FY 2012 Budget Submission. It says a lot about the Agent Orange effect on the budget as well as the general increase in all claims for all causes in the 21st century.

"Over the past ten years, disability rating claims received from Veterans have grown at a tremendous rate. Although the workload in the last ten years has doubled, additional employees, advanced technologies, and training enabled VA to complete an unprecedented number of disability claims – nearly 1.2 million during 2010. The growth in received disability claims is driven by improved access to benefits through the joint VA and DoD Pre-Discharge Program, increased demand as a result of nearly ten years of maintaining a wartime footing, the establishment of new disabilities that are presumptive of herbicide exposure in Vietnam and other new regulations, and the impact of a difficult economy prompting America's Veterans to pursue entitlement to the benefits they earned during their military service. These influences are still present and, as a result, VBA is forecasting continued high levels of growth in disability claims volume. The claims growth, with the new Agent Orange-related presumptions, is expected to increase disability claims by 24 percent in 2011. Included in this growth is the influx of claims due to the addition of Ischemic Heart Disease

(IHD), Parkinson's Disease (PD), and Hairy Cell Leukemia (HCL) and other B-Cell Chronic Leukemias (BCL) to the list of conditions subject to the presumption of service connection as a result of exposure to Agent Orange. The majority of the Agent Orange-related claims (for these 3 issues) will be received in 2011, so receipts in 2012 will be less than receipts in 2011. Of these claims, approximately 93,000 are covered by the Nehmer settlement, in that they were previously denied. These claims are very complex and can be completed at a rate of production that is less than half the normal expectation. However, we anticipate that 2012 claims receipts (exclusive of Agent Orange claims for the new presumptives) will increase 10 percent over 2010 non-Agent Orange claim receipts."

As an interesting side note, in the VA budget request for 2012, VA justified needing more money because more bypass surgery was being performed at the VA medical centers due to coronary artery disease. This was the most commonly granted new herbicide-presumptive condition under the new law of 2010, but the reason VA said there are more bypass surgeries being done was this: *"The predominately male, older VA population with its high incidence of high cholesterol, high blood pressure and cigarette smoking represents a highly susceptible population for this disease."* Ah ha, just like I thought.

NEHMER IMPACT

The history of the *Nehmer vs. VA* law suit was discussed in my previous section "Agent Orange Litigation and Legislation" and I mention it again here only to note that *Nehmer* is what most significantly busted the budget when it comes to Agent Orange. Not all Agent Orange claims are affected by *Nehmer*, only the ones for which a condition had been diagnosed, claimed, and denied prior to that condition being added by law as a Agent Orange presumptive disease. New diagnoses and new claims for herbicide-presumptive diseases come in every day the claimant won't get retroactive pay to any earlier than the date of claim (or the date a newly added condition is added by law if he had the diagnosis prior to that date and he files the claim within a year of that new law date).   But *retroactive* payments for these Agent Orange conditions, authorized as a result of the *Nehmer* lawsuit, can be paid back to 1985, per the Nehmer consent decree, if the veteran claimed it that long ago and had the condition that long ago. Compensation can only ever be paid back to the date the original claim for a particular issue was received, or date of initial diagnosis, whichever is later. Still this is atrocious that we would go back and pay a person for 30 years' worth of having a disease. He obviously survived without the money (either worked or was supported by another federal program), and the condition wasn't too severe if it didn't kill him in 30 years; but how are we making it up to him by now giving him a lump sum of $300,000?

I just feel that there should be some consideration for where this money comes from: taxpayers, many of them poor or struggling. I think it is enough that we will pay this veteran $3,000 or more a month for the rest of his life. We taxpayers didn't get to vote on this and I don't think we would have agreed on these lump retroactive sums. Yes, it was in accordance with law, but laws can be changed, and should be changed. Our children who will bear the burden of the $21 trillion national debt won't even know about the $2.8 trillion VA portion of that debt unless they read this book.

"THE VIETNAM EFFECT"

I am not unsympathetic to Vietnam veterans. Although I didn't approve of the war, many of them didn't either, and they didn't volunteer to go, but they served as their country demanded and they deserve to be commended, not necessarily compensated.

The Vietnam Veterans are always quick to note in their statements, "I personally was never spit on, but I've heard of others who were spit on and had things thrown at them when they returned from Vietnam."

I did see one claim wherein the veteran claimed he and his fellow soldiers had been spit on and called "baby-killers" upon their return from Vietnam. It turned out that guy had never even been to Vietnam. He was drafted during the Vietnam era but was never sent to Vietnam due to his crazy behavior in boot camp and he was discharged from service after only three months. He subsequently filed numerous claims over and over for the next 40 years. He sent letters to several congressmen and the president. In his letters he claimed to be a Vietnam vet and he discussed how disgraceful it was that the Vietnam veterans were getting treated so badly by the VA, how the VA kept denying all their claims after their great sacrifice to this country.

In reality, the Vietnam vets get practically everything they ask for. Every few years a few more conditions are getting added to the list of herbicide-presumptive diseases.

It may be true that Vietnam vets were not given proper respect when they returned from war because there were certainly plenty of Americans opposed to that war. But if that's what we're paying them for then let's call it what it is and treat all Vietnam veterans equally.

I'm not the first who has suspected that those who served in-country Vietnam were exposed to many things that probably posed a greater risk and had a more likely or greater effect than exposure to Agent Orange. Besides the horrors of war, seeing dead and mutilated bodies, and night and day fearing the vicious Vietcong with their knives and punji sticks, our soldiers lived in harsh jungle conditions of high heat and humidity, trudged in wet boots for days on end, and were exposed to many infectious diseases due to insects and parasites. Many became addicted to the readily available illicit and impure drugs. They were exposed to smoke, consumed unsanitary food and water, and had little and poor medical treatment for their daily minor injuries. The seriously wounded and dead were medevac'd out but those who were "lucky" really bore the brunt of the misery and spent a year there. Many spent two or three tours there.

In 2000, VA convened a group to discuss possibly granting service-connection based on the "in-country effect" considering the wide range of Vietnam War risk factors. But the committee determined this approach would not likely change the outcome of compensation policy, because the law still required VA to identify specific diseases related to exposure, and required VA to obtain the NAS reviews of all relevant scientific and medical literature for each disease. Besides they noted there were *no ongoing long-term health studies of Vietnam veterans* to provide input for such approach.

I for one, would have preferred to pay all these Vietnam veterans based on the "in-country effect" rather than picking and choosing between specific conditions. Not only would it have saved a tremendous amount of tax dollars spent on the studies, and the re-opening of claims year after year, it would just be easier to stomach. I don't mind paying Vietnam vets. I just don't like granting benefits for things such as type II diabetes and coronary artery disease when we know these things are prevalent in this age-group of people regardless of whether they served or not. And the basis of establishing these granting laws is nothing more than a finding of some degree of possible *"association."* Association is not causation. Association simply means that more veterans have a disease than non-veterans have. This could be due simply to the fact that veterans have more access to free health care and diagnostic testing than does the general public! And they have more motivation to get themselves diagnosed with these things because they stand to gain big monthly bucks for it!

If you read veterans' files, their statements to doctors and to the VA, many of them clearly want to be sick and worsening, and they will do whatever it takes to make themselves sicker, so they can get their benefits increased. They will deliberately not take their medications in order to increase their symptoms; i.e., not take their daily hypertension or diabetes or thyroid medications. They will demand non-critical surgeries in order to get the 100% temporary compensation. Many of them will go in complaining of diabetes twenty times before they ever get diagnosed with it. Anyone, if tested enough, will eventually turn up a little high on their creatinine,

BUN, or A1c results, and they will immediately claim this and be granted before they ever get a follow-up test. In many cases the subsequent tests were normal, but VA could not reduce because "sustained improvement hasn't been shown." All one can do is set him up for another future exam a few years down the road. I have also seen many diagnoses when the lab reports really weren't clearly supporting of a diagnosis of diabetes, but the doctor prescribed Metformin, so the veteran will forever carry that diagnosis and 20% based on the medication; his next tests will be normal and it will be considered that the medication is controlling it. Other times, there's a diagnosis but the condition is "controlled by diet and exercise" and that condition is also granted forever.

***

Veteran X served 18 months in the late 1960's in Vietnam. After that he smoked three packs a day for more than 50 years. At age 72 he developed lung cancer, and VA granted him 100 percent compensation for lung cancer, presumably related to exposure to Agent Orange in Vietnam.

***

Veteran X served from 1972 to 1973 in Vietnam and at age 52 he claimed CAD (coronary artery disease). His father had a heart attack in his 40's and bypass surgery in his 50's. His brother had heart stents at age 47. It is clearly a congenital disease for this family but that does not matter to the VA. He is granted for CAD (as ischemic heart disease) presumptive to herbicide exposure.

***

Veteran X didn't step boots on the ground in Vietnam, but he did serve on the USS Cony for the two days of November 6 and 7, 1967, the only 2 days this ship was in the waterways of Vietnam. VA maintains a "ship list" and if the veteran was on that ship when it went up in a waterway, or if he went ashore from a ship that docked in the blue water, his exposure is conceded. The veteran is granted 100 percent disability for diabetes, with complications of kidney failure and neuropathies, attributed to exposure to Agent Orange in Vietnam.

***

Veteran X served honorably from November 1967 to October 1971. Vietnam Era, right? Right! And guess what! In his 60's, more than 40 years after service, he developed diabetes mellitus type II that is now requiring insulin three times a day. Very serious. But can he be granted service-connection? No. He served on a Navy ship throughout his entire career; he never set foot on the land in Vietnam. Never mind the fact that those who were in Vietnam came aboard the ship with their rucksacks and gear that they had dragged through the jungles, and with their boots that had trudged through rice paddies and jungles saturated with Agent Orange. He and thousands more RVN veterans like himself with diabetes or ischemic heart disease or prostate cancer have been denied because they were not physically in Vietnam. But they got their diseases the same, at the same time in life the others did! Maybe it's because they too were exposed and VA is cheating them, but more likely it's just that they would have developed the cancer or diabetes anyway. It's the age, lifestyle, and environmental hazards that a generation has been exposed to for 50 years, not just one little year in Vietnam, on or off the ship!

***

Veteran X was an airplane mechanic stationed in Taiwan. He had a TDY trip to Vietnam to work on a plane, so he was in-country, on a runway for about 2 hours until he completed the job and got back on his plane (same runway) and returned to Taiwan. He filed a claim for REM sleep disorder that he feels is a precursor to Parkinson's disease. It's a wasted claim for now because he has no diagnosis of any of the presumptives. But VA must develop for medical records and rate/deny the case, telling the veteran that if he can provide medical evidence of the association it will be reconsidered. If he does provide something, such as a bogus internet blog about sleep disorders, VA will then require an exam and a VA medical opinion, and another rating decision must be issued. Meanwhile, Parkinson's is on the herbicide-presumptive list, and he will be granted for Parkinson's if he ever gets a diagnosis of that. And if REM sleep disorder ever gets added to the list, he could potentially get thousands in retroactive pay, unless Congress puts an end to this foolishness!

***

Veteran X has diabetes mellitus, prostate cancer, and Parkinson's disease, all diagnosed and treated at his local VA medical center. He served 4 years in the military from 1965-1969, the peak of the Vietnam War; however, he was never in Vietnam. As a Navy sailor he spent the 4 years on various ships. They were near Vietnam, and they were involved in battle, firing from the ship and taking on fire, but he never stepped on Vietnam soil, and never went up into any of the inland waterways. He has been denied over and over again and has appealed to BVA which has also denied him.

***

Veteran X is a Vietnam veteran who filed his first claim at age 92. He'd never been to a VA medical center. While seeing a private physician he reported a few mild symptoms of neuropathy of his extremities. The physician did not diagnose Parkinson's, but he wrote in the medical notes this remark: "Since this man is a Vietnam vet, I'm referring him to the VA and perhaps they can evaluate him in their Parkinson's clinic, and he may qualify for benefits." When the man reported to the VA Parkinson's clinic, the records were erroneously established (before any exam at all) that he had been diagnosed with Parkinson's by a private doctor and referred to VA for treatment. After completion of the Parkinson's questionnaire, they told him to file a claim and sent him to a VSO for help in submitting the claim.

His case was rushed through as a priority due to his age, and the claim was granted with a minimum evaluation based the VAMC record showing "Parkinson's" on the Problem List. Then to determine the current severity of the condition he was set up for an "at-once" exam by a contract examiner who filled out a DBQ, noting the condition already diagnosed by VA, all he had to do was check boxes per the veteran's responses. The veteran was never seen by a physician in the Parkinson's clinic until *after* he was granted service-connection. Not only did this veteran not have to wait two years for his unsupported diagnosis, he was also given preferential treatment due to his age. Veterans over 85 years old require "priority processing" which means their cases are worked first, and raters are encouraged to grant them as much as possible. It's a bit ironic that by that age they're settled down and don't have big plans or needs for the money; even their children and grandchildren are grown. So some unrelated entity such as a nursing home or charity will reap the benefits we pay.

***

Veteran X was granted compensation for diabetes as 10% disabling for the past 10 years. A 10% is assigned whenever there is a diagnosis but the condition isn't severe enough to require medication; it's considered to be controlled by diet and exercise. All lab tests for the past 10 years have been normal. So he's given a VA exam to evaluate for an increase, and on exam he expresses a whole range of symptoms. Based on his totally subjective complaints he is now granted 20% for the left arm, 20% for the right arm, 20% for the left leg, and 20% for the right leg, all diagnosed as peripheral diabetic neuropathy. He's also granted erectile dysfunction and special monthly compensation for loss of use of a creative organ. The problem with all this is that the new conditions are granted based totally on his subjective complaints, and any diabetes that is not even serious enough to require medication is probably a misdiagnosis and is certainly not going to cause any of these complications! It's fraud.

***

Veteran X has been granted for diabetes and is seeking an increase. He has no kidney or urinary complaints. Tests show his creatinine is above 1.2 so the doctor reported a "definite decrease in kidney function" and per regulation an additional 60% disability evaluation is granted. This veteran is over 80 years old and the lab finding may be normal due to his age and other conditions/treatments, besides creatinine alone is not enough criteria to diagnose kidney failure, but that is not to be considered or questioned by a "non-physician" rater.

***

Veteran X has a long family history of diabetes, but his diabetes is granted based on Agent Orange exposure. The treatment records show that he was diagnosed with diabetes after a bout of pancreatitis which was caused by his most critical condition, alcoholism. It is extremely common to see this medical history in the veterans' VA Medical Center records if anyone would bother to do a study: repeated cycles of treatment for alcoholism, often emergency hospitalization for acute congestive heart failure, followed by a diagnosis of pancreatitis, then followed (on day of discharge from the hospital) with an initial diagnosis of diabetes!

***

Veteran X has been granted 40% for his prostate cancer residuals. He now comes in for an increase exam. He tells the doctor, *per the examiner's remarks on the report*, "They're trying to take my money. I just don't want my benefits reduced." So the doctor shows him what all the check-box choices are on the DBQ and helps him choose the most severe symptoms to support the highest rating, grossly exaggerating the number of pads he uses and the number of times he urinates daily.

***

Veteran X has recovered from prostate cancer surgery and was previously granted 40% for residuals, but now claims an increase so he gets another VA exam. He's also now claiming erectile dysfunction (ED) and depression secondary to the ED. Instead of being happy that his life was saved from the cancer, he supposedly became depressed. His treatment records show he had been treated for ED (had been prescribed Viagra) for many *years* before he was diagnosed with prostate cancer. But no one cares about that; the ED will be automatically granted effective the date he underwent prostatectomy, because it is an expected residual of prostatectomy. He understands the rating schedule now because it was explained to him on the last rating decision. So now he claims he is changing his pads more than 4 times per day. This ups his evaluation to 60% for one issue, which is enough to qualify for schedular individual unemployability (IU), and he has the new service-connection for depression secondary to his ED. So the week after he receives that new rating, he submits the claim for IU, claiming that his depression (due to ED) prevents him from working. Although the depression is minor, and ED is 0%, he does qualify for IU now based on the 60% for voiding dysfunction. I agree that no one should be expected to work if they are changing Depends more than 4 times a day, but he didn't even mention that as a reason for why he can't work. I don't feel that depression about erectile dysfunction is a good enough reason for not working, or for VA to grant IU, but he got it.

***

Veteran X served about 2 years during the Vietnam Era. On discharge he was hired by General Motors and he worked there for 32 years before retiring due to age, and he started drawing a nice GM retirement. Seven years after his age-based retirement, about 40 years after returning from Vietnam, he filed a claim for service connection for PTSD. He had never in all those years been diagnosed or treated for PTSD, nor had he exhibited any symptoms at home or work to make anyone think he had PTSD. However, his VFW representative convinced him that anyone who served in Vietnam must have PTSD and just doesn't know it.

The PTSD stressor was conceded by VA based on the "fear and easing standard" because he served during the Vietnam War. He was initially granted 30 percent for PTSD (the normal minimum anyone gets if they can show a diagnosis). The VA letter that explained the payment amount also explained what symptoms he would need to report in order to qualify for a higher level of disability. So he came back in with a claim for increase, reported all the required symptoms to the VA examiner (who had never seen him before), and the resulting exam warranted an increase to 70 percent. Then the VFW rep explained to him that when a veteran has at least 70 percent, and at least one condition was 40% or more, he qualifies statutorily for Individual Unemployability (IU). The evidence must still state that the veteran cannot work, but all that's needed to show that is one sentence of the VA exam where the doctor says this condition would affect his ability to work. So he filed for IU, total disability, claiming that he cannot work due to PTSD.

Meanwhile, VA noticed in reviewing his file that he had been treated for coronary artery disease (CAD) many years prior, so since he had Vietnam service, the VA invited a claim for service connection for the CAD, because ischemic heart disease is associated with herbicide exposure in Vietnam. He filed and VA granted service connection for his ischemic heart disease. He had undergone a CABG (open heart surgery, coronary artery bypass grafting) and stents, all while maintaining the job at GM.

At the time of his claim for IU, the heart condition was totally asymptomatic (no symptoms) as it has been ever since he had the stents placed several years before his retirement. The heart condition had never prevented him from maintaining gainful employment. The PTSD is also bogus in that he was never occupationally or socially impaired, and he never even thought he had a mental problem. In addition to his successful career, he had the same wife all those years, multiple children and grandchildren, all with whom he reportedly had great relationships. He also belonged to a community club where he enjoyed participating in charitable events (demonstrating admin and interpersonal skills) at the time of his claim for IU. No occupational or functional impairment, but 100% compensation is paid.

***

Veteran X served two terms. The first was an "honorable" period of one year during the Vietnam war. We'll never know whether he actually behaved honorably during that period because a lot of things soldiers are court-martialed for in peace-time, are often overlooked in a war-zone. The mission is to stay alive, and often what happens in Vietnam stays in Vietnam, although there are many PTSD claims about friendly fire incidents and regrettable treatment of the enemy. There are also plenty of claims requesting service-connection for alcoholism, drug abuse, and lung cancer (from cigarette smoking) due to proliferation of substances during Vietnam.

This veteran served a second term during which he was ejected from the Army after being convicted of grand theft larceny, and he properly received a dishonorable discharge for that period. VA will not pay benefits for the 2nd period of service, but it doesn't matter. He is being paid 100% for diabetes and prostate cancer based on his service in Vietnam. The examiner asked him why he got out of service and instead of telling the doctor he was kicked out with a bad conduct discharge, he said, "because the young kids coming into service were so immature and had no military pride." Wow.

***

Veteran X filed a claim for a plethora of current conditions that he came down with later in life, that were not shown in his military records, and have never been associated with any type of exposures. He was denied for everything except tinnitus, a subjective condition that is practically automatically granted to anyone who was ever in a combat zone. He reopened the claim and gave this statement. *"What more proof do I need as a combat veteran of the Vietnam war to prove that I am combat disabled? I only received 10% for tinnitus and everything else is 0. Again, let me stress I was a combat vet in that war in Vietnam and today I am a sick vet. All I am asking for is what I am entitled to as a combat veteran who served in the Vietnam War under orders of the US government. I just want my just dues in compensation at the 100% rate. Please expedite my claim as soon as possible."*   He didn't provide any new medical records, didn't explain why he thought any condition was due to service in Vietnam, just clearly noted that as a Vietnam vet he feels "entitled."   VA disability compensation is a highly abused "entitlement program" and it's time someone explained this to veterans, politicians, and taxpayers.

GULF WAR CLAIMS

For VA benefits purposes, anyone who served on active duty from August 2, 1990 to the present is considered a Gulf War Veteran. For example, any of these veterans will qualify for war-time pension even if they never left the mainland U.S. But for compensation purposes, specific diseases or symptoms have been recognized by the VA as associated with service in specific foreign war zones, when that service is verified by their DD214 (military discharge) or other military records. Those who get the special "Gulf War" considerations include anyone who served in Southeast Asia (Iraq, Kuwait, Saudi Arabia, Bahrain, Qatar, United Arab Emirates, Oman, Gulf of Aden, Gulf of Oman, waters of the Persian Gulf, the Arabian Sea, the Red Sea, and the airspace above these locations) from August 2, 1990 to the present. Anyone who served in Afghanistan from September 19, 2001 to the present is also considered for certain presumptive diseases, although not for all of the Gulf War illnesses. The Gulf War veteran can wait years after service (after many other jobs and experiences) before filing his Gulf War claim, and will still receive a full Gulf War General Medical Exam, which will end up showing a dozen general complaints and issues to grant, whether or not related to Gulf War exposures.

The whole Gulf War thing needs to be either eliminated from the rating schedule or revamped because the policies are not being applied consistently, and simply serving in the Gulf does not (should not) qualify as a disability. Gulf War claims are very difficult to rate. The regulations and manual procedures are so convoluted, and training is so poor, that no one wants to develop or rate them. The issues are inconsistently granted or denied, and many errors are noted on quality reviews, but additional training of the same old content does not help. Many veterans are getting high evaluations without supporting evidence, just because they went to the Gulf. Others are getting nothing because the doctors don't understand how to complete the exams and opinions, and those claimants keep coming back in again and again with appeals until they are finally granted. Most of the claimants do not even know what they're asking for; their POAs are writing things on their claim such as chronic fatigue syndrome, fibromyalgia, and Gulf War syndrome.

The Gulf War veterans are already being granted for their PTSD and their TBIs more than any group before them, and they get all the regular subjective aches and pains granted such as their joints, headaches, and foot problems. But the VA wants to go an extra mile for them. Gulf War General Medical Exams are being erroneously given to everyone who ever served in the Gulf War arena even if they just claim a few simple issues, not a Gulf War syndrome, and anything that shows up on that exam is likely to be granted. It's a big waste of money and VA examiners' time, and each exam opens up a can of worms, raises lots of issues the veteran never thought of but then decides to claim. An examiner cannot initiate a claim, so the VA must send a letter to the veteran inviting a claim for the newly raised issues, and there you have another unnecessary claim in the system.

Practically every veteran who has returned from service in any Southwest Asia region, Iraq, or Afghanistan has filed a claim based on "Gulf War illness," "Gulf War syndrome," or one of the symptoms established as possibly related to Gulf War environmental exposures, *just because they can.* The most common complaints attributed to Gulf War exposures are respiratory problems, gastrointestinal problems, skin problems, chronic fatigue syndrome, and fibromyalgia. But if nothing can be diagnosed, that's ok, it can still be granted as an "undiagnosed illness."

The Gulf War regulation provides a whole list of bacterial and viral diseases that if diagnosed (by lab findings) will be automatically granted, and of that list I am fully supportive. These include malaria, brucellosis, campylobacter jejuni, coxiella burnetiid, mycobacterium tuberculosis, nontyphoid salmonella, shigella, visceral leishmaniasis, and West Nile Virus. I personally never saw a single claim for any one of these diseases by any Gulf War veteran. They are truly serious conditions that deserve service-connection, but if a soldier gets one of these he will be treated by the military, medevac'd to Walter Reed just like the serious combat-injured cases, and his file will be case-managed through to service-connection.

The soldiers who have returned from Iraq and Afghanistan complain of all sorts of ailments, although actually very few of them ever reported a symptom during service in the desert. They wait until their separation exam or until after service to file a VA claim for all this miscellaneous bull. They have learned that they can claim almost any symptom and attribute it to "exposures." Most don't even list any symptoms on their claim, they are simply claiming they are sick due to exposures to sand or burn pits, because they've been told by the military to claim this! But "exposure" in and of itself, is not a disability if no disease resulted. When asked to clarify their conditions, they'll come back in claiming the whole list: respiratory conditions, gastrointestinal issues, skin conditions, chronic fatigue, and fibromyalgia. They claim because they can, and because they are encouraged to do so. They often put "Gulf War Syndrome" on their claim not having any idea what they are claiming and then they don't know what to say when the examiner asks for symptoms. Some learn that they can make up any sort of symptoms and attribute them to Gulf War exposures and they just might get granted because the regulation says the list of diseases is "not limited" to those specified. But the veterans must say they believe their symptoms are due to exposure to something like sand, high temperatures, or burn pits.

Before attributing a symptom to any Gulf War illness, the VA examiner is supposed to rule out any other possible diagnosis that may be responsible for the symptomatology presented, but how can they do that other than by asking the veteran? The examiner does not see the veteran's treatment records if there ever were any (don't need any for a GW claim), and the doctor has never treated this veteran. He simply asks the template questions, checks off the boxes, and VA grants the money.

BREATHING COMPLAINTS

A common complaint on Gulf War claims is "difficulty breathing" but rarely is there any impairment shown on the pulmonary function tests (PFTs). In many cases, the truth comes to light that the individual had actually been treated for allergy and asthma symptoms as a child. They were not undergoing any specific treatment at the time of entry to service, so they were considered "whole." Now when allergic or asthmatic symptoms re-appear during service, it gets attributed to service exposures, and disability is granted. The fact that the veteran is no longer exposed after service, and therefore no longer experiencing symptoms, doesn't seem to matter for GW vets, even though the regulation clearly says that service connection is not warranted if symptoms improve when removed from the allergen, because then it's not a chronic condition. Many veterans continue taking medications or using inhalers, then say that the medications are the reason the symptoms are not present on exam.

The fact that medication is taken for a condition is often one of the ways of confirming a diagnosis as well as a basis for determining the level of disabilities. When the veteran goes to the VA C&P exam, the examiner has never treated him before and generally has not seen his records (not required to look at them unless there's an opinion requested). The examiner simply asks the questions on the DBQ checklist. The claimant replies, "yes, I use an inhaler every day." The doctor checks that off on the DBQ (without even verifying there is an active prescription) and the VA grants 30 percent disability.

The regulations indicate the importance of considering pulmonary function testing (PFTs) when assigning an evaluation, but the PFTs are often totally normal, and the condition is granted anyway because the examiner diagnoses it anyway. The regulations also say that asthma must not be granted unless there is documented evidence of asthmatic attacks, but there is rarely any documented attack in any record, and it is granted anyway because the veteran served in the Gulf.

GASTROINTESTINAL COMPLAINTS

As for gastrointestinal disorders, the veteran claims he has stomach pain or acid reflux after eating, or he claims he has intermittent periods of diarrhea or constipation. How is one to verify this? The examiner has no way to confirm these symptoms during a 15-minute exam. The records don't show anything, but because he reports it to the examiner, it gets put on the exam report, and the VA grants 30% based on the exam.

The only way to properly diagnose gastroesophageal reflux disease (GERD) is by an EGD (esophagogastroduodenoscopy), but very few veterans granted compensation for GERD or acid reflux have ever had an EGD, or if they did the test was negative. The veteran is prescribed Omeprazole anyway to abate the claimed symptoms and many foolish veterans are taking it on a daily basis for no good reason. Over the years, continued use of this drug causes true stomach and intestinal damage, then the VA medical center really has something to treat.

Over and again I have seen GERD granted as related to Gulf War exposure, or even after a negative EGD "acid reflux" was granted as an "undiagnosed illness" based on digestive symptoms because some doctor gives a positive opinion, and it's just wrong! Rarely, but occasionally, a doctor will say it is *not* likely due to Gulf War exposures, with rationale. *"Based on this examiner's review of current peer-reviewed medical literature, the passage of gastric contents into the esophagus (gastroesophageal reflux) is a normal physiologic process. Most episodes are brief and do not cause symptoms, esophageal injury, or other complications. Gastroesophageal reflux (GERD) becomes a disease when it either causes macroscopic damage to the esophagus or causes symptoms that reduce the quality of life. Based on this examiner's review of current peer-reviewed literature to include the Institute of Medicine's report, Gulf War and Health: Volume 10: Update of Health Effects of Serving in the Gulf War released on February 11, 2016, there is inadequate or insufficient evidence to determine whether an association exists between deployment to the Gulf War and structural gastrointestinal diseases. Therefore, the claimed disability pattern or diagnosed disease of GERD was less likely than not (less than 50 percent probability) related to a specific exposure event experienced by the Veteran during service in Southwest Asia."*

OIL WELL FIRES AND BURN PITS

At certain times during the Gulf War, Iraqi forces ignited oil well fires producing dense black smoke, and many veterans have claimed illnesses due to that exposure. According to a VA website, http://www.publichealth.va.gov/exposures/gulfwar/sources/oil-well-asp#s, the Institute of Medicine (IOM) Gulf War and Health report, "Health Effects of Serving in the Gulf War" found that *"the current available evidence is not sufficient to establish a causative relationship between chronic multi-symptom illness and any specific drug, toxin, plume or other agent, either alone or in combination. Burning oil fields may cause temporary skin irritation, runny nose, cough, eye-nose-or-throat irritation, but irritation is temporary, resolves once the exposure is gone. Research shows no long-term health problems from exposure."* But time and again this stuff is granted anyway.

Meanwhile "burn pit exposure" is the new Agent Orange. I guess every war has to have something so these veterans can be paid forever after leaving service. Yes, Gulf War veterans are all "exposed" to burn pits in the desert because that is the current proper sanitizing method of destroying stinky rotten garbage and waste in a war zone. There is no proof that this exposure to burning is causing any illness. Thank goodness they are able to have burn pits. If all this waste was lying around unburned every one of them would truly be sick. That would be true exposure to contaminants. The soldiers have dust masks to wear whenever they have to approach the pit or if winds are blowing their direction. Current news stories note that over 155,000 Gulf War veterans have signed the "Burn Pit Registry." So what? Every Gulf War veteran asked to sign the registry has signed the registry. Where is the illness? Where is the medical evidence linking burn pit exposure to any disease or impairment?

GULF WAR SYNDROME

The VA had to develop its own condition, Gulf War Syndrome, and a special exam, "Gulf War General Medical Exam" because civilian doctors were not finding anything wrong with the Gulf War claimants, and now Gulf War exams can only be done at the VA medical centers. If the claimant reports a respiratory, gastrointestinal, skin, or fatigue problem, the examiner tries to discover any objective evidence of a problem that he could diagnosis. If he can diagnosis something, then that issue will be granted on a direct basis. If there is no diagnosis but the claimant does a good job of reporting symptoms, the examiner may decide there is an "undiagnosed illness" due to specifically stated exposures; then this can be granted on a presumptive basis. There are not a lot of "undiagnosed illnesses" being granted because first it's too confusing for examiners, the no-diagnosis bit. Then if an examiner does concede an "undiagnosed illness," the rater doesn't know what diagnostic code to grant it under, because the rating schedule is arranged by diagnosis, and raters are trained not to grant for symptoms that have not been diagnosed! But usually the examiner says that anything found has been attributed to a diagnosed disability, not related to GW exposures, and that there is no evidence of any "undiagnosed illness" or diagnosed illness with no etiology, so the condition gets granted on a direct basis.

CHRONIC FATIGUE SYNDROME

Chronic fatigue syndrome (CFS) is one of those magical conditions that cannot be seen by the physician, cannot be measured by any test, and cannot be scientifically related to any exposure or event in service. And yet, in honor of our great Gulf War veterans, the regulations have been written to allow any who have been in Southeast Asia to be granted service connection for CFS if they can find a doctor to diagnose it. CFS in and of itself is ridiculous, but veterans are claiming plain ole "fatigue" and having it granted as CFS. The regulation stipulates that CFS will not be diagnosed unless there is a "new onset of debilitating fatigue severe enough to *reduce daily activity to less than 50 percent of the usual level for at least six months*" but I've never seen such symptomology shown in records, despite many diagnoses of CFS. The diagnosis also requires *six* or more of a list of very specific symptoms but these symptoms, if reported, are usually already supporting another service-connected condition such as fibromyalgia, headaches, and sleep disturbances. Per regulation, a symptom must not be used to support more than one diagnosis, but you will see it on GW ratings.

FIBROMYALGIA

Fibromyalgia is another magical condition with no scientific testable symptoms. The Institute of Medicine in 2016 reported there was *"limited/suggestive evidence of an association between deployment to the Gulf War and fibromyalgia."* Association (even if it was definite and not just limited or suggestive) is not good enough for me; association is not causation. Fibromyalgia is defined as a disorder characterized by widespread musculoskeletal pain accompanied by fatigue, sleep, memory and mood issues. Fatigue, sleep, memory and mood issues are common to every human! The key to this condition is that "widespread musculoskeletal pain" must be shown. "Widespread pain" is defined by VA as pain in both the left and right sides of the body, that is both above and below the waist, and that affects both the axial skeleton (i.e., cervical spine, anterior chest, thoracic spine, or low back) and the extremities. The examiner looks for "tender points" and if the claimant reports tenderness in the areas noted above, then Voile! A diagnosis is given, and service-connected compensation is granted.

***

Veteran X has 6 children under the age of 9 years old, and she is claiming "fatigue" due to service. Really? A working mother with even 2 or 3 children under 9 years old should feel fatigue. She didn't even say "chronic fatigue syndrome due to Gulf War exposures." Just fatigue. But as a Gulf War vet she is sent to the full GW general medical exam with special review and comments required from the examiner regarding the various potential Gulf War illnesses. It is unethical for the rater to question this claim. The reason the rater knows about the children is that the physician thought it was important enough to include it in his remarks. Hint, hint. But a rater is not allowed to use common sense in this case. He has to consider the condition as service-related because she first complained of fatigue in service.

***

Veteran X filed for "chronic fatigue syndrome" and on his VA exam when asked to describe his symptoms he explained "sometimes I feel tired." Well, quite a symptom. Do not we all sometimes feel tired and fatigued? CFS should only be granted to someone who had a sudden onset of fatigue so debilitating that he was reduced to 50% or less of his prior physical ability. Such a person would probably be confined to bed or a wheelchair, not running around to his exams appearing normal.

***

Veteran X is a Gulf War veteran, discharged in 2007, now claiming fibromyalgia. The examiner goes down each part of the body, various muscles and joints of the neck, hips, knees, etc. If the veteran claims any point is "tender" or painful then this is considered a positive "trigger point". No complaints or injuries or treatment was shown in the service records, and nothing was shown for 8 years after service. In 2016 she filed the claim, got the GW exam, and was granted 40% for fibromyalgia related to exposures in the Gulf War. She also claimed irritable bowel syndrome (IBS) with *subjective* symptoms of alternating diarrhea and constipation. There was no documented medical evidence of this anywhere in service or after. She has never been treated for such symptoms, but because she's a Gulf War veteran she was diagnosed with IBS and granted 30% for this as presumptive to Gulf War. *Any* Gulf War veteran who knows how to properly answer questions on a Gulf War exam can and will be granted up to 100% disability, regardless of the fact that they have appeared perfectly healthy over all the years since they returned from the Gulf. There's no time limitation on filing these claims, and that must change!

***

Veteran X claims service-connection for fibromyalgia because she served in Iraq. On her general medical exam she has no specific complaint and has never sought treatment. She just says, "I hurt all over. All my joints hurt." Everyone feels that way at some point in time, especially when they are overweight and out of conditioning, or if they have the flu. But if you've been in Iraq, and you haven't had any actual injuries to your joints, that is pretty much all you have to say to get granted 20% or 40%. Then you'll get another 50% or 70% for your PTSD and you're home free.

***

Veteran X is a Gulf War veteran whose fibromyalgia claim was denied because the evidence shows she has previously been diagnosed with rheumatoid arthritis. She has a real condition, diagnosed by blood tests! But that has not been linked to Gulf War so it is denied. The examiner noted that the Institute of Medicine's report stated there is limited/suggestive evidence of association between Gulf War and fibromyalgia, but that there is inadequate/insufficient evidence of association between Gulf War musculoskeletal system diseases (including rheumatoid arthritis). So if she didn't have the rheumatoid arthritis diagnosis (a real thing that must be denied) she would have been granted (for the fake thing)!

***

Veteran X is a Gulf War veteran claiming respiratory illness due to fire pit exposure in Iraq. On exam he reports that he had been treated for asthma before service. But the military records show he came into service with no mention of asthma on his entrance exam so he was considered whole with no disability. Then he tended a fire pit in Iraq and started coughing, and the field clinic prescribed Albuterol inhalers. When he returned from overseas he continued to have the prescriptions refilled whether he needed them or not. And who knows whether he has used them or not. The VA examiner diagnoses asthma based on fact he has been prescribed an inhaler, and reports that he is symptom free. He has now been removed from the allergens that caused his respiratory flareup and has no symptoms, but that regulation is ignored; we will pay him forever.

CAMP LEJEUNE CONTAMINATED WATER

In January 2017, VA published regulations to grant "presumptive" service-connection for diseases associated with exposure to contaminated water at Camp Lejeune, N.C. Historical records show that various chemicals, including perchloroethylene (PCE), a dry cleaning solvent, and trichloroethylene (TCE), a degreaser, were dumped on the grounds of Camp LeJeune and may have sunk into the wells providing water used for bathing and drinking by the military troops and their families living on post. Some veterans who served at Camp LeJeune subsequently (*many* years later) developed various cancers (but no diseases that haven't been also experienced in the general population). These veterans had read the news reports of contaminated water at Camp LeJeune so they filed law suits and claims for service-connection.

VA has now conceded that any serviceman or woman who served at Camp Lejeune for at least 30 days between August 1953 and December 1987 "may" have drank contaminated water there, and they will be granted service-connection for any of the following eight diseases: adult leukemia, aplastic anemia and other myelodysplastic syndromes, bladder cancer, kidney cancer, liver cancer, multiple myeloma, non-Hodgkin's lymphoma, and Parkinson's disease.   This is ridiculous because there's no proof that they wouldn't have come down with their disease if living somewhere else, like all the other people, veterans and non-veterans, who have these diseases and never lived near Camp LeJeune. It's all purely political; a way to make America think VA is doing wonderful things for veterans.

In the VA Congressional Budget Submission for 2018, VA estimated that this issue alone would increase VA compensation obligations by $285.3 million in 2017.

All "Camp LeJeune" cases are handled by a special team, so I had little experience with them. The cases I saw were all just claims for "exposure" to the water with no specific diseases listed, and these claims just waste manhours and resources, and delay the processing of legitimate claims for sick veterans.

SLEEP APNEA

Sleep apnea is the hot new "tinnitus." It's well known that tinnitus will be granted to almost every veteran who claims it, so when the word got out, that issue started appearing on every new claim. Sleep apnea now also appears on almost every new claim. In 2001, only 983 veterans were service-connected for sleep apnea but by 2014 that number had increased to 114,000, and compensation for sleep apnea alone now costs us over $2 billion dollars per year. The numbers are raising exponentially since most soldiers are now asking for a sleep study to be done in service so that it's guaranteed to be granted by VA when they get out.

Sleep apnea is generally manifested by snoring and daytime sleepiness, but not all snoring is sleep apnea, and most daytime hypersomnolence is just due to not enough hours spent in bed. There are two kinds of sleep apnea, one of which is Central Sleep Apnea, pretty rare. Central sleep apnea results when the brain is causing the problem and fails to signal the muscles to breathe during sleep. Some medical literature suggests that using a CPAP (continuous positive airway pressure machine) prescribed for obstructive sleep apnea for too many years could lead to dependence and actually cause central sleep apnea (as machine overtakes the natural response, one may eventually not be able to sleep normally without a CPAP). Anyway, most veterans don't seem to have the central type yet (give it a few years); right now they are all claiming Obstructive Sleep Apnea.

Obstructive sleep apnea (OSA) occurs when there is a blockage of the airway in the throat, when soft tissue in the back of the throat collapses and closes during sleep to interfere with breathing. The tissues in the back of the throat become flabby with aging, just like all body tissues get flabbier with age and especially when there is reduced physical activity (deconditioning) and when obesity is involved. Obesity is the number one risk factor for developing obstructive sleep apnea. Almost every sleep study report I've seen notes obesity and age as likely factors for why the person has tested positive, and the report goes on to recommend dietary changes as the best treatment.

The American Academy of Sleep Medicine, as reported on *aasm.org* in 2018, estimates that more than one in four adults have sleep apnea, and they report that this is increasing yearly due to the rise in obesity. A FAIR Health study, reported in March 2018 issue of *Sleep Review*, found that from 2014 to 2017, insurance claims for sleep apnea treatment rose 850% nationwide and 911% in rural areas. It's not surprising that 74% of patients were between the ages of 41 and 70 (the age when we get overweight and flabby).

Sleep centers are popping up in every city as doctors are recommending sleep studies about as often as they order urinalyses. I won't be surprised if we someday find out the whole sleep apnea thing is a hoax, a way for sleep study centers and medical equipment supply companies to get rich on selling CPAPs (continuous positive airway pressure machines) and BPAPs (bilevel positive airway pressure machines). How many of our forefathers died from sleep apnea or were 50% disabled by some unexplained cause now discovered as sleep apnea?

For the military and veterans, the rate of sleep apnea diagnoses is rising even faster than in the general public, because their sleep studies are free!   Already, one in every 11 veterans drawing compensation is service-connected for sleep apnea! This bothers me and others because a grant of sleep apnea with CPAP warrants 50% disability even though there is no obvious evidence of any disability. Even if the claimant had hypersomnolence (daytime sleepiness) before, supposedly the CPAP is eliminating those symptoms, so where is the disability?

All the soldier has to do is get a sleep study while in service, or ask for it in service and get the test shortly after discharge, and he is set up for 50% disability for the rest of his life! Even though this condition is usually not disabling at all!   The VA won't grant myopia (weakened near vision) because it's an age-related condition corrected by reading glasses. Why does VA grant sleep apnea that is supposedly corrected by use of a CPAP?   If one uses his CPAP as prescribed he will supposedly get a good night's rest and will not have hypersomnolence the next day. The people with sleep apnea who are using their CPAPs each night are walking around at work and driving down the road like everyone else and you never know which ones have sleep apnea and which ones don't. How is this a disability? Even if it is a disability, it certainly does not warrant 50%, because it does not reduce the ability to work by 50 percent. It warrants no more than a 0%, or perhaps a 10% if you want to consider the nuisance of having to be treated by CPAP.

But over and above all that, what does this condition have to do with military service? Nothing! This person would have been diagnosed regardless of whether he ever spent a day in service. Nothing that happened to him in service could possibly have caused his sleep apnea. When a person gets old, everything gets flabby. One thing that gets flabby is the tissue in the back of the throat; therefore, the older you get the more likely you will develop sleep apnea and snoring. Overweightness is the major risk factor in development of sleep apnea, and often if a person loses a lot of weight, a subsequent sleep study will show the condition resolved.

So everyone in service is getting a sleep study done now, and the lucky ones will test positive for sleep apnea! Some won't be positive now because they're still young and non-flabby, but the complaint is in their military record now so when they do test positive 20 years from now, they'll just reopen the claim and say, "see, I had the symptoms in service." If they don't get the sleep study done in service, they'll claim it within a year of discharge and get the sleep study from the VA. The VA examiners are especially generous on diagnosing sleep apnea even when the study report shows little or no apneas. Many soldiers have had a negative sleep study in the private sector (before the military started doing them a few years ago) but they now go to the VA and get another one done, and if there is only one tiny hypopnea on the test, the VA examiner will diagnose sleep apnea. A private physician with the same results would have said there is no diagnosis. Some of the veterans go again for another sleep study every couple of years until they finally get a diagnosis. This is expensive, and you and I are paying for it.

So what if the sleep apnea symptoms did first start in service, the snoring and gasping for breath at night; the condition still was not *caused by* military service. The law should be changed so that it is never granted. Or if you must grant it just so that the veteran can get free CPAPs, then grant it at 0%. Just reducing evaluations for this one condition would save the government (us taxpayers) over $2 billion per year, and that's not even counting the cost of sleep studies and C-CRAPs, I mean CPAPs.

Many claims for sleep apnea are coming in from people who have been out of service many years and just now getting diagnosed (because they are old and fat now).   These are initially denied because the condition was not shown in service.   However, the new trick is to claim sleep apnea "secondary" to any other service-connected condition they may have.   The most common one is to claim sleep apnea secondary to PTSD, since practically every veteran who submits any claim has been granted PTSD.

Time after time the VA wastes my tax dollars on obtaining a *competent* medical opinion that explains the following regarding PTSD. *"Sleep apnea is characterized by recurrent collapse of the velopharyngeal and/or oropharyngeal airway during sleep, resulting in substantially reduced or complete cessation of air flow despite ongoing breathing efforts.   This pathophysiologic mechanism is unrelated to the pathophysiologic mechanism of PTSD.   Although many individuals have both PTSD and sleep apnea, there is no causative relationship between the two."*   Still the VA will not issue just a simple ruling that there is no relation between PTSD and sleep apnea.   Therefore, every time someone claims it, we have to pay for the medical opinion all over again. Waste of tax dollars, waste of doctor's time, waste of VA employees' time.

The funny thing is that occasionally some idiot doctor will actually say, "Yes, the sleep apnea *is* likely secondary to PTSD" with no logical rationale, and one old veteran gets granted. It has to be granted if the doctor says so!   As a result, many veterans who were denied for sleep apnea have come back in on Appeal citing one of the rare cases where it was granted as secondary to PTSD.

Therefore, the Board of Veterans Appeals is currently dealing with this nightmare rather frequently.

The veterans come up with all sorts of causes for their sleep apnea and many of them think it is the same thing as insomnia or sleep deprivation. Many claim it occurred because they had to pull night shifts in the military and often didn't get enough sleep day or night, and many say they didn't get enough sleep because they had to remain constantly alert during their deployments. Lack of or limitation of sleep has nothing to do with sleep apnea! There is also a current flood of claims for sleep apnea "caused by Gulf War exposures" because VA has added "undiagnosed respiratory illness" as something to look for in Gulf War exposure claims. Fortunately, sleep apnea is a diagnosed illness so most doctors when asked to relate it to the Gulf War are giving a negative opinion because there is no undiagnosed illness here.

In 2012, one brave government official raised the issue of potential "fraudulent" sleep apnea claims to the House Veterans Affairs Committee, based on the significant increase in sleep apnea grants, and the high evaluations being granted for no obvious disability. That prompted a review and the VA "tightened" the sleep apnea regulations in 2016. But the only change was to stress that the evidence must show a breathing treatment device (CPAP or BPAP) is required in order to grant the 50% evaluation. The change changed nothing! Raters were already required to verify that a CPAP or BPAP had been issued. Big waste of time.

The VA criteria for granting sleep apnea needs to be more tightly defined. Normal blood oxygen levels are 95-100, and hypoxemia by definition is below 90%. An apnea is when one actually stops breathing, and a hypopnea is an event of "reduced" breathing, very shallow breathing, or a low respiratory rate. I'm not convinced that shallow breathing is a bad thing when sleeping comfortably; the person breathing gently certainly looks more peaceful than one breathing heavily. Anyway most VA sleep studies are showing no apneas at all, just a few hypopneas. With as few as five hypopneas an hour, the VA will diagnose sleep apnea and prescribe a CPAP, and that will entitle the veteran to 50% disability.

It is worth noting that the Social Security Administration (SSA listing 3.10) does not even consider sleep apnea as a disability unless the claimant's test shows he has a mean pulmonary artery pressure greater than 40 mm Hg, arterial hypoxemia with required arterial blood gas values, significantly decreased FEV1 or FVC values, or chronic impairment of gas exchange due to clinically documented pulmonary disease with decreased single breath DLCO values or decreased arterial blood gas values as required. These are the things that would warrant *100%* disability per the VA schedule, but I never saw such a bad case of sleep apnea in any VA record.

What I have seen far too much is VA granting sleep apnea based simply on any poorly supported diagnosis. Sometimes a CPAP is not even prescribed because the symptoms are so slight, and even that will get a 30% evaluation. But generally the veterans will demand a CPAP because they know that will get them 50%. It also doesn't matter if the subject refuses to wear/use the CPAP. Just like medication, if it is prescribed, an appropriate evaluation is given just as if he is using it.

***

Veteran X has been diagnosed with "mild obstructive sleep apnea" for which he will get 50% disability compensation. His sleep study shows that 0 of his recording time was spent at arterial oxygen saturations of less than 90% SaO2. Periodic limb movements were 0 with and index of 0. The electrocardiogram demonstrated sinus rhythm. In supporting the diagnosis there were no apneas or hypopneas mentioned. Based on the sleep study findings reported, there should be no diagnosis, and yet the doctor diagnosed sleep apnea. But a rater is not a physician and cannot dispute a doctor's diagnosis.

***

Veteran X is another veteran whose sleep study showed no sleep apnea but showed he had difficulty getting to sleep. So the doctor diagnosed "insomnia," a mental condition which has nothing to do with sleep apnea. The "symptoms" were claimed during service, so insomnia was granted, even though this is totally subjective and frivolous, and not necessarily a chronic condition. Difficulty falling asleep during a sleep study is totally normal because you are in a strange room with dozens of probes all over your body and an extremely tight band around your chest to hold the wires in place, and you're being watched. Diagnosing insomnia in this setting is preposterous.

***

Veteran X says he's had trouble sleeping for three years. He says he's not sleepy during the daytime, he does not nap, but he just doesn't get enough sleep because he goes to bed at midnight and gets up at 5 am. His sleep study showed: Sleep efficiency was 92.8%. Sleep latency was 7.5 minutes. Wave sleep was 27 minutes. REM sleep was 74 minutes. Snoring was noted. There were 0 obstructive apneas and a total of 26 obstructive hypopneas all night for an overall apnea/hypopnea index of 5 events per hour. There was 1 central apnea and 0 central hypopneas. Respiratory events were typically associated with arousals from sleep. This *barely* meets the criteria for "mild" sleep apnea, diagnosed when there are 5-10 apneas or hypopneas per hour. The fact there are no daytime symptoms (no impairment) should also be considered when giving this diagnosis, and paying this veteran, but that's not happening.

***

Veteran X files a claim right after discharge so he gets a full general medical exam. He claims back and neck problems, radiculopathy, migraines, carpal tunnel, heart condition, respiratory condition, digestive condition, foot problems and knee problems. There was absolutely nothing found on the exam, no diagnosis of anything except sleep apnea, which was granted because he had a sleep study before discharge. He has no apparent symptoms of it, but he gets 50% disability, for life. No functional occupational or social impairment.

TRAUMATIC BRAIN INJURY (TBI)

A traumatic brain injury (TBI) results when the head is struck by an object, or the head strikes an object, or the head is affected by a nearby blast or explosion. Most TBI's happen to toddlers (learning to walk, falling, pulling something onto their head) and teenagers (sports, driving, fighting), people who abuse drugs and alcohol (falling, fighting), and elderly people (falling). For these injuries in the private sector the patients almost always fully recover and have no symptoms later in life. The third cause of TBI, being close to an explosion, is most often experienced by servicemen in combat in Iraq and Afghanistan. It's the latest and greatest thing on a long list of conditions all Iraq and Afghanistan veterans feel they are obligated to claim, regardless of documented injury or symptoms, and for them, the symptoms reportedly just get worse, never better.

Traumatic Brain Injury (TBI) is the injury event itself, not a diagnosis or disorder or symptom. The severity of a TBI injury is determined immediately after the event based on the length of loss of consciousness, length of memory loss or disorientation, and how responsive the patient was after the injury. Although you can read this on the VA website, VA raters are not trained this way, and compensation is not assigned this way. A severe TBI injury, or one with unconsciousness, disorientation, or impaired responsiveness will be treated immediately, will go in the soldier's records immediately, and he will likely be shipped to Walter Reed for further studies and evaluation. The claim will be "case managed," flagged as special and processed expeditiously.

Medical literature says that TBI will never get worse with time. If symptoms were not shown on the initial examinations right after the injury, they will not develop later. Symptoms reported 5 to 10 years later are *not* likely due to a TBI in service. Yet VA continues to grant "TBI" to veterans claiming subjective symptoms first claimed many years after serving in Southeast Asia. There'll be no report in the claimant's records of any blast exposure or injury in service but VA will concede it just because he was there and it *could* have happened. Typically, if a blast happens near a soldier and it knocks him to the ground, even if he didn't lose consciousness, he'll be checked out by the field medic and this goes in his record. Even those who actually did get checked out in service, at the most suffered a "mild" TBI, because there was no unconsciousness or disorientation. Per medical literature, *mild* TBI's improve, heal, and do not cause chronic life-long symptoms. But most TBI claimants never had a scratch and were not knocked to the ground. In fact, they thought nothing about the incident at the time. Years later someone tells them if they were in Iraq they should claim TBI, so they do, and they report that they were near blasts.

Medical literature also says that a TBI condition will *not* worsen later. Not that it probably won't or usually won't, but that it just *will not*. Yet in case after case of TBI claims, VA granted 40% in 2008, then increased it to 70% in 2012, then increased it to 100% in 2017. Why? Because the veteran learned the tricks. He learned what to say on exam, and if the examiner checks the boxes, the rater must assign the increased evaluation with no question.

* * *

Veteran X claims he was near an explosion in Iraq, and there's no evidence in his medical records, but the personnel file shows he was in Iraq where it *could have* happened, so he has been granted PTSD and TBI based on all purely subjective symptoms, and he has a total evaluation of 90%. The only symptom he claimed was memory loss, says he often forgets where he is (spatial deficits facet of the TBI template), but the examiner completed the exam template to show deficiencies in every single facet of TBI except consciousness; he is admittedly conscious. He works full time as a security guard in a federal facility. Should he really be allowed to be serving in this capacity considering his alleged condition? He's conscious, but other than that, the report shows he's a walking mental wreck, 90% disabled.

* * *

Veteran X was hit in the head with a baseball while in service. He wasn't on any kind of Army team or anything, just having fun on the weekend. He has no symptoms to indicate there was any damage done but he is claiming service connection for it.   VA considers this in the line of duty and will grant.

***

Veteran X is 25 years old.   Immediately after discharge he had a police academy exam done which found he was in perfect health, no deficiencies noted, and he was accepted into the police academy. Within a few months he submitted a VA claim for multiple joint conditions: shoulders, knees, ankles, and since he was within a year after discharge he was given a full general medical exam. The only thing found on the VA exam was bilateral shoulder pain, 10% disability for each shoulder, and lumbar spine condition 0% disabling, totaling 20% disability.

A year later, being not happy with 20%, he came back in with another claim, this time for PTSD and TBI.   He says he believes he has TBI due to exposure to explosions in service.   During his first year after service he had been to the VA medical center and had all sorts of screenings and assessment, none of them reporting any mental problems or TBI symptoms. The VA records clearly show "no depression", "no sleep problems," and no evidence of any impairment on cognitive testing.   But since he was stationed in an area where he could have *potentially* been exposed to explosions, VA gave him a TBI exam, and based on his subjective complaints the examiner diagnosed TBI and he was granted 40%.

The next year, after reading the rating criteria which the VA provided him, he came back in for an increase, and after complaining more diligently on the increase exam, he was increased to 70% for his alleged TBI.

This is disgraceful, disrespectful and humiliating to the soldiers being treated at Walter Reed for true TBI, suffering real head scars, memory loss and cognitive impairment, besides PTSD from coming so close to death in the explosion, soldiers who may never be able to function normally in society again.   When TBI happens, it happens immediately upon impact of the explosion. It knocks the person out, and they are gathered up on a stretcher and medevac'd

292

out to Walter Reed.   Yes, there are football players who had so many minor concussions that they now have a diagnosis of TBI, and they didn't know it for years.   But when you're in battle and you have a concussion from an explosion you know it!   You don't come down with it two years later, or 30 years later.

HEADACHES

Headaches are not migraines, and the Rating Schedule only provides compensation for "migraines" but that doesn't stop VA from granting headaches. Headache is a common symptom of colds, flu and many other acute illnesses. It is a totally subjective symptom that cannot be confirmed by any test. Compensation is supposedly allowed only for *chronic* illnesses, not acute illnesses. Nevertheless, thousands of veterans are receiving compensation for "headaches."   Totally subjective, rarely documented, acute headaches.   Ten percent wouldn't be any worse than giving 10% for subjective tinnitus; but no, VA gives much more. These ordinary acute headaches, lacking any diagnostic code or criteria of their own because they're not chronic diseases, are being evaluated based on *migraine* criteria, and that is totally wrong in my opinion. Even veterans with true migraines are also being grossly over-compensated.

Migraine is a serious illness that *can* cause social and occupational impairment, and it is a condition that can be objectively verified by brain scans and should only be diagnosed when such a brain scan has been done. The VA rating procedural manual, MR21-1, says that "medical evidence is required to establish that the reported symptoms are due to *migraine* headaches," but nevermind that. The manual also says "evaluations depend primarily on the frequency of attacks and the degree to which symptoms are prostrating. The extent to which the headaches cause work impairment is also a factor and is considered for the 50-percent evaluation." The manual says, *"Prostrating,* as used in 38 CFR 4.124a, DC 8100, means 'causing extreme exhaustion, powerlessness, debilitation or incapacitation with substantial inability to engage in ordinary activities. *Completely prostrating* as used in 38 CFR 4.124a, DC 8100, means extreme exhaustion or powerlessness with *essentially total* inability to engage in ordinary activities.'" The manual says that the "frequency" must be a "factual determination," supported by such evidence as medical progress notes or incident journals kept by the claimant. The claimant's subjective report of frequency *can* be accepted "as long as those symptoms have been competently identified as symptoms of *migraine* headaches" So if the claimant simply has a log of headaches, and the headaches have only been diagnosed as "tension headaches" this frequency should not be used to support a 50% disability!

The regulation allows 10% disability if a prostrating migraine attack occurs only *once every 2 months*! It allows 30% if a prostrating attack occurs once a month, and 50% is applicable for "very frequent completely prostrating and prolonged attacks productive of severe economic inadaptability."

"Prostrating" according to Webster means that you are "stretched out with face on the ground" or "lying flat." In other words, the pain of the headache is so severe that the only way to deal with it is to lie flat. The regulation is clear that no compensable evaluation should be assigned unless the evidence shows "prostrating attacks" and yet that is *not* how raters are instructed to rate. They are instructed to assign high evaluations based on DBQs showing very frequent headaches.

The first problem is there is no documentation available or required to show that the person has ever had a "prostrating" attack, such that he had to lie down in a dark room. And secondly, it doesn't matter. Raters are told to give the 10, or 30, or 50% for any headaches, based on the number of headaches the person is reporting. A headache is a headache, and since it's not in the regulation, it has to be rated "analogous to" migraines.

Commonly a claimant explains that his headaches last a few minutes and resolve with Tylenol. He says nothing about needing to lay down or having any of the other symptoms which accompany true migraines, such as vomiting or vision problems. But this must be ignored by the rater. If the examiner indicates on the DBQ that the claimant reports having *very frequent* headaches, the evaluation builder will generate a 50% disability evaluation. A rater can take the time to drop this to 30% by adding an explanation that there is no "economic inadaptability" shown, but the "best" being the "fastest" raters will never do that.

I've seen a few cases of true migraine disability, a condition that actually affected the claimant's attendance at work. The condition can be legitimate, but the vast majority of claimants being granted for this have never really had a single migraine headache. If they do have real migraines, shouldn't we look at whether this was really caused by battle or other military activity, or just genetic?

The most preposterous thing is that even if the examiner diagnoses the condition as "tension headaches" it still gets granted the same way! That is just not what the regulation very clearly intended!   The regulation even explains in footnotes that when headaches are a subjective symptom of such conditions as traumatic brain injury or cerebral arteriosclerosis, that no more than 10% will be assigned for the headaches. So how can VA go on granting 30% and 50% for common subjective headaches?

JOINTS, FUNCTIONAL LOSS, & PAINFUL MOTION

The VA regulations say that disability compensation is to be paid commensurate to functional loss. When it comes to joints, VA has chosen to equate a subjective complaint of pain as a functional loss, when there is no actual evidence of any injury or residual disability. This is wrong. Millions of dollars are being paid out based on 10% disabilities for various joints, major joints and minor joint groups. The major joints are shoulder, elbow, wrist, hip, knee, and ankle. Minor joint groups are cervical spine, thoracolumbar spine, hands, and feet. Some veterans list every single joint and joint group on their claim, despite there being no record of any injury in service. Many veterans are receiving 10% for each of multiple joints or joint groups, totaling as much as 90% with no record of any injury and no objective evidence of any true chronic disability. And for conditions rated 10% there is no requirement for a future exam to see if the condition ever improves, even if the current exam looks a little fishy with no objective evidence.

For any joint or joint group, 10% disability will be assigned to a veteran by his simple statement of "pain" even if there is no record of any injury and no objective evidence of any damage, infection, or painful motion. Objective evidence would be something seen by a physician during the exam (such as limited motion on the range of motion testing or abnormal gait or a wincing of pain when the joint is moved) or objective evidence could be findings on an x-ray, MRI, or other test. The regulations are as follows.

> "38 CFR 4.40, Functional Loss. *Disability of the musculoskeletal system* is primarily the *inability, due to damage or infection* in parts of the system, *to perform the normal working movements* of the body with normal excursion, strength, speed, coordination and endurance. It is essential that the examination on which ratings are based adequately portray *the anatomical damage, and the functional loss*, with respect to all these elements. The functional loss may be due to absence of part, or all,

of the necessary bones, joints and muscles, or associated structures, or to deformity, adhesions, defective innervation, or other pathology, or *it may be due to pain, supported by adequate pathology and evidenced by the visible behavior* of the claimant undertaking the motion. Weakness is as important as limitation of motion, and a part which becomes painful on use must be regarded as seriously disabled. A little used part of the musculoskeletal system may be expected to show evidence of disuse, either through atrophy, the condition of the skin, absence of normal callosity or the like."

"38 CFR 4.45, The Joints. As regards the joints the factors of disability reside in reductions of their normal excursion of movements in different planes. Inquiry will be directed to these considerations:

(a) Less movement than normal (due to ankylosis, limitation or blocking, adhesions, tendon-tie-up, contracted scars, etc.).

(b) More movement than normal (from flail joint, resections, nonunion of fracture, relaxation of ligaments, etc.).

(c) Weakened movement (due to muscle injury, disease or injury of peripheral nerves, divided or lengthened tendons, etc.).

(d) Excess fatigability.

(e) Incoordination, impaired ability to execute skilled movements smoothly.

(f) Pain on movement, swelling, deformity or atrophy of disuse. Instability of station, disturbance of locomotion, interference with sitting, standing and weight-bearing are related considerations. For the purpose of rating disability from arthritis, the shoulder, elbow, wrist, hip, knee, and ankle are considered major joints; multiple involvements of the interphalangeal, metacarpal and carpal joints of the upper extremities, the interphalangeal, metatarsal and tarsal joints of the lower extremities, the cervical vertebrae, the dorsal vertebrae, and the lumbar vertebrae, are considered groups of minor joints, ratable on a parity with major joints. The lumbosacral articulation and both sacroiliac joints are considered to be a group of minor joints, ratable on disturbance of lumbar spine functions."

"38 CRF 4.59, Painful motion. With any form of *arthritis*, painful motion is an important factor of disability, the facial expression, wincing, etc., on pressure or manipulation, should be carefully noted and definitely related to affected joints. Muscle spasm will greatly assist the identification. Sciatic neuritis is not uncommonly caused by arthritis of the spine. *The intent of the schedule is to recognize painful motion **with** joint or periarticular **pathology** as productive of disability.* It is the intention to recognize actually painful, unstable, or malaligned joints, *due to healed injury*, as entitled to at least the minimum compensable rating for the joint. Crepitation either in the soft tissues such as the tendons or ligaments, or crepitation within the joint structures should be noted carefully as points of contact which are diseased. Flexion elicits such manifestations. The joints involved should be tested for pain on both active and passive motion, in weight-bearing and nonweight-bearing and, if possible, with the range of the opposite undamaged joint."

These regulations do say that painful motion is an important factor of disability, but also clearly say that the painful motion should be *carefully noted* and *definitely related to the affected joints*. It also says that the intent is to recognize painful motion *"with joint or periarticular pathology"* as disability. This means first you need to have a pathology, then if there's evident painful motion clearly related to that pathology, it is a disability. But the current VA interpretation uses the *subjective* complaint of pain *as the pathology*, when there is no evidence of any pathology.

Time and again a VA examiner states that *subjective* pain (not *objective*) was shown on exam but *"it does not result in or cause functional loss."* Right there on the exam, clear as day, NO functional loss. Such cases should be granted as 0%, but no, they are granted as 10% due to VA interpreting things any way they can to grant more, more, more.

Even though the examiner has reported no evidence of painful motion and no limitation of motion, a 10% evaluation is still assigned for each joint, based on the current *interpretation* of 38 CFR 4.59, as clarified in the claims processors' working manual, M21-1MR. Not only is the law interpreted too loosely, these examples given in the manual also demonstrate how the various sections of law are contradictory, so the VA just goes with whatever is more favorable to the veteran. The VA procedures manual gives the following examples.

> (From M21-1MR) "The following are examples of considering a minimum compensable evaluation under 38 CFR 4.59:
>
> Example 5: On examination, a claimant reports current symptoms of regular pain of the right knee (particularly when fully (straightening the knee) that is worsened with increased activity. The examiner finds normal ROM (range of motion) without pain on examination. Repetitive motion testing produces no evidence of pain or loss of motion. The assessment is right knee strain. Assign a 10-percent evaluation under 38 CFR 4.71a, DC 5261. The claimant's reports of joint pain are found to be credible. There is no basis to reject the complaints of pain as lacking in credibility. 38 CFR 4.59 does not require objective evidence of painful motion. The claimant's statement establishes that there is actually painful motion of the joint, even though it was not objectively verified on VA examination.

> Example 6: On examination, a claimant reports constant pain of the left elbow (particularly when bending the arm). The examiner finds normal ROM without pain on examination. Repetitive motion testing produces no evidence of pain or loss of motion. There is no swelling or spasm. The assessment is degenerative arthritis of the left elbow corroborated by x-rays. Assign a 10-percent evaluation under 38 CFR 4.71a, DC 5003-5206. The claimant's reports of joint pain are found to be credible. There is no basis to reject the complaints of pain as lacking in credibility. Although 38 CFR 4.71a, DC 5003 requires noncompensable LOM (limitation of motion) and objective confirmation of LOM by spasm, swelling, or satisfactory evidence of painful motion, 38 CFR 4.59 provides an alternative basis for a compensable evaluation and does not require objective evidence of painful motion. The claimant's statement establishes that there is actually painful motion of the joint, even though pain was not objectively verified on VA examination."

If you look at old rating decisions from the 1980's or earlier you'll see that joint conditions were rated with some common sense back then and were often denied. If the claimant had a back strain or a knee strain during service in the 60's or 70's, then later claimed osteoarthritis/DDD (degenerative disc disease) which manifested in the 80's, this would *not* be granted. If he had no problem with the knee or back through all his working years, but then developed osteoarthritis after he was 60 years old, then this condition was attributed to aging and was not granted secondary. Now, medical opinions are received in all such cases, and the examiner almost always says, YES, it is at least as likely as not that the current condition was incurred in service. In a few exceptional cases I've seen an examiner say NO, because osteoarthritis is an age-related condition and there are no medical studies showing it results from strains that occurred many years earlier in life. The regulations need to be changed to incorporate this medical opinion as VA guidance, so as to save the trouble and cost of millions of medical opinions.

In addition to the abuse of the system by "joint pain" complaints, joints also lend easily to other forms of fraud.

Many veterans seem to be getting knee replacements simply so that they can get 100% compensation for 13 months. I say this because they are often only 10% disabled (for a knee condition) when they *request* surgery from their orthopedist. Often the doctor will not do the replacement the veteran requests but will agree to cortisone shots or less invasive (and less compensable) arthroscopic surgery. These minor procedures do not warrant more than two or three months of convalescence, but often it will be dragged out to six or nine months, just because it takes VA that long to pull the case again and obtain a follow-up exam. Then within a year or two the claimant is again requesting a total knee replacement.

A common way veterans try and succeed in increasing their overall compensation through joint conditions that were not present in service, is by claiming them as "secondary to" or resulted from other service-connected joint conditions. It is common to claim one knee secondary to the other, or one ankle secondary to the other, or a leg condition secondary to a back condition.

The doctors will often opine that one condition resulted from the other even though there is no supporting evidence or medical literature, and even though the doctor has not read (or acknowledged) the records which show the veteran has had other recent injuries or intercurrent cause for the newly developed conditions.

Very rarely but sometimes a doctor will provide a logically supported medical opinion that says he finds no association between the two joint conditions, and he will quote supporting medical literature. For example, *"A study at the University of Toronto showed no relation of one knee joint causing another corresponding joint issue **unless**: (1) There is prolonged altered gait due to the* *first leg problem. This would be from some sort of permanent condition such as a steel rod in the leg, or a leg that cannot move the knee at all forever. It would not typically result from an ACL or meniscal tear or from patellofemoral joint syndrome because these conditions heal before an altered gait develops. (2) If one leg is shorter than the other then this will put undue pressure on the other leg."* If you pull a hundred files where one knee was granted secondary to the other, you are not likely to see one of these two scenarios. What you will see is positive opinions based on nothing.

***

Veteran X claimed bilateral ankles, bilateral knees, and bilateral shoulders. He says it all started in basic training in 2006. His service treatment records show no injuries and never a complaint of any joint problem, pain or otherwise. In 2016 he filed a pre-discharge claim which means he was still in service when he filed it, and the VA exam was also conducted while he was still in service, so this claim document became his evidence (and only evidence) of a complaint of the conditions *during* service, and the VA exam became his medical evidence of the condition in service. The VA examiner diagnosed strains and sprains of all claimed joints. When there is nothing on X-ray and no limitation of motion, and no objective evidence of a problem, but only complaints of "pain," the examiner will diagnose "strain" or "sprain." Thousands of these are granted every day when in fact, if they exist at all, they are "acute" conditions, not chronic disabilities subject to service connection. This veteran worked in the military for 10 years after the alleged sprains/strains occurred in basic training, so where is the functional impairment?

***

Veteran X had 5 minor surgeries on his left knee. After the first surgery he received 100% for 6 months, after the 2nd surgery another 100% for 6 months, after the 3rd he got 9 months. Obviously, the surgeries were destroying the knee, at least he kept claiming that it was worse each time. He finally got his total knee replacement,

100% for 13 months, and after that an automatic 30% was assigned for life, or until he figures out that if he reports severe symptoms still exist, then he will get 60% for the knee forever.

***

Veteran X served two months in basic training in 1992 before being discharged with an "uncharacterized" discharge. He never went to AIT (advanced individual training) to learn an MOS (military occupational specialty). He injured his right knee during basic training, just a minor injury, common to many in basic training, and that was not the reason he was put out of service. He was granted service-connection for it anyway. Fourteen years later he claimed the left knee secondary to the right knee. The evidence shows he injured the right knee in 2004 while working at Macy's, had required meniscal tear surgery, and had received payments through a workers' compensation claim. When that expired, he filed with the VA and the VA granted the right knee secondary to the left knee, so taxpayers will pay this cheater for the rest of his life.

***

Veteran X had a minor left wrist injury in service in 1972, no fracture. He now, more than 40 years later, has arthritis and tendonitis of the wrist. The VA medical opinion says the left wrist is as likely as not a progression of the condition that started in service. The same exam shows that the right wrist has exactly the same diagnosis and findings of arthritis and tendonitis. There was never a right wrist complaint in service. Only the left is granted service-connection, but neither should be!

***

Veteran X fell off a bicycle during service and injured his left shoulder, so he has been granted service-connection. Since discharge he has had 2 surgeries and was paid temporary 100% for convalescence for 3 months each time. He staggered the surgeries so that the 100% periods would be back-to-back rather than overlapping. On the new post-surgery exam, he reports that he still cannot lift his arm above his head so he continues to get the 20% disability for each shoulder. Odd how VA surgery never seems to improve any service-connected condition.

***

Veteran X has been service-connected for a right knee condition since service. He is now undergoing a total right knee replacement. The VA will pay him 100% compensation disability for 13 months from the date of the surgery.   Not only will he be back to work within 6 months, but even during those 6 months that he is out of work he is actually still getting his full normal pay, because as a federal employee he has accrued thousands of hours of sick leave just for this purpose, and he'll be using sick leave. The whole purpose of the "100% temporary evaluation" for convalescence is because the person is presumed unable to work during that time. For any regular surgery, the temporary 100% is only paid as long as the veteran is unable to work. If the doctor says he can go back to work after 2 months, then the temporary 100% is paid for 2 months (actually rounded up to 3 months).   Why should the federal government pay a salary *and* a duplicative 100% for convalescence during the same period?   Just another example of double-dipping, and in the case of military retirees, triple-dipping.

BACK CONDITIONS

Everything in the prior section on Joint Conditions applies to back conditions, but back conditions are the most often claimed and most abused joint issue, only behind hearing loss, tinnitus and PTSD. The fraud results because almost everyone will have a little back pain once in a while after overexerting or heavy lifting, and especially in activity such as military training. It's called an acute back strain or sprain. No abnormality seen on X-rays. The symptoms resolve within a few hours, days, or weeks and there is no further complaint or treatment shown in the military records or on the military separation exam.

Many years later, the claimant uses a reference from his military records to show a back condition was treated in service. Then the claimant shows that he had another back sprain or other back condition many years later after service, and the VA requests a medical opinion as to whether it is a continuance of the in-service condition. Almost inevitably the examiner will say yes it is at least as likely as not that it's the same condition. Well I beg to differ. It is the same back, and the same diagnosis (strain), but the latter manifestation is a new injury, new strain, probably due to deconditioning.

The issue will start out being granted and rated at 10% based on subjective pain only (as explained in the prior chapter). The exam shows no limitation of motion, no swelling, no altered gait. Later the veteran will file an increase, will pretend on exam that he can only bend over half way, and his evaluation will be raised to 20%. Later with more exaggerated symptoms he'll be increased to 40%, even if there's still nothing shown on X-ray or MRI.

This is wrong. An in-service strain/sprain is merely subjective anyway with no evidence of any fracture or ruptured disc. IF he does have an after-service condition, then it clearly is a new condition, and it's usually just another subjective strain also. It can often be directly related to the type of work the claimant is currently performing. Often he will report that he was lifting a heavy box, or helping move furniture, or he slipped on the sidewalk, and that same condition from service recurred! Well no, it's a new injury and should not be granted. But VA will grant.

Once a strain has been granted, more serious back issues in the future will continue to be service-connected as a complication of the prior strain, when actually they're not. The VA will just change the name of the condition from strain/sprain to degenerative disc disease or osteoarthritis and increase the rating.

In the past, back strains and sprains were denied because they are "acute" conditions and VA service connection is reserved for "chronic" conditions. Here's an example of how conditions were rated (denied) in the 1960's, even with a defect shown on x-ray.

"Residuals of the back injury diagnosed in service as lumbosacral contusion and low back strain left no permanent residuals at the time of discharge from service and none were found on the current VA examination. The condition therefore is rated as acute and transitory. The x-ray findings suggestive of a posterior arch defect in L-5 are indicative of a developmental abnormality."

On the rating code sheet, the issue was noted as, *"0000 – posterior arch defect L-5 (by x-ray), constitutional or developmental abnormality, not a disability under the law. Residuals of low back injury, contusion and/or residuals of low back strain, not shown on last examination at discharge from service or on the current VA examination."*

Somehow, over the years since that rating, the whole system has become lenient and lax. If a person had the slightest one-time back complaint in service, and there is anything seen on a current X-ray or even a comment noted on the exam, or subjective report of pain by the veteran, he *will* be granted for that condition. No logic required. Then as years go by the claimant will begin to report pain or numbness in his lower extremities and this will be granted as radiculopathy secondary to the back condition. It's not uncommon to see a simple back strain in service turn into a 60% disability at age 70, that would be 40% for the back and 20% for radiculopathy of each leg. And this being all one related condition would qualify for IU, 100% compensation.

On an extremely rare occasion a medical examiner will opine that the older-age condition is *not* related to the in-service strain. This should be the rule.

"The Veteran does have clinical findings that show evidence of bilateral lower extremity radiculopathy. Based on this examiner's review of current peer-reviewed literature along with a Cochrane Database Systemic Review, this examiner could not find any literature that reports any objective evidence that lumbar strain alone leads to lumbar disc herniation, lumbar degenerative disc disease, or lumbar radiculopathy. However, the veteran's back conditions of lumbar disc herniation and facet arthritis associated with neuroforaminal narrowing can cause bilateral lower extremity radiculopathy. Therefore, in regards to the requested medical opinion, veteran's bilateral lower extremity radiculopathy is less likely than not (less than 50 percent probability) proximately due to or the result of the Veteran's service-connected condition of thoracolumbar spine strain."

This same type of unwarranted service-connection is granted on thousands of claims every day for every different major joint or minor joint group of the body. I won't write a chapter on every joint; they're all the same. A minor sprain or strain occurs in service and it later gets linked to any and everything that ever happens to that body part for the rest of the veteran's life. That is fraud and misuse of government funds, allowed, encouraged, and perpetrated by the VA.

FOOT CONDITIONS

The most common foot condition claimed is Pes Planus, otherwise known as "flat feet." Pes planus is usually a congenital condition (you're born with it) and is not disabling unless it causes symptoms. The front page of every military entrance exam has a box where the examiner indicates pes planus (flat feet) or not, and if so, indicates the condition as "asymptomatic" meaning normal, no problem. If it was symptomatic the person would not be allowed into service.

Many people have flat feet that have caused them *no* problems prior to service, and if they made it 18 years without problems, they probably won't have a problem in service unless there is some specific foot injury. In many cases the pre-existing condition is never mentioned again throughout their service treatment records or on their separation exam. But when it comes time to file that all-inclusive VA claim, it is noted by their POA that their service treatment records showed "pes planus" so that is picked up as a disability to claim!

The only time pes planus should be granted is when a veteran comes into service with normal arches (as would be shown on the first page of his military entrance exam) but then suffers "fallen arches" due to some strenuous incident or after wearing ill-fitting boots through a long march, and then is treated in service for this. In that case, I admit it does warrant service-connection because it was truly caused by a military service activity preparing for battle.

Not only is pes planus too often granted, it is grossly over-evaluated, and the same goes for plantar fasciitis or heel spurs which are evaluated by the same criteria. If an examiner only knew what evaluation VA is going to assign based on the little boxes he has checked on the Foot Condition DBQ I believe they would think twice. Often an examiner reports that there is no objective evidence of any problem. The gait is normal. There is no evidence of pain on use of the feet. There is no pronation and no characteristic calluses. But the examiner notes that the veteran answered yes to "extreme tenderness on bottom of both feet." The examiner is supposed to manipulate the feet in order to make this determination, but instead he just asks the veteran, "Are your feet tender on the bottom?" This is totally subjective and of course the claimant says "Yes." For a positive answer to this one question, the veteran will receive 50% disability.

Another common foot condition over-rated is Achilles tendonitis. It certainly deserves service-connection if it was due to injury in-the-line-of-duty. The problem is the regulations, DBQs, and evaluation builders do not clarify whether this should be treated as a foot or an ankle condition. As a result many veterans are granted two evaluations, one under a foot code and another under an ankle code (two different body parts is OK); however, it's wrong because it's all one condition and one symptom of pain, and it is not a foot or ankle joint condition, but a tendon condition! Tendons and muscles are never rated consistently because the muscle section of the rating schedule was written for evaluation of bullet wounds, something most raters will never see on a claim.

***

Veteran X was noted to have asymptomatic pes planus (flat feet – no symptoms) on his military entrance exam, but shortly into service he began to report problems with his feet as well as many other physical complaints. The military provided surgery to fix his pes planus, noted by the surgeons as a congenital condition he had prior to service. After surgery he complained even more and in less than a year he was honorably discharged due to a foot disability that prevented him from full performance of duties. After service the veteran moved back in with his parents and made a life of filing VA claims. By age 28 he had already filed 17 claims, each with multiple issues, and he was receiving 100% compensation.

PERIPHERAL NERVE CONDITIONS

The biggest error in granting nerve conditions is that the complaint is simply "pain" in the extremity and it's probably not a nerve condition. An examiner must diagnose the pain as either a joint, muscle, or a nerve problem, and usually it will be granted as a joint condition, especially if there's any reduction in range of motion, or objective pain on joint motion. But when the claimant specifies a nerve problem, then often he will be granted for both the joint and the nerves of that extremity.

There is rarely any ECG (nerve testing) done. Wrist complaints will frequently be diagnosed as "carpal tunnel syndrome" (median nerve impairment) without any nerve conduction study. All the nerves of one arm must be evaluated together, and that often adds up to 30%. A claimant can be given separate evaluations for the nerves of a leg. Even if the condition is not severe, just moderate, he can receive 20% for the femoral nerve impairment and 20% for the sciatic nerve, for a total of 40% for the leg all based on subjective pain, the same evaluation he would get if his foot had been amputated! What an insult to amputees!

Service-connection is too often granted for nerves as secondary to some other service-connected issue. If service-connection has already been granted for diabetes, then any complaint of nerve pain or numbness will be diagnosed and granted as diabetic peripheral neuropathy. If service connection has been granted for a lumbar spine condition, then lower extremity peripheral nerve complaints are granted as radiculopathy secondary to the lumbar spine. Complaints of the upper extremities will be granted secondary to any cervical spine condition. Radiculopathy is too often diagnosed and related to a cervical or thoracolumbar spine condition based on subjective complaints only even though the spine condition is only a "strain." When there is no X-ray or MRI evidence of any chronic spine condition, the spine is probably not really causing any complications, and certainly not long-term chronic radiculopathy. But once 10% is assigned for any extremity, it is not likely to ever be re-evaluated or reduced.

SKIN CONDITIONS

Skin conditions are frequently over-rated and I question whether most of them should not be considered congenital issues anyway, not subject to service-connection. Oily skin subject to acne, light unpigmented skin subject to sun damage, and sensitive skin subject to allergic allergies are congenital. Other skin problems such as venereal disease and nail fungus are more due to willful misconduct or poor hygiene, not due to military battle. I do agree that service connection may be warranted for a few skin conditions such as "jungle rot" from trudging through Vietnam rice paddies, or skin cancer from exposure to radiation, if these conditions manifested shortly after exposure in service, but you won't see these in the normal workload of claims. What you will see is claims for acne, ingrown toenails, actinic keratosis (sun spots), and PFB (pseudofolliculitis barbae, ingrown facial hairs).

Superficial acne should not be granted compensable unless it is affecting other parts of the body besides the face, and yet almost every time you see it granted you will see it was only on the face and was granted based on the percentage of the "exposed areas" noted by the doctor. "Deep acne" may be granted compensable but you will rarely see that diagnosis. A compensable evaluation may also be granted based on "disfigurement" for acne scars if the examiner fills out the DBQ to indicate scars.

The common acne claim is from a young 18- to 20-year-old who is having a little acne due to sweating in basic training or in the desert. Perfectly normal for age and conditions. It is not a chronic condition and there are no life-long scars. The condition should not be granted. If 10% is granted it will most likely continue forever, long after the claimant outgrows the acne; future exams are not generally required for anything at the 10% level. When you have enough of similar acute conditions, 10% each, they add up quickly to develop a "disabled" veteran.

Many veterans are getting 60% disability for PFB (pseudofolliculitis barbae). This is a common condition that occurs in the beard area of the face when a black man shaves his curly beard. As the hairs grow back, if a hair ingrows into the skin it causes a pimple. If one shaves every day, the hairs don't get long enough to get the curl anyway. But once the condition does develop, the military issues a profile, or "shaving chit," which allows the soldier to grow a short beard rather than shaving. Then his pimples can be treated, the condition resolves, and he should not have the problem again if he refrains from shaving. Thousands of veterans are claiming this condition. Many of them never shaved again until after they got out of service, and since the condition had been present once in service, and is present now again, they are granted service-connection for this skin condition.

The skin regulation allows skin diseases to be evaluated based on the amount of area caused by skin problems. If any one condition, or any combination of multiple skin conditions, is affecting 40 percent of the whole body area, or is affecting 40 percent of "exposed" areas, then a 60% evaluation is applicable. Many veterans are getting 60% for PFB because it affects 40 percent of the exposed areas, but really it couldn't possibly be, because the entire beard does not cover 40% of all exposed areas. The whole PFB thing is absolutely ridiculous because the PFB is not affecting employability at all! The person only needs to wear a beard to eliminate the problem. The military is the only job in America that cares whether you wear a beard or not, and even they grant waivers for this condition!

A veteran cannot receive separate evaluations for his PFB, one based on skin disease and another based on the measure of scarred area. However, he can be granted 40% for his PFB and still receive an additional 30% for having 5 or more scars that are painful, and if one of more of those scars is elevated or depressed on palpation he can receive an additional 10% for that.

Many veterans have been granted 60% for tinea versicolor, a skin condition that was *not* caused by service although it may have started during the service years, and in any case it is *not* preventing him from working. The condition affects the trunk and extremities, usually not the face or any exposed body parts! It is a condition caused by a fungus that is present on most everyone, but it occasionally flares up into a problem on some people.

Go to any big-box-store and you will see employees with serious skin conditions, sometimes repulsive looking. Yet they have to work, because they are not veterans. These workers are providing security, stocking shelves, or interfacing with customers as cashiers, and the fact that they have a skin condition is not impairing their work. There are plenty of other employment opportunities for factory workers, construction workers, computer operators, and call center workers who do not even interface with the public. It is shameful that we are paying veterans to sit at home because of minor appearance issues not truly disabling them.

Meanwhile thousands of Americans are working while suffering from debilitating diseases such as hidradenitis suppurativa which could be treated except they can't afford the cost of over $5,000 for two pens of Humira! What if some of this $90 billion of compensation money per year, maybe just one or two billion of it, could be diverted to the working class who need help with their medical care…

RESPIRATORY CONDITIONS

There's very little reason for respiratory conditions to be attributed to military service, but thousands of veterans are granted for things like asthma and allergic rhinitis which were certainly not caused by service. Most issues are granted because the condition was incurred in service, meaning it was first diagnosed or first treated during service. I don't consider that a good enough reason because even if it did first start in service it was not caused by battle or by any required military duty, except for the rare condition of asbestosis. It is a fact that many Navy veterans have developed asbestosis from their duties of working around asbestos in the hulls of old Navy ships, and this is a legitimate claim that warrants compensation.

Most older veterans claiming respiratory conditions are claiming chronic obstructive pulmonary disorder (COPD) which is caused pure and simple by their smoking 3 packs a day for 30 years. COPD is also frequently diagnosed in conjunction with alcoholism and congestive heart failure.

The claims for asthma should not be granted because this is a congenital/developmental disorder. The records show for almost every claim of asthma, the veteran had a history of childhood seasonal hay fever and asthma, many even had several hospitalizations pre-service. And many were on medication up until entering service. But on entrance exam they do not report it and nothing is noted about it, so the new recruit is accepted as "whole" with no defects. Within a week of basic training he or she is at sick call being issued an inhaler, and they will keep the prescription going throughout their military service just in case they need it. Upon discharge, he or she will be granted service-connection for asthma, incurred in service. Such claims should be considered as fraud because the veteran clearly knows that the condition was not caused by military service. It was pre-existing. The entrance records were falsified and that should be punished the same as if he had falsified records of his age or high school diploma.

Another common finding is "exercise-induced asthma" which is not a chronic condition and should never be service-connected, but it is granted over and over. The diagnosis is given when the pulmonary function tests (PFTs) are perfectly normal. Such a condition is never seen on examination because the claimant is not exercising during the exam, and I never saw any physical test on a respiratory exam; it's all just subjective. The regulation says that for any asthma, "in the absence of clinical findings of asthma at time of examination, a verified history of asthmatic attacks must be of record." Time and again there is no documented (medical or lay) evidence of the claimant ever having had an attack, and yet they are assigned a ridiculous evaluation based on a ridiculous report of attacks.

Thousands of veterans are erroneously service connected for allergic rhinitis. I have never seen a case where a chronic disability resulted from being exposed to any allergen in service. The cases are granted because the claimants lie on entrance to service and don't admit having any allergies so they are accepted into the military as whole, and then the condition manifests itself during service whenever they get around certain grasses or animals or foods.

The VA regulation is very clear that service connected compensation is not warranted for allergies if symptoms subside when removed from the offensive allergen. The claims should be denied with a statement like "Allergic conditions are considered acute and transitory conditions. Seasonal and other acute allergic manifestations typically subside in the absence, or removal, of the stimulating allergen and resolve without residual disability. Therefore, service connection for allergic rhinitis is denied since this condition is considered acute and transitory in nature." Period.

Lung cancer is one of the many herbicide-presumptive conditions that will be granted without question to any veteran who stepped foot in Vietnam during the Vietnam War era. There will be no questioning about how much he has smoked, or where he has worked since service (coal mines or steel foundries), or whether his parents had the disease.

The latest and greatest respiratory claim is for "any undiagnosed respiratory condition" related to exposures in the Gulf

War, specifically exposures to burn pits or oil fires. This issue is discussed more in the Gulf War chapter, but the bottom line is that there is no evidence of any chronic respiratory condition being caused by exposure to burn pits or oil fires. It's all fraud.

***

Veteran X served three years on a ship from 1971 to 1973. He did not work down in the hull or in the engine room or boiler room, did not work on the pipes or electrical system, and did no painting or scraping or refurbishing of that ship. VA conceded his exposure to asbestos on the ship because all old Navy ships in those days had asbestos to insulate the pipes and electrical system, and sometimes had it in the flooring. Exposure should not be conceded unless the veteran's MOS or general ship duties required him to get his face and hands into asbestos covered areas such as the boiler room and engine room.

After his discharge from service this veteran (as many other Navy veterans like him) worked in the Norfolk Naval shipyard for 30 years, stripping out and refurbishing old ships before he retired in 2010. In 2016 he was diagnosed with pulmonary asbestos. The VA examiner opined that it was at least as likely as not caused by service. It was clear by the doctor's writeup that he didn't even know the difference between active duty service in the Navy versus post-service working in the shipyard (it was all military to him) because he attributed the disease to more than 30 years of exposure to asbestos. But because he said it was at least as likely as not caused by service, service connection was granted without any dispute to the doctor, as disputing the doctor is not allowed. Medical literature shows that 30% of people with mesothelioma are veterans, but what the studies don't show is how many of those worked at the Naval shipyard *after* service.

HYPERTENSION AND HEART DISEASE

A person who is diagnosed with hypertension during service probably either had it before service or would have developed hypertension in the same year regardless of whether he had been in service or not, because there is no record of any military incident causing the hypertension. I've never heard of anything that could happen to someone in service to cause them to develop hypertension other than alcohol abuse, but alcohol abuse is considered willful misconduct and not supposed to be granted service-connection. However, VA will grant any hypertension diagnosed in service or within one year after discharge, no questions asked.

"High blood pressure" is something everyone may experience at one time or another due to various acute illnesses, substance abuse or drug interactions, or even stress or excitement. But "high blood pressure" is not a diagnosis of hypertension and service-connection should only be granted if there is a true and supported diagnosis of hypertension.

The VA regulations are very strict about how hypertension should be diagnosed. It requires a series of blood pressure readings to be done, two or more times a day, on at least 3 different days. A blood pressure reading is expressed as systolic pressure over diastolic pressure, such as 120/80. For a diagnosis of regular hypertension, the readings must show diastolic blood pressure is predominantly (more than half of the readings) 90mm. or greater. A diagnosis of isolated systolic hypertension would be given when the systolic blood pressure is predominantly 160mm or greater with a diastolic blood pressure of less than 90mm (something I never saw diagnosed).

But time and again, hypertension has been granted simply because the word hypertension or HTN was shown once in a military record, and with no evidence of the 3-day blood pressure check. Also, often when it is claimed on separation or within a year of service the VA will do checks to determine a diagnosis but they do it only on two separate days, and try to make up the difference by doing 3 checks on each day. It's not the same thing, and it's not correct, but when the VAMC records give a diagnosis of hypertension, it cannot be disputed by a peon rater.

Many servicemen and women are diagnosed with "white-coat hypertension" when in service. This is high blood pressure manifested whenever the patient is in a doctor's office, but at home it always tests fine. It's just a matter of being nervous around medical procedures and examinations. This is a "temporary" elevation of blood pressure and is not supposed to be granted! But it is granted over and over again because there is a "diagnosis" of some kind of hypertension in service.

Then there's the problems of "hypertension" versus "hypertensive heart disease" versus other types of heart disease (valvular, arrhythmias). If he has both "hypertension" and "hypertensive heart disease" then he gets two separate evaluations, because the heart and the blood vessels running through the heart are two separate things! If the veteran already has a diagnosis of hypertension, any other abnormal symptom or findings shown on exam (other than the blood pressure readings) requires returning the exam for the doctor to address a possible heart condition diagnosis and it should require an opinion too but that is generally skipped. Often the treating physician has not diagnosed or treated "heart disease" and has only prescribed medications for the hypertension, but the VA clarification request forces the one-time examiner to give the additional diagnosis.

It's also peculiar that hypertensive heart disease is not the same as ischemic heart disease and for purposes of ratings related to Agent Orange exposure, the rules are very strict; only the ischemic types of heart disease can be granted, not hypertension or hypertensive heart disease. And yet, if a veteran with hypertension comes down with any sort of heart disease, including ischemic, valvular, or arrhythmic, it will be granted as secondary to the hypertension!

By definition, coronary artery disease (CAD) may be manifested by "left ventricular hypertrophy" which is enlargement of the left ventricle, and that's the most common symptom used in providing a 30% evaluation. Time and again you will see cardiac tests showing "no hypertrophy, no dilatation," but yet showing mild left *atrial* enlargement. Raters are not doctors and they are taught that if there is any enlargement of any part of the heart, it is to be considered "hypertrophy" which justifies 30% disability as a separate grant, in addition to whatever percentage he has for hypertension.

***

Veteran X is service-connected for hypertension and now he has been diagnosed with coronary artery disease (CAD) so VA will automatically grant that as a separate issue secondary to his hypertension, without getting a medical opinion. His hypertension is only 0% disabling because his systolic pressure has never been above 160 and his diastolic has never been above 100. He probably doesn't even have hypertension, it was just high one time during an acute illness. It is highly unlikely that this slight degree of hypertension, if present, could have possibly caused a new serious heart condition to develop. Typically, complications of hypertension, to include heart disease and kidney disease, occur only when the patient has had uncontrolled or untreated severely high blood pressure for a long time. But the VA doesn't even consider that. Just grant, grant, grant.

***

Veteran X was first noted to have high blood pressure by his dentist in service, so he was sent for a 5-day series of blood pressure readings, but readings were all normal. He was never diagnosed with hypertension in service, as clearly he did not have a chronic problem. After service he filed a claim for multiple issues (not including hypertension) and his blood pressure was found to be high during his general medical exam, so the VA examiner diagnosed hypertension (without a 3-day test). Hypertension was granted on a presumptive basis because it manifested to a compensable degree within one year after discharge. In fact, it should never have been granted because a properly documented series of blood pressure readings, twice a day on three separate days, is not of record to support the diagnosis. It's pretty clear he has only white-coat hypertension.

***

Veteran X was diagnosed with hypertension in service and kept it under control with medication prescribed freely by the military. After service, he stopped taking the medication. After one year he filed a claim for hypertension and his blood pressure was so high on VA exam that he was granted 40% disability. Due to the circumstances (he had not been on medication so it was extra high) a routine future exam was diaried. On the exam 2 years later he was found to have normal blood pressure. He said he was now maintaining a healthy lifestyle and had no symptoms. Since everything was normal and he stated he was no longer taking any medications, his evaluation was appropriately reduced to 0%. This infuriated him and he requested reconsideration. The medical records over the year following his reduction show that his blood pressure gradually increased to levels that would warrant 10%, then 20%, then 40% because he refused to take any medications, although they were free to him through the VA pharmacy. His 40% evaluation was restored. As long as the condition is controlled with meds it warrants only 10%, but whether he takes the meds or not is no business of the VA benefits office. The rater is not allowed to apply logic to assigning an evaluation, nor may he give any warning to the claimant about a potential heart attack or stroke due to deliberately letting his blood pressure run high just for the money.

SURGERY IN SERVICE

Many veterans take advantage of the fact that the military performed surgeries, and often the surgeries were to correct problems they were born with or that were not caused by service. Any time a surgery is performed in service for any reason, the condition is subject to service-connection, and at the very least the scar will be granted.

Many "elective" surgeries are performed in service for congenital pes planus (flat feet), congenital genu valgum (knock knees), breast reductions, vasectomies, reverse vasectomies, deviated septum (crooked nose), ptosis (drooping eyelids), flap ears (ears stick out), removal of moles, and anything else you can imagine. The military is currently considering that they may perform surgeries for transgender conversions.

Each of these surgeries should make the person "better" and there should be no residual other than a surgical scar, stable and nonpainful which would be service connected at 0%. Unfortunately, veterans will repeatedly claim other residuals such as ongoing pain in the area of surgery, and especially painful scars even when the scar looks great. Subjective pain cannot be denied so compensable evaluations will be paid. Often the veteran tries to profit from surgeries that were done to help him or her, instead of being thankful they didn't have to pay for it themselves. I have seen numerous cases of vasectomies, followed by reversed vasectomies, and then the veterans claim the procedures caused them to be impotent, so they get granted for erectile dysfunction and loss of use of a creative organ. The women who have elective breast reductions will almost always claim it has left them with painful tender scars.

Some surgeries are performed for legitimate treatment for medical conditions that "occur" during service whether or not they were "incurred" in service: cataracts, retinopathy, heart bypasses, kidney removal and transplants, knee replacements, spinal discectomies, emergency appendectomies for appendicitis, cancer removal, and Cesarean sections to deliver babies of female soldiers. Some of the most common surgeries are for hallux valgus (to correct bunions on the feet) and hysterectomies done for various gynecological conditions.

Many of these post-surgical conditions warrant an automatic minimum evaluation from the VA, even if there are no symptoms; for example, 30% after bypass surgery, 30% after a kidney removal, 30% after a knee replacement, and 30% after a partial hysterectomy or 50% after a complete hysterectomy, and 80% after a radical double mastectomy.

If a condition that started in service has been granted as service-connected then any surgeries performed later in life for that body part or disease will also be granted as an increase in the condition. A temporary 100% will be granted for a period of convalescence/recuperation from surgery, and then the condition is again evaluated based on residuals or in many cases a minimum evaluation is dictated by the rating schedule.

These conditions, after recovery from surgery, do not necessarily prevent a person from full-time gainful employment, and especially when the problems were not caused by battle or military-related injury, compensation is simply not justified.

AMYOTROPHIC LATERAL SCLEROSIS (ALS)

If amyotrophic lateral sclerosis (ALS), also known as Lou Gehrig's Disease, is diagnosed in any veteran who served 90 days or more continuous active military service, it will be presumed related to their service, and 100% disability compensation will be granted, permanent and total.

According to the ALS Association's official website, "Amyotrophic lateral sclerosis (ALS) is a progressive neurodegenerative disease that affects nerve cells in the brain and the spinal cord. Motor neurons reach from the brain to the spinal cord and from the spinal cord to the muscles throughout the body. The progressive degeneration of the motor neurons in ALS eventually leads to their death. When the motor neurons die, the ability of the brain to initiate and control muscle movement is lost. With voluntary muscle action progressively affected, patients in the later stages of the disease may become totally paralyzed."

I'm not saying this is not a serious disease. It is a death sentence and as such, the person should be considered 100 percent disabled. But there's no reason to find it service-connected. It used to be considered related to Agent Orange, but then someone noticed that the odds of developing ALS are just as good for any veteran who ever served in any branch anywhere, so now it's granted to any veteran who gets the diagnosis.

The problem is there are no studies to prove this condition was caused by any event or exposure in service. The medical literature only shows a "correlation" not causation. ALS has been more frequently diagnosed in veterans than in the general population. But how long will it take for common sense to prevail? Clearly veterans, who have access to free treatment and free diagnostic testing, are of course more likely to be diagnosed with this or *any* other condition, because they more frequently will complain of miscellaneous symptoms and will be tested and diagnosed with something!

Stage 1 or 2 symptoms could actually be a number of other possible diseases, or nothing chronic, so how many of these diagnosed ALS cases will be confirmed by progression beyond stage 1 or 2? Only time will tell.

The ALS Association says that 90 to 95 percent of cases are sporadic and can affect anyone, anywhere. The other 5 to 10 percent of cases are familial, meaning hereditary, so there is 50 percent chance of passing the disease to any children. Onset is usually between the ages of 40 and 70. The symptoms are twitching, cramping, or stiffness of muscles; muscle weakness affecting an arm or a leg; slurred and nasal speech; and/or difficulty chewing or swallowing. Who among us has not had some of these symptoms such as stiff muscles or muscle weakness? Eventually the disease will affect the diaphragm (muscle that supports the lungs) so in advanced stages the person will have trouble breathing. ALS is granted 100% from the start, so a case needn't be reopened for increase. Has anyone checked the veterans' ALS cases to see how many of them ever progressed into stage 5 ALS, and if so, how do these numbers compare with the general population?

ALS is a horrible disease and if Americans want to pay 100% disability to every American who has a confirmed diagnosis in the advanced stages of ALS, that's fine, let our Social Security system take good care of it. But it not a condition limited to veterans, and there is no evidence that it was caused by any specific military activity or exposure. Such grants by the VA, especially 100% for stage 1 symptoms, are insulting to veterans who were actually injured in war.

***

Veteran X, a 70-year-old man, went to his private physician with a single symptom of "tremors" in his hands. Slight decreases were shown on EMG (nerve testing). No other symptoms or findings. Tremors can be a symptom of Parkinson's or other nerve disorders. ALS is a muscle disease. The private doctor noted in his report that he was personally aware that a diagnosis of ALS would warrant automatic service-connection with 100% disability compensation, as well as free medical care for the rest of his life, so he requested that the patient be referred to the VA. And he was. There was no actual diagnosis of ALS, the referring doctor simply noted that some of the claimed symptoms could be early symptoms of ALS. (Ironically, tremors are not noted as an early symptom by the ALS Association.) VA accepted the referral and entered ALS in the Problem List. The VA could not have otherwise treated the man, unless he had some service-connected condition, or at least something he was claiming to be service-related, and what were they going to do, turn him away? Of course not, so now the VA medical records show ALS, and the rater must automatically grant it, without requesting any exam or verification of the disease. And it must be granted Permanent and Total so there will be no future exams. ALS is a terminal illness, a hot topic, a rush job, it must be granted immediately, within a few hours after receiving the claim, and no questions asked!

SEXUAL DYSFUNCTION (ED, SMC-K, AND FSAD)

MALE ERECTILE DYSFUNCTION

Erectile dysfunction (ED) is one of the easiest issues to get granted because unless there's a rare case of penile injury ED is purely subjective, and thanks to the internet the veterans now all know it. In 2010, there were 366,581 veterans receiving special monthly compensation (SMC-K) for ED. By 2016, that number had risen to 605,573.

Is anyone at the VA or any doctor completing the DBQ going to actually do a test to see if the condition exists? No. The best trick is to claim it before you get out of service, then you'll be able to claim it continues after service. It doesn't matter how old a veteran is; veterans of all ages are claiming ED. They claim it's due to stress and marital problems and drugs they're taking for other issues. The funniest thing is that even if the veteran reports his condition is helped or resolved by taking Viagra or Sildenafil, he still gets granted anyway!

If it's not claimed during service, there's a chance it will be granted after claiming it on the general medical exam if the claim is received within one year of discharge. That's wrong, but it's a common error to grant everything noted on a general medical exam including issues that were not shown in service.

The Rating Schedule doesn't even have a diagnostic code for erectile dysfunction (ED), so ED is rated under DC 7522 as analogous to penile deformity. But the regulation doesn't even list any criteria for impotence, and that's why it's granted as 0%, besides for most occupations it does not occupational impairment. The code simply provides that 20% will be granted for penile deformity, and there are other codes for greater physical losses. Deformity is very rarely shown on VA exams because the claimants have an option to skip the penile and rectal exams if they wish, and those with deformity are apparently electing not to be examined. In 10 years I only saw one case in which the veteran claimed penile atrophy (deformity) due to diabetes, although it is not uncommon.

Another common way to get ED granted is on a secondary basis when the veteran is service-connected for diabetes or prostate cancer. ED is a common complication of diabetes and will automatically be granted if it's claimed. ED will also be automatically granted effective the date of a prostatectomy.

Service connection for ED is sometimes *erroneously* granted as secondary to posttraumatic stress disorder (PTSD). For example, one examiner gave this positive opinion of a link between conditions. "When compared to the general population, veterans with PTSD are at increased risk of sexual dysfunction. A review study published online in the *Journal of Sexual Medicine* on February 9, 2015, found that male veterans with PTSD were significantly more likely than their civilian counterparts to report erectile dysfunction or other sexual problems. Therefore, the veteran's erectile dysfunction is at least as likely as not due to or the result of PTSD." This rationale only notes a *correlation*, it does not provide any evidence of a "causal" relationship between the two conditions. *Of course* the problem is more commonly reported by veterans with PTSD, than by civilians! *Every condition in the world* is more commonly reported by veterans with or without PTSD, than by their civilian counterparts, because veterans are trying to increase their disability compensation. What does a non-veteran gain from reporting ED? This is a totally bogus rationale and yet the rater must accept it and grant this secondary condition. Why? Because VA raters are not doctors and have no right to question a competent medical examiner. Common sense is not allowed.

SPECIAL MONTHLY COMPENSATION (SMC) - K

Special Monthly Compensation (SMC) is a supplemental benefit, additional money paid on top of whatever they get for the total compensation evaluation. SMC is a very complex system which must have taken years to develop. It provides an extra benefit, on multiple possible levels from $105 to $9,000 a month, to veterans who need Aid and Attendance, or who have loss of limbs, or total blindness, or certain other very serious impairments.

The lowest level of this benefit is SMC-K, which pays for loss, or loss of use of, a "creative organ" and we're not talking about the brain. SMC-K is a benefit that was intended to compensate soldiers who had their penises either blown off or their testicles destroyed by punji sticks. One may not be too disabled to work (which is the basis for compensation) but a soldier with damaged sexual organs cannot reproduce, so this supplemental benefit compensates for that.

Although erectile dysfunction (ED) usually only warrants a noncompensable 0% evaluation, whenever ED is granted, the veteran is also granted SMC-K for loss of use of a creative organ, and that pays $105 or more per month forever. In the past, SMC-K was not automatically granted, it required some supporting medical evidence, and it wasn't paid if ED was resolved by medication, but as for everything else, the VA has loosened the slots. Grant, grant, grant. Also, no one sets up a routine future exam to confirm that the ED is continuing, because it's 0%, and it's all based on the veteran's subjective report anyway. I have seen many cases of veterans drawing SMC-K and fathering several children after the date of award, and of course getting extra compensation for each dependent child. Furthermore, for those without children, SMC-K will be granted even if the claimant had an elective vasectomy during service!

ED is also being granted a thousand times a day based on the complaint that "sex isn't as great as it used to be." Even if they are using Viagra and having fully satisfactory results with the Viagra, they are still being granted for the ED and the SMC-K. The veteran opts to waiver the penile exam in most cases, but he still gets 0% for ED. Then he gets the SMC-K, $105 per month even though he's doing fine with Viagra. Can you imagine what an insult this is to a veteran who actually had his private parts destroyed by an IED?

SMC-K is also granted to any veteran who has had a sexual organ removed. This includes men who have had a testicle removed and still have one perfectly good testicle for procreating. It is also granted to female veterans who have had a hysterectomy or even one ovary removed, even though they could still bear children with one ovary. If they've fathered or borne children, I'd say they've not lost their creative capacity and it probably shouldn't be granted.

A female veteran who has infertility due to hypothyroidism that was first diagnosed during service will also be granted SMC-K. The hypothyroidism has nothing to do with service; she would have that even if she'd never been in service. But it has to be granted because it was first discovered or diagnosed during service. Now because she is granted for that, and has infertility presumably related to the hypothyroidism, she can also be granted for the infertility; therefore, she is entitled to SMC-K based on loss of use of a creative organ. !

FEMALE SEXUAL AROUSAL DISORDER (FSAD)

A relatively new law (2015) now allows female veterans to get service-connection and SMC-K for Female Sexual Arousal Disorder (FSAD), which is exactly what it sounds like, female ED, and there is no need to have any missing sex organs when that is diagnosed. The intent was apparently to provide equal rights to women since so many men were getting SMC-K for ED.

FSAD is commonly granted as related to endometriosis or any gynecological condition, and many are also granted FSAD secondary to Military Sexual Trauma. It doesn't matter one bit if the veteran has given birth to 5 children all subsequent to the claimed incident. A finding of FSAD is entitlement to SMC-K, special monthly compensation for loss of use of a creative organ. Any time any gynecological condition is considered, the examiner is now required to ask the female veteran whether she has symptoms of FSAD related to the condition diagnosed, basically encouraging and soliciting this additional claim. And if she knows what's good for her pocketbook she'll say Yes.

SUMMARY OF SEXUAL DYSFUNCTION

There is so much fraud and abuse of this SMC-K benefit by men and women! I believe SMC-K for loss-of and loss-of-use-of a creative organ was intended to pay those men who had their sexual organs blown off by gunshot or bombs, or mutilated by punji sticks, during "battle." Young men, some who had never even married yet, would not be able to father children when they returned from war. The condition now sometimes occurs when a soldier steps on an IED in Iraq, and he fully deserves this benefit! It could also be applied to a woman if she had her uterus destroyed by a mortar wound. But those are the types of cases it should be applied to now, and no other! Imagine what the mutilated soldier feels about all these other people who are getting the benefit while still having sex and raising kids!

***

Veteran X has been diagnosed with ED, and the doctor says the etiology (cause) of the condition is the claimant's "relationship with his wife." In other words, he has problems with sex because he's not getting along with his wife. But can he get an erection and ejaculations without medications? The doctor notes YES he can. So apparently he can do it alone or with other women, just not with the wife. We have to grant service connection for this issue because the doctor has given a diagnosis and it started in service and was shown on his pre-discharge exam. ED is granted at 0% so there will never be another future exam to see if he still has the problem after he divorces and remarries. The 0% grant leads to automatic grant of SMC-K based on loss of use of a creative organ, for which we will pay the veteran $105 per month for the rest of his life, with never a future exam.

(18) FIXES HAVE MADE THINGS WORSE

General Allison Hickey, the Under Secretary for Benefits at the VA who resigned under pressure in October 2015, was a nice enough lady, a bit dramatic, but she meant well. Secretary of VA, Eric Shinseki, had also recently been fired in May 2014. It appeared to me that these two truly wanted to do and give everything possible to our great veterans. From what I can understand Shinseki was an excellent leader but as the highest authority he had to take the fall for problems uncovered in the VA medical centers such as unacceptable backlogs in patient appointments, nothing he personally did wrong. Hickey, as second in command, was "fired" for actions she took in trying to get some effective leadership in place at the VA medical facilities that were failing miserably. To this day, no one has acknowledged that VA hospitals can't keep up the demand anymore due to being overrun by veterans abusing the system in order to beef up their files for compensation purposes. VA may fire more leaders and disgruntled employees and they may hire a slew of new medical workers (if they can find any willing to work there) but VA hospital performance isn't likely to improve until someone realizes VBA needs fixing. VHA will then fall into place.

Hickey was working hard to fix the VBA problems as well, specifically the backlog of disability claims. Unfortunately she didn't have a clue as to what was causing the problems, but she was working on the director's commitment to get claims processed within 125 days. Changes were coming down the pipe so fast the worker bees couldn't keep up.

It seems to me that around 2006 to 2010, perhaps in adherence to the new Veterans Claims Assistance Act (VCAA), VA was going in the right direction on rating claims by hiring better educated claims processors and requiring them to write more detailed letters developing for evidence, and more detailed explanations in their rating denials, a policy that would have reduced reopen claims and appeals. But all that took a 360 degree turn when the VA decided to de-personalize claims by adopting new automated programs that spit out form letters and cookie-cutter ratings with minimal explanation of decisions. This caused more reopens and appeals.

Meanwhile, perhaps also in adherence to the new VCAA policies of "helping" more veterans get more benefits, the claims workload grew because VA began making many issues easier to grant, thereby encouraging more new claims and reopens of previously denied claims. New "fear and easing standards" allowed granting of PTSD to veterans with no verified stressor as long as they had served in a war zone. A new list of MOS's with "probable" exposure to excessive noise allowed veterans who claimed hearing loss and tinnitus to get exams and opinions regardless of having any history of hearing loss. More Navy veterans could file Agent Orange claims based on a growing "ship list" of vessels that docked or entered Vietnam waterways. Vietnam veterans were invited to file claims for more new Agent Orange presumptive conditions, and thousands of previously denied claims for those issues were reopened. New policies for Gulf War presumptives and undiagnosed illnesses due to Gulf War exposures stirred claims from every Gulf War veteran who'd been discharged since 1990.

And all kinds of conditions previously denied for lack of continuity of symptoms since service could now be granted by obtaining a medical opinion linking current conditions to whatever happened in service decades ago. Medical opinions slow down everything.

Meanwhile, the claims process kept getting easier for veterans as the claim forms got simpler and they were able to file claims on-line. Furthermore, veterans were getting more educated on the claims process and their rights to file and they were getting lots of "tips" on the internet. As VA regulations and policies got laxer, and veterans got wiser, the claims increased and started piling up.

It was obvious that Under Secretary Hickey had done her homework as far as reading all the claims statistics. She knew that VBA had a big problem making their quotas such as the number of claims being processed each year and the number of days it was taking to process a claim. Despite VA hiring thousands more claims processors, by 2010 there had accrued a huge backlog of compensation claims and lots of complaints were coming in from all levels: veterans, POAs, congressmen, and the President. It was taking about two or more years for a claim to get rated. At the same time, a greater number of claims were coming in, and the claims had more issues than ever before.

The solution at that point would have been to crack down on frivolous claims that VA shouldn't be paying anyway; i.e., stop paying them (start denying them) so that future veterans would stop claiming them. Start requiring medical evidence to support increases and start reducing evaluations when warranted instead of just continuing until the next exam; these things would reduce the number of fraudulent increase claims. Start requiring examiners to provide proper rationale for their opinions so they won't be so quick to link every ridiculous claim. Make rating decisions based on the entire record and require evidence for granting as well as for denying. Tighten up across the board by taking a stricter adherence to the regulations and rating schedules, thereby not granting every new issue and every increase claim, and explain each denial to the veteran in words he can understand, specific to his claim. That would have reduced the workload for the future and led to more legitimate claims being processed more accurately. But no attempt to reduce the number of claims or number of issues was even considered. Instead, all the new ideas implemented were just tricks to process claims faster and grant more, thereby encouraging more claims and more issues.

The new goal that had been set by President Obama and Secretary of VA Shinseki was that a VA compensation claim would be completed within 125 days of receipt. I believe that is still the current goal for new claims, and in fact VA has made great strides in reaching that goal! Per the VA website (www. benefits.va.gov/reports) the average number of days for completing a Fully Developed Claim is now 100 or less. And under a new program of Decision Ready Claims, certain increase claims are being completed within 30 days.

Unfortunately, as everyone actually working the claims said from the beginning, any increase in speed is going to mean a decrease in quality, and I believe quality of decisions is now worse than ever, regardless of Quality statistics. In the past, at least a rating decision was composed by the rater, with some semblance of justification for the decision. Now, the processing has become more and more automated to speed things up. There's no time for thinking about a logical decision or for writing a justification and a rater who can't keep up the speed will be demoted to some other job. Besides, the VA wants a decision to be the same no matter which rater does it or which of the 56 offices across America may have produced the decision. To accomplish that, the VA turned to automation.

Hickey knew that the reason for the increasing backlog of claims was that there were increasingly more claims each year, and longer claims with more issues. So she and others at the top set out to *fix* the system. Unfortunately, they didn't ask for input from the people working the claims (at least they certainly didn't ask me). Whoever she reached out to for advice told her that the way to get more claims done faster was to make the claims submittal and processing simpler and more automated.

For veterans there came the VA website, www.ebenefits.gov, where the veterans upload their own claims and evidence. And there came simplified claims forms, the Fully Developed Claims (FDC) and the 526 "EZ" forms.

For the claims developers and raters, there first came the SNL program which stood for Simplified Notification Letter, but we called it Saturday Night Live.   With SNL we rated more issues faster, not better but faster.   Instead of the rater writing up an explanation for the decision, he just entered a few letters of "code" and the system generated the text, canned text, suitable for any common or unique situation, and with absolutely no explanation to the claimant about his specific claim.   Practically every decision done under SNL has been reopened or *appealed* causing more work for the raters and Appeals Department.

Then came the Disability Benefits Questionnaires (DBQs) which are exam worksheets with a list of symptoms and a bunch of little boxes for the physician/examiner to check; these took the place of actual written examination reports.

Corresponding to these DBQ's, they came up with the "Evaluation Builder" which is basically computer software with a bunch of little check boxes.   The rater checks these boxes corresponding to the boxes that were checked on the DBQs, and that generates an Evaluation, with no brainwork needed.   Not only are the DBQs totally inadequate anyway because they don't match the Rating Schedule, in many cases they also do not correspond adequately to the Evaluation Builder. When Hickey came around to visit, we tried to tell her the DBQs were horrible, but she insisted that we must *not* return the DBQs to the examiners for dispute or clarification, but just go with whatever the physician checks off, and "grant, grant, grant."   Grant whatever and as much as you can, and *never* develop to deny. In other words, don't ask for clarification of an exam that looks funny, and if you suspect there could be some medical records out there that would contradict the DBQ, do *not* request those records unless the claimant has asked you to get them.

Due to complaints from veterans, VSOs, and claims raters, investigations of the DBQ program have been done by the Office of Inspector General (OIG) in 2012 and 2016 but as far as I know the VA has not fixed any of the problems such as fraudulent reports and erroneous ratings that result from the use of DBQs. Many DBQs are fraudulent in that they are not completed by real physicians! Although there's a box on the form for the physician ID number, no one verifies that it is a legitimate number as there's no time for that. Also there are certified physicians available through the internet who will talk to a veteran on-line or on the phone, and never treat or see the veteran in person, but will then fill out the DBQ with whatever the veteran wants it to say! Even legitimately completed DBQs, done by VA physicians or contracted examiners, are being completed by doctors who have never *treated* the veteran and who are meeting him for the first time on the day of exam. They fill out the DBQ based on whatever the veteran wants it to say! Even with all the fraud aside, the DBQs are just a bunch of checked boxes and they do *not* explain the true unique condition of each claimant. The multiple-choice selections on the template frequently do not adequately describe the claimant's condition. The exams frequently contain contradictory information in different sections or provide a diagnosis with no actual supporting symptoms. Or they'll describe a condition as "severe" but all the measurements and tests show mild or no symptoms!

The latest program to speed up claims processing is the Decision Ready Claims. The POA submits on-line a new or increase claim for the veteran after the veteran gets a DBQ completed on his own somewhere or the POA must order one for him. This encourages more DBQs from non-VA doctors, from doctors who are completing it because they're being paid to complete it, not in conjunction with treatment, and they check whatever boxes the veteran wants them to. Often the veteran completes it and the doctor just signs it.

So the rater has to try to enter all those little DBQ check-box responses into the automated system "Evaluation Builder" which will generate the appropriate level of disability, 10 to 100%. Frequently, the multiple-choice answers on the DBQs do not match the corresponding condition in the Evaluation Builder. The exam may indicate something quite serious but it comes out with a low evaluation, or more often it is vice versa. The rater does not have time to deal with this and is not supposed to use his own best judgment. Theoretically the DBQ should be sent back to the examiner for clarification, but raters are advised over and over again to not do that. The best a rater can do is try to find other medical evidence in the file that better represents the true picture of disability, and then explain the modified decision, to include why the other evidence is more probative than the DBQ. But very few raters will even read the other evidence much less take a chance on getting an error. Every decision is expected to be primarily based on the DBQ and there will be no error issued if the Evaluation Builder is used and the rating was based on the DBQ. But more importantly, the rater doesn't have time to invest in making an accurate decision. The rater has "quotas" to meet, a number of ratings to be completed, a limit to how long cases can stay in his queue, and *everything* depends on that production record, to include promotions (or not being demoted), performance awards, and more work-from-home days.

So the result of all the automations since 2010 is that the ratings became worse, less clearly understood, and more erroneous the more automated they became. Automation led to granting more and granting higher evaluations. The people who invented these "improvements" were only concerned with greater production, i.e. more claims being processed faster; they had no concern about quality of decisions being made. And they tried to compensate for the lack of quality by just erring in favor of the veteran. You might get in trouble for *not* granting but you're not likely to get an error for granting. No one will complain about the system if everyone is getting granted.

The people who invented these automations were just computer geeks who had no inkling about what was truly wrong with the compensation program, why the case load was overwhelming and production times were increasing. The true problem was that we were paying way too many veterans too much money for too many wrong reasons. And the more it happens, the more they tell their friends, and the more bogus claims are submitted, and the longer the list of claimed issues on each claim.

(19) WHAT CAN BE DONE?

I've always believed that if you're going to complain about the way anything is done, you must also be ready and able to provide an alternative better way to do it. I've tried to do that throughout this book by providing very specific cases, how they were decided wrong, and what the more logical alternative decisions might be. But in addition to the way certain specific issues are granted, many broad general changes in regulation and policy must be implemented.

The granting of VA disability compensation has gotten entirely out of control. A veteran who was diagnosed with hypertension six months after military discharge later develops heart disease and we pay him 100% disability for life, and we pay his wife after he's dead. A Vietnam vet comes down with diabetes 40 years after service and we pay him 100% disability for life for all the complications of diabetes, and we pay his wife after he's dead. A vet who served less than two years was paralyzed in a car accident while he was home on leave from service and we are paying him 100% forever with special monthly compensation totaling more than $9,000 a month, plus special housing adaptation and automobile allowance. A vet serves 20 years honorably, gets full military retirement, then works a federal civilian job for 20 years and gets full retirement for that. Meanwhile he files a claim for 40 minor issues, many granted 10% each based on subjective evidence only, plus sleep apnea is granted at 50%, so he's receiving 100% disability although he's never been physically, occupationally, or socially disabled at all. And he's triple-dipping the federal government (us, the taxpayers).

All these veterans are already getting help from our government (us, the taxpayers) through retirement or social services in addition to any private earnings or pensions, but we also pay them VA disability compensation.

American taxpayers should not be funding the lavish lifestyles of many veterans, especially when the taxpayers don't even know and understand it. All we hear in the news is, "We've got to take care of our great veterans." Most assume that means those who suffer from battle injuries, and most of us are in agreement that we are willing to compensate them. The VA medical centers with their free care and medicine is another thing we are willing to bite the bullet and pay for, even though a great majority of the care being given is not related to any war injury. But these monthly "disability compensation" checks to non-disabled and to non-battle-injured veterans is a whole other story. It's wrong, it's unjustified, and it needs to stop.

The VBA is doing everything it can for veterans in accordance with existing regulations, and is stretching those regulations ridiculously in favor of the veteran. I'm proposing that the regulations need to be changed, not just amended but totally revamped.

The most important change is to clarify and stipulate that the first and primary requirement for "service-connection" is that the condition was incurred in battle or during a required military activity, such as a physical fitness test, a road march, a training exercise, a military plane crash or military ship on fire. If it happened while off-duty, or if it's some kind of disease or condition he would have developed in the private sector, it is *not* service-related. Do away with service-connection for any disease attributed to any "exposure" in Vietnam, southeast Asia, Camp Lejeune, or anywhere else. If the symptoms weren't manifested during that exposure, or within a month or some other reasonable manifestation time after that exposure, it's not due to that exposure. We should put a time limit on any "exposure" claim. If a Vietnam veteran doesn't have it by now, it wasn't due to Vietnam exposure, but if we don't halt them, these claims will continue coming in stronger than ever for the next 40 years as more of the general public develop diabetes and heart disease. We can't do anything about claims already granted, but we can put the brakes on for the future.

Yes, there will be an uproar of veterans and VSOs. And of course any congressman with guts enough to tackle this issue will be scorned and labeled as disrespectful and unpatriotic, just like me. Veterans are the sacred cow of America!

But indeed, I'm extremely patriotic; I love my country and that's why I'm willing to speak out against governmental fraud and abuse. I believe in paying taxes to support our schools, infrastructure, firemen, policemen, and garbagemen. I'm even willing to give some of my hard-earned taxdollars to help Social Security and Medicare pay for those unable to work, veteran or non-veteran. I am willing to contribute to a strong U.S. military. And I'm also willing and glad to contribute to VA disability compensation for those veterans who were *injured while in battle or another required military activity*. But I am not willing to contribute to paying trillions of dollars to all veterans simply because they are veterans. They were paid for their service, they receive numerous veteran benefits, and they were never promised life-long compensation payments simply because they served. Besides placing an unjustified financial burden on current (us) and future taxpayers (our children) with this growing $2.8 trillion deficit, this current VA entitlement program is destroying a lot of our able-bodied young veterans, squashing their morals and self-esteem, turning them into players, partiers, freeloaders, couch potatoes, when they should be the pride of our working class. Our country will suffer from this reduction in the work force and increase to the "welfare rolls."

But my strongest opposition to the current VA policies of granting every petty claim, and huge monthly payments for conditions not caused by service, is that this is a great insult and disservice to our truly *war-injured* veterans. The VA disability compensation program was created for them and it needs to be restored and returned to them.

The VA problem is multi-faceted and it will require a task force of *knowledgeable* and *motivated* individuals to fix this broken system. Choose a team of people who have *worked* at the claims processing level under the current regulations and policies so they know what's wrong with the system. But don't choose the perfectly contented "yes man" or the workers with the highest production levels because they don't know or care what the regulations say; they're just doing as they're told and letting automation do the job. Choose the disgruntled complaining whistleblowers and give them a chance to submit their ideas for change. You don't have to accept all their ideas but it's a place to start, and this book is a place to start.

The fixes cannot be done overnight or even in a year. The changes will not affect those who have already been granted. The $90 billion in compensation payments this year will have to be paid by us. The $2.8 trillion of unfunded liabilities, increasing every year, will have to be paid by our children. But it's time to start pulling in the reins instead of getting looser and looser with granting more issues and at higher evaluations every year, as has been the trend over the past 10 years.

(20) CHANGES IN ATTITUDES & POLICIES

The attitude of the VBA from the top is that we all must do everything humanly possible to support our great veterans. It doesn't matter how long they served or what they're claiming, just grant, grant, grant, as fast as you can and as much as you can. There is no focus on making reasonable, quality, fair decisions; all that matters is quantity and speed of processing. This approach is offensive to our truly war-disabled veterans and results in gross misappropriation of American taxpayers' dollars.

A rater who tries to question the granting of a fraudulent claim will be quickly reminded of 38 CFR 4.23, *Attitude of the Rating Specialist*, as if that law said a rater must always rule in favor of a veteran. In fact it only says that even when a veteran is rude or threatening or sends a 300-page letter full of vulgarities aimed at the VA, you must not let that influence your decision on the claim; a claim should always be decided fairly based on all the facts of evidence.

At the VBA claims processing offices, greater automation has de-personalized the individual claims. More personal attention should be given to each claim, and the rater should be able to take as much time as needed to decide it correctly and explain it, not just grant it and go for the sake of making his daily quota.

One would assume that a veteran's case goes before a group of people known as the "rating board." After all, a veteran's claim is nothing more than a law suit against the federal government, requesting compensation for injury incurred on the government job he performed. So the rating board would seem to be a type of hearing committee or judge and jury of sorts. In reality, there is no "board" for each case. There is only one single individual reading the case and judging the case as fast as he can. No one else knows whether he has read the evidence or not. He has not spoken to the claimant or heard any evidence unless the veteran requested a formal hearing and drove hours to attend it; that's very rare. The single rater may be very inexperienced. Anyone who has done this job will admit that it takes at least three years to learn the job, and the only way to learn is through experience because every case is different, and yet you must start doing it as soon as you return from the formal training. Many raters are extremely stressed to the point of contemplating suicide, but rarely do they quit. Over and over I heard raters say they wanted to leave and needed to leave for the sake of their nerves and sanity, but they just couldn't find any other job anywhere that would pay this much money and provide equivalent benefits: sick pay, vacation pay, and excellent retirement benefits.

The rating job is not one easy to attain. The applicant has to be an honor scholar or veteran and compete with thousands to be selected, then go through the hell of months of formal training as a VSR. Ideally one should work as a claims developer (VSR) before ever being considered for a rating position (RVSR). Then he goes through more hell months of formal training to learn the rater's job and serves on a training team for 6 months to a year where he learns by the trial and error method instead of one-on-one teaching and mentoring. It's an extremely stressful job because a veteran stands to gain or lose a lot of money based on that one little inexperienced rater's decision.

One difficulty for a new VA rater is that they have no "rating board" to consult with when deciding whether to grant or deny. Some cases are straight forward and can be decided with some self-assurance, but many others are so convoluted the rater is uncertain. He is told, "Just give it your best shot. If the veteran doesn't like it, we have an appeal process. If you messed up, it can be granted on appeal, and with retroactive pay back to the same date as if you had granted it." Each rater simply needs a "mentor" during the early years of rating, someone he can double-check a decision with, or someone to send him in the right direction in the massive bulk of regulations. After a few years, the rater still needs a go-to partner, someone equal or a little more experienced, to consult with on the difficult cases. And if that partner is also confused on the case, then it would go to that rater's assigned go-to, and so on, getting as many raters involved as necessary until some kind of comfortable decision can be made by the original rater. I don't mean that they will be sitting around a table together for hours on this case, but one on one, the rater will move on to discuss with another rater until a justifiable decision can be made.

That type of thing rarely happens at the VA. There is no time for this because each rater is "on production" and will only get credit for cases assigned directly to him. If he helps a friend or even if he helps someone he's been appointed to assist as needed, he will get no credit for that time. Each rater is on his own, and it's "sink or swim." If he sinks he goes back to claims development or transfers to the Education department or becomes a supervisor. The required production quota a rater is expected to meet daily is preposterous, and if one exceeds that quota, you can rest assured the evidence in his cases has not been properly reviewed or addressed.

In recent years, a great improvement was implemented at some stations, and that is the "Quality Review Board" consisting of experienced raters who now just review the work of others. A rater is now allowed to send an email (not speak in person) to the Quality Board, to ask a question, and depending on who was assigned to answer the questions that day, sometimes some assistance is provided (by email), although often it is a waste of time. Most often the question is answered with a few quoted manual references which the rater has already reviewed. The problem is that the regs and working manual are so massive that each often contradicts itself and/or the other.

When a rater first starts he is so overwhelmed with the everchanging procedures and massive regulations and pressure to produce that he works by rote without much contemplating. He spends months learning the regulations but then sits at the computer and has to let most of it go out the window because VA policies don't match the regulations. It's even harder for those of us who once rated claims during the time when exam reports were written and ratings were "written." We could at least pick what we felt was relevant from the exams and we could tweak or add some explanations to our rating decisions. Now ratings are not "written" by the rater; they're just punched in like a multiple choice quiz where none of the answers really fit. It frustrates the heck out of an old rater. It all seems amazing and strange and questionable to a new rater but he keeps doing as he's told, thinking it'll all make sense someday.

But over time, a rater starts to see the fallacies of the compensation program. After reading enough files he begins to readily spot the fraudulent claims, the lies on exams, erroneous markings on DBQs, and unjustified positive medical opinions. By the time he has reached journeyman level and understands what he is doing, he sees the big picture and gets more disgusted every day. The rater is earning $80K per year with great work hours, facilities, and benefits. But the crazy thing is that the government spends all this money on him and does not let him do his job. The rater was hired based on his intelligence and demonstrated ability to learn and make decisions, and yet he is not allowed to make a judgement call or use common sense or logic in rating a case. The ratings are done by rote, and a monkey could do them the way the VA wants them done; just look at checkboxes on the DBQ and mark the corresponding checkboxes on your computer, and spit it out. They should hire idiots for the job so there'd be no complaints. Intelligent people are insulted and humiliated by having to create ratings they don't agree with, and by being an accomplice to this big counterfeiting ring.

The problems at the claims processing offices are vast and nobody wants to hear them. The supervisors/management team will not entertain questions or problems because they don't know the answers and they have problems of their own, trying to meet the production quotas handed down to them from higher levels, all way up to the President's Secretary of Veterans Affairs. By the way, the Secretary of Veterans Affairs, at least in this century, has never been anyone who has ever rated a case or even worked in the disability benefits department and doesn't even have to be a veteran. They have absolutely no idea what is going on in the lower levels of this agency. And they never will because this is a typical U.S. government trickle-down agency. Everything starts at the top and trickles down, most of it never getting to the stream of employees at the bottom, not that anything from the top would be of any use to anyone at the bottom anyway. The directors and managers in the VBA offices also know very little about the actual claims processing, and the lowest level supervisors spend all their days keeping attendance, granting leave, and reviewing Excel spreadsheets (production quotas and statistics).

I believe that for all the specific claims developing and rating problems I've discussed, just as in any organization or corporation, the problem solving and improvements *must come from the lower echelons*, must come from the worker bees at the very bottom of the ditches, and must go UP. Only those people at the bottom see the actual claims, use the software, and process the decisions. Only those people know what the problems are, and only those people can present some possible viable solutions or changes. The VA, like many U.S. government agencies, from time to time *pretends* to ask for input from the bottom. But they do it by collecting *surveys* where employees have checked little boxes or answered on a scale of "not likely to highly likely." There is no meat to these surveys. There is no place to submit a viable solution. If there's ever a space provided for typed comments, it it limited to a few characters/words, not enough to explain the problem, much less the solution. I always said that the best way to get honest suggestions is to have an old fashioned "Suggestion Box," an actual box with a slot in the top and a lock on the bottom, nailed outside the director's office, where employees could place "anonymous" suggestions. It worked 50 years ago when people really cared, but now everyone just laughs when I mention this. Everyone knows that even if a good suggestion were entered, it would never go any further up the line. Management at the regional office level is too chickenshit and brownnosing to make any suggestions to the higher echelons regarding policy change, procedural changes, regulation change, or law change. If any discontent or uprising from subordinates is shown, the supervisor/director may easily be relieved of his position.

I worked for some other federal agencies where suggestions were encouraged; I made my share and even received awards for some of them, so I know it's possible. But the VA does not encourage suggestions from the peons, only from their highest levels, the ones who don't know enough to suggest anything logical. Other agencies also invited employees of all levels to meet with the Inspector General (IG) whenever they came to town, but during my 10 years at VA the employees at my level (the workers) were never even notified when the IG would be in the office, and we certainly weren't invited to visit them for any discussion.

Generally, a regional office director has no experience in VA compensation benefits and if he did it was 30 years ago when procedures were totally different, and ratings were totally different. These directors usually get this job to spend the last "lame duck" 18 months of their career before retiring. They have no idea what their office is doing, and the employees have no idea what he is doing, because they never see him and cannot even imagine any use for him.

Administrative problems at the rating level of the VA office is a whole book into itself. I could spend a year writing suggestions for improving the way employees are treated and the way claims are processed at the VA, but that is not the primary purpose of *this* book. The main point I want to make in this chapter is that "the attitude of the rating specialist" is overblown, and the attitude of the VA administration chiefs and lawmakers is what needs tweaking. First the focus should be less on spitting out more decisions faster, and should instead be on producing a correct, fair, and quality decision, one that is "fair" for the veteran and for the American taxpayers supporting him. We want to support our war-injured veterans, not the malingering beat-the-system freeloaders. A lot of money is going out for these claims; we deserve to have each claim properly slowly and thoroughly reviewed, and conscientiously decided. I believe that if claims were being properly decided and decisions explained clearly to the claimants, this would in time lead to fewer new claims, fewer reopen claims, and a reduction in fraudulent claims.

(21) CHANGES IN FEDERAL REGULATIONS

Don't tell me "it's federal law, so it can't be changed." We American taxpayers are supporting 535 congressmen, each paid no less than $174,000 per year to do *nothing but* change laws. Laws affecting "our great veterans" and/or affecting our tax dollars should be top priorities.

Changes must be made to the laws, regulations, and working manual used in deciding VA disability claims, specifically, U.S. Code Title 38, Veterans' Benefits; Code of Federal Regulations (CFR), Title 38, Book B, Chapters 3 and 4, and Book C; and M21-1MR (VBA's working manual). Not only do the laws and regulations need to be *tightened* instead of loosening them more each year, but the implementing policies and procedures (M21-1MR) need to be revised to reflect a tightened or at least a *strict* interpretation of these laws. Each year and with every new decade of VA secretaries, directors, supervisors, quality review specialists, and appeals officers, they just keep stretching and loosening the interpretation of the existing regulations.

The Government Accountability Office (GAO) function is to make recommendations to Congress about issues regarding the spending of our tax dollars. Regarding VA disability claims, they've issued a recent report (2017) about the backlog of Appeals and the only advice therein was that BVA should hire more employees; well, that might speed it up but won't fix anything. Their last report that dealt with the problems of rating VA disability compensation claims was issued in 2012. The recommendations were that VA must revise the old rating schedules to better reflect the impact of impairments on earning. I agree with the premise because in accordance with the general regulations and purpose of compensation, each assigned evaluation (10%, 30%, etc.) is supposed to represent the degree to which that disability affects the person's earnings, i.e. ability to work. An evaluation of 50% would be applicable if the person is only able to do half and earn half of what he could have without the condition.

VA has supposedly implemented the GAO recommendations by starting a review/revision process on the entire rating schedule, one body system at a time, and they have committed to doing regular periodic reviews/revisions to each section of the rating schedule once every 10 years. I saw a few revisions to the rating schedule over the past few years since that report but I can't say that has fixed any of my concerns. Some sections were improved, some were worsened, and it angered me that whenever changes were made, raters weren't informed until the changes were solidified. I felt it would be prudent to put the "proposed changes" out there for all raters to look at (if they cared to) so that maybe some more experienced raters who had seen a greater variety of symptoms reported would be able to give some input to something so critical to their daily work. But so what, the schedules are being tweaked, to bring them out of Old English into modern day prose, but I've seen no indication of a change that now better reflects the degree of impairment to earnings. The problem still exists. The evaluations are too high for conditions that are not preventing the veteran from working. But even if you assigned a straight 10% (the lowest compensable rate) to every granted condition, these veterans are claiming so many petty issues that they would all still result in a combined evaluation of 90% disability. The rating schedule is by no means the biggest problem, and revamping it will not stop the avalanche of bogus fraudulent claims. The solution is to stop soliciting, encouraging, and granting claims for petty subjective not-incurred-in-battle conditions.

I gave examples throughout this book of specific issues that are frequently decided in ways that I just don't think President Lincoln intended when he committed us taxpayers to support those who have borne the battle. A committee for improvement could take each specific issue and do a brief review of current medical literature on the condition. Then pull a sample of 100 rating decisions that have granted that issue in the past year and review those entire files including all military service records and all post-service evidence to get a true complete picture of the case, not just what was noted on a recent DBQ. VA rates a million claims a year, but on those 100 claims alone (for each specific issue) the committee would have enough data to revise the applicable regulations and rating policies (interpretations), to include revision of the rating schedule, DBQ/exam template, and evaluation builder for that issue.

But before the evaluation of specific issues can be corrected, there are several general/core rating principles that must be clarified.

Start with the very first paragraph of the VA regulation regarding disability compensation, *38 CFR 3.4 (b)(1) Disability Compensation*, and clearly define "in line of duty." The regulation says that entitlement exists if the personal injury or disease, or aggravation thereof, was "incurred or aggravated in line of duty." The definitions regulation, 38 CFR 3.1, defines "in line of duty" as "injury or disease incurred or aggravated during a period of active duty." But what does "incurred" mean? *If* it means anything that ever happened to a soldier while he was on the military payroll, and any disease that the soldier was first diagnosed with during service, then that needs to be *changed.* It should mean only injuries that resulted from military activities (not basketball injuries and motorcycle accidents), and only diseases contracted in service due to specific exposures (such as malaria in Vietnam, or chloracne due to herbicides), only things that happened to a soldier while he was performing an assigned military task, whether that was in a battle, in a road march, or in a maintenance shop. The VA uses "in line of duty" correctly when considering claims from Reservists and National Guard members who are attending required training. During those few days or weeks, the member is considered to be on active duty and can be granted service connection for injuries that happen to him while he is actually training, but not if he's out on the town that evening. But when deciding regular claims from regular active duty members, "in line of duty" is disregarded, despite that being the foremost regulation!

A primary VA policy I would implement is to start making the veteran more accountable for *supporting* his own claim, rather than just giving him the benefit of the doubt. Years ago, if the evidence was not there in the military file, then the case was denied. Certainly with today's electronic records and with the military helping soldiers stack their in-service file, if it's not in the military file, then it wasn't incurred in service. But today VA is laxer than ever on requiring any real evidence; lay statements and subjective reports are as good as a police report.

It all started falling apart with the Veterans Claims Assistance Act of 2000 (VCAA) which prompted VA to promote and encourage more claims, develop for all manner of evidence not mentioned by the veteran, to do everything in its power to help develop a claim, and to grant every issue at the highest evaluation possible. A disability claim is a law suit against the VA, not a little courtroom tort claim that might result in a one-time retribution, but a law suit that will result in monthly payments for the rest of the veteran's life! Ironically, while the claim is against the VA, the VA is the entity who has to develop and support and grant the claim! The VA workers work *for* the claimant, and *no one* is there for the government (us taxpayers who must pay the decided settlement). Veterans have always contended that the VA is out to deny them; rumors are that VA will always deny a claim the first time and that you have to fight for it with reopens. But that's all a crock of bull, couldn't be further from the truth. VA's goal is to grant as much as possible. Unlike a private corporation where employees are directed to be thrifty, no one at VA thinks any of this money is coming out of their pocket. But it is! It is our tax dollars now and our children's debt for the future.

It has become very easy now for a veteran to support his own claim. He can go on-line and submit his claim, review his file, and upload more crap every day, and believe me he does, all manner of duplicate stuff that is not helping but that is overshadowing the legitimate pertinent records. The reviewer no longer has time to read all this mess. The rater, due to pressures to produce quantity and not quality, looks at the claimed issues and looks at the DBQs and grants the most he can, and I do mean he stretches that evaluation to the highest possible level. The other evidence means nothing. The goal for many VA employees is to get each veteran to the maximum benefit as quickly as possible so as to limit future reopen claims. Grant, grant, grant.

Every time the VA gets exposed in the news (a lot lately), the VA solution is to relax standards, grant more, and do more more more for the veterans. The solution to the problem is not to do MORE, but to try to start doing things RIGHT for the veterans, which at the same time will be doing what's right for the American taxpayers and our country.

The Social Security Administration (SSA) is no agency to be proud of. Anyone who has worked there will attest to what a mess the SSA is also, and many of those employees transfer to VA for higher wages. But from the SSA files that I have reviewed in conjunction with VA claims, it appears to me that they have a better system for determining disability. Simpler, more primitive, and more just. The case is assigned to a particular person who will take responsibility for that claim, not to a computer system of thousands of raters. The claim and the medical evidence is actually reviewed by that person. A medical exam is done by and for the SSA and the results are a pertinent part of the decision. The decision is often a denial; they do not try to grant disability to everyone who asks for it. The decision will frequently be something like this, "After careful review of the evidence, we have decided that we cannot grant your disability claim at this time because the evidence does not show that you are too disabled to work. Although some of your conditions may prohibit certain work activities, you are still able to perform some form of gainful employment, to include sedentary employment." Wow, if the VA could get on board with that.

(22) JOINT EFFORTS NEEDED

Repairs to this failing VA disability program will require joint efforts from the military departments, the VA Benefits Administration leadership, the VA regulation/policy writers, the VA physicians and contract examiners, and the Veteran Services Organizations (VSOs).

First the military departments must stop giving honorable discharges for misconduct, bad conduct, nonproductive service, drug/alcohol abuse, and personality disorders. Veterans benefits are for veterans with honorable discharges, and when the military lets the criminals slide out as honorable, VA has no choice but to grant them equal benefits, but these claimants present some of the most fraudulent claims. Furthermore, VA must stop converting dishonorable discharges to "honorable for VA purposes."

Next, the military departments must stop *encouraging* claims. Currently the last 30 days of a soldier's term is spent going to clinics and looking for issues that can be put on his VA claim. He can also submit the VA claim pre-discharge if he's within 6 months of discharge, and he can have his VA examinations done pre-discharge, so he can start getting VA benefits immediately after discharge. All this is great for seriously injured soldiers, and that's what it was intended for, but for a soldier still in the field, with no noticeable disability, it's an abuse of military time we're paying for. Whatever the soldier puts on that claim form becomes evidence that the condition was "present during service" because he reported it during service, even though he has never complained before or been treated for the problem. The pre-discharge procedures are being abused by soldiers who are creating bogus claims in order to continue receiving paychecks after their service ends.

VA compensation was never intended to be a continuance of military pay, and the federal taxpayer has never agreed to pay a healthy soldier all his life-long days just because he served a few months in the military. This practice is causing healthy young men and women to become bums, dependent on an entitlement program for the rest of their lives, at the hardworking taxpayers' expense.

VA, by federal funding through our taxpayer dollars, provides plenty of great benefits to veterans including home loans, educational assistance, medical care, insurance, vocational and recreational rehabilitation. Communities, private agencies, and private businesses, profit and non-profit alike, also provide multiple benefits and discounts to veterans. It's time we returned VA disability compensation to our battle-injured veterans, for whom it was intended, as they are the ones truly deserving of this financial support and recognition.

The Veteran Service Organizations (VSOs) such as VFW and American Legion (and dozens of others) must stop *encouraging* claims and preparing/submitting *bogus* claims. They've taken on a mission of helping all veterans prepare and submit claims, in pretense of fighting for the veterans against the evil VA. The fact is there are very few legitimate claims, for injuries incurred during battle, which have not already been submitted for those veterans before they ever left Walter Reed. The VSOs need to get back to their original purpose of providing social activities and comradery for veterans, and stop promoting fraud.

The VA Medical Centers must retrain their examiners, as well as all the contracted examiners, and explain to these doctors the ramifications of the DBQs they are completing. More honesty and accuracy would require a return to the old-style exam where the examiner actually wrote up what he saw and what he thought, but with the push for more modern technology VA is not likely to give up the automated DBQs with the little check boxes. The doctors need to know that they should not be checking boxes of symptoms unless there is some *objective* evidence seen on exam, *or* medical records showing ongoing *treatment* for the subjective complaints. Every DBQ should have a mandatory remarks section at the end for the doctor to explain just how mild or severe this condition really is and those remarks should be considered more probative than the check-boxes of subjective complaints.

The VA Medical Center physicians who are "treating" patients must stop diagnosing conditions just because a veteran comes in and rattles off a bunch of subjective symptoms, all for the purpose of a future claim. If there's nothing on x-ray, or CT, or blood test, or EMG, or EKG, or echocardiogram, then there is no injury/disease! Service connection should not be granted for subjective "pain" or for any claimed condition that cannot be properly diagnosed.

Veterans Benefits Administration (VBA) must submit changes so that 38 CFR 3 and 4 can be rewritten in accordance with Lincoln's promise, if that is indeed the VA's motto and mission. Service connection should be granted only for *service-caused* injuries or illnesses, conditions that resulted from battle or military training activities, conditions that never would have developed if the claimant had not been in service. Injuries due to after-duty sports and private vehicle accidents should not qualify for compensation. For diseases, perhaps a new 50/50 probability standard could be adopted like this: "If there is at least a 50/50 chance the condition would have presented anyway had the claimant never been in service, then the condition must be denied." The whole Agent Orange presumptive debacle needs to be reviewed and reversed because it was a political decision not supported by medical evidence. The whole Gulf War presumptive-exposures debacle needs to be reviewed and reversed because it is unclear, contradictory, unsupported by medical science/literature, inconsistently examined, and inconsistently rated.

Will any private company in America pay workers' compensation because a worker came down with diabetes, venereal disease, or depression/anxiety, or was injured in a car accident on the way home, while he was employed there? VA disability compensation should be paid the same way workers' comp is paid, only for injuries that were actually incurred in the course of performing the required job duties.

The VBA needs to *activate* a FRAUD department and encourage those who develop and rate claims to submit fraudulent cases for review. Submit corrupt POAs for review (those submitting fraudulent claims for the veterans.) Submit corrupt physicians for review (those preparing fraudulent exams, and those writing letters or completing DBQs for veterans they've never met). Suspicious cases should be investigated. Insurance agencies and workers' compensation claims offices employ investigators to go out and spy on claimants to see if they are really disabled or if they were just faking it on interview/exams. Although this sounds like more work, or more employees to hire, it would actually greatly reduce the workload because many of the crooks would be discouraged from filing their false claims if they thought they might get caught. Those who are caught lying or exaggerating on a VA claim or VA exam should be fined at least $5,000, and any benefits already awarded should be stopped.

The Office of Inspector General (OIG) might as well be dismantled. They haven't caught the problems in the past and they are not likely to ever see or understand the problems if they have never rated claims. They have addressed some problems in the past such as DBQ fraud and erroneous reporting of income (for pension and IU) but nothing was done at the VA working level to correct the noted deficiencies. I have witnessed OIG inspections at many federal offices, and employees were invited to visit with the OIG if they had issues to raise. But in 10 years working at a Veterans Benefits Office I never once witnessed an OIG inspection, and was never informed that they would be in the building in case I desired to meet with them. I'm sure there were OIG visits with management, but they certainly weren't meeting with the employees at the working level. Furthermore, VA employees would not dare raise the issues I have discussed. In fact, VA employees will be muter than ever now that employees can be fired "at will" under the *VA Accountability and Whistleblower Protection Act of 2017.*

The purpose of the Whistleblower act was to "ease restrictions on the discipline and termination of bad VA employees," and VA Secretary Shulkin praised it as a way to improve morale at the VA, but it had the opposite effect. Apparently, the whistleblower portion was meant to encourage employees to report crimes being committed or hidden by their superiors, but in fact it serves to stifle any reporting of the types of problems I'm noting in this book. More than 1700 VA employees have been fired since the act, and recent articles in *The Washington Post* and *The National Examiner* have reported that retaliation against whistleblowers has increased since the act. If an employee dared to voice opinions like mine (shared by many) he would be promptly fired as "disloyal" to the VA, and "undermining the mission of the VA."

Veterans benefits are a sacred cow, considered "untouchable." It is blasphemous, unpatriotic, and suicidal to even insinuate that we may reduce benefits for our great veterans. I could never suggest it while I was an employee. I had to bite my lip and do as I was told. But now that I am beyond the fear of dismissal, I am willing to suggest exactly that. Veterans' disability benefits are greatly abused and greatly overpaid and are a major silent contributor to America's $21 trillion budget deficit.

I propose that a special committee be established to examine one or many or all of the issues I have raised. I have given examples but the committee should pull random case files and see for themselves. The VA rating system uses a 4-digit diagnostic code for each specific disability, i.e., DC 6020 is tinnitus and DC 7911 is diabetes. So it is easy to pull a sampling of ratings for any particular issue. But don't just review the files to see if the rating decision matched the DBQ and the Evaluation Builder. We already have local quality reviewers and STAR reviewers doing that all day long and reporting that rating quality is high!

I am proposing that the review go a few steps deeper. Review all the veteran's history. Review his employment and social activity the same way SSA would do for a disability claim or a corporation would do for a workmens compensation claim. Then review the actual regulations. Did the level of disability spit out by the Evaluation Builder actually meet the level of disability specified in the regulation, specifically is there any true functional impairment? Also analyze the cause of the disability. Was it really incurred in the line of duty, or was it something the veteran would have experienced anyway as a congenital condition or from a non-military accident? It's not simply a matter of rating the claims in a different light with different considerations. It's not simply a matter of requiring the rating specialist to use common sense and to rate a claim based on the whole record and to write a justification of the decision, whether granted or denied. It's not a matter of making sure the raters do what they're taught. The regulations and policies need revision! The whole system of granting disability needs to be reviewed and regulations revised to clarify that disability benefits will be provided only to veterans who were injured or diseased *in-the-line-of-duty* and that this condition would not have beset him if he had not been performing a required military action.

Such a new mind-set and new regulations/policies cannot be written or implemented over night. It may take a year for a revision or clarification of a few primary sections of 38 CFR 3. The rating schedule itself does not need to be immediately changed, only the primary principles which determine "service-connection." Once service-connection for an issue is conceded, then the existing Book C criteria could be used to assign an evaluation, although evidence in support of the evaluation should come from medical treatment records and even job-performance records, not just a DBQ from a single-time examination for the condition.

Any "changed" policies and procedures of course could not affect any veteran who has already been granted, except to perhaps prevent his future increases. The same way any regulation change is implemented, a date in the future must be set for new procedures to take effect, applicable to all claims received after that date.

Every VA rater would need re-training to reverse the mentality of "grant, grant, grant" and to reverse the fear of denying. The goal is not to deny. The goal is to make a true, honest, fair decision. If the veteran has a truly disabling medical condition that was caused by his military performance of duty, then grant! Otherwise, no. And if granting, then set an evaluation based on the degree of disability actually shown by objective evidence! VA already hires highly educated persons to be raters, trains them extensively, and pays them extraordinarily well. Let them use their brains, logic, and reason, and let them explain their decisions!

Automation has destroyed the credibility of this program. Check-box DBQs and Evaluation Builders could still be used as the *tools* they were designed to be, but the final decisions must be based on the entire file of evidence, with consideration of contradictory evidence, and consideration of *lack* of objective evidence, and above all, each decision must be based on logic and reason! A return to rational decisions, written and justified, is imperative if we are to put an end to the abuse of this entitlement program, an end to *The Greatest Fleecing of America.*

References

"A Closer Look at Sleep Apnea." *American Academy of Sleep Medicine*, accessed Aug 2018, aasm.org/private-insurance-claims-sleep-apnea- rose-steeply.

Crawford, Neta C. "US Budgetary Costs of Wars through 2016: $4.79 Trillion and Counting." *Costs of War*, Brown University, Sep 2016, watson.brown.edu/costsofwar/files/cow/imce/papers/2016/ Costs%20of%20War%20through %202016%20FINAL%20final%20v2.pdf. (Updated a similar report first released by Neta C. Crawford, Boston University, on June 25, 2014.)

Davidson, Joe. "Victims say VA whistleblower retaliation is growing under Trump, despite rhetoric." *The Washington Post*, 30 Oct 2017, www.washingtonpost.com/news/powerpost/wp/2017/10/30/victims-say-va-whistleblower-retaliation-is-growing-under-trump-despite-rhetoric/?utm term =.e702d7cc9a84.

Davis, Scott. "VA launches criminal investigation against whistleblowers." *Washington Examiner,* 14 May 2018, www.washingtonexaminer.com/news/va-launches-criminal-investigation-against-whistle blowers.

"Fair Health Study Delves into Sleep Apnea." *FAIR Health*, accessed Aug 2018, www.fairhealth.org/article/fair-health-study-delves-into-sleep-apnea.

"High Stakes Health Care." *The Government Standard*, Vol. LXXXVI, No 5, American Federation of Government Employees, AFL-CIO, September/October 2017.

Johnson, Paul M. "A Glossary of Political Economy Terms." *Auburn University*, accessed August 2, 2018, www.auburn. edu/~johnspm/ gloss/entitlement_program.

Krause, Benjamin. "VA Awards Medical Disability Examinations Contracts For $6.8 Billion." *Disabled Veterans.org*, 21 Sep 2016, www.disabledveterans.org/2016/09/21/va-awards-medical-disability-examinations-contracts-6-billion.

Kujawa, S. G. and Liberman, M. C. "Adding Insult to Injury: Cochlear Nerve Degeneration after 'Temporary' Noise-Induced Hearing Loss." *J. Neurosci, The Journal of Neuroscience,* 11, 29(45) 14077-14085 (2009), www. jneurosci.org/content/29/45/14077.

Larson, Emily. "Fact Check: Has the Trump Administration Fired Over 1,500 VA Employees?" *CheckYourFact*, 01 Feb 2018, checkyourfact.com/2018/02/01/ fact-check-has-the-trump-admin-fired-over-1500-va-employees.

May, Caroline. "VA Disability Claims for Sleep Apnea Skyrocket in Recent Years." *Veterans Today,* 6 Jun 2013, www.veteranstoday.com/ 2013/06/06/va-disability-claims-for-sleep-apnea-skyrocket-to-over-1-2-billion-per-year-read-more-httpdailycaller-com20130604va-disability-claims-for-sleep-apnea-skyrocket-in-recent-years.

Noise and Military Service: Implications for Hearing Loss and Tinnitus. Institute of Medicine, Medical Follow-up Agency, Committee on Noise-Induced Hearing Loss and Tinnitus Associated with Military Service from World War II to the Present, The National Academies Press, 2006.

Philpott, Tom. "Attorney urges Congress to end sleep apnea claims 'abuse'." *Stars and Stripes,* 30 May 2013, www.stripes. com/news/veterans/attorney-urges-congress-to-end-sleep-apnea-claims-abuse-1.223588.

Preslin, Patricia, et al. "Proportionate Mortality Study of US Army and US Marine Corps Veterans of the Vietnam War." *Journal of Occupational Medicine*, 30(5):412-419, May 1988, journals.lww. com/joem/Abstract/1988/05000/ _Mortality_Study_of_US_Army_and_US.7.aspx.www. disabledveterans,org/2016/09/21/ va-awards-medical-disability-examinations-contracts-6-billion.

"Prostate Cancer." *American Cancer Society*, accessed Aug 2018, www.cancer.org/cancer/prostate-cancer.

Proxmire, William Sen. *The Fleecing of America.* Houghton Mifflin Company, 1980. (only as noted in the Preface herein)

"Rural Diagnoses of Sleep Apnea Up 911% from 2014 to 2017, Finds Analysis of Insurance Claim Lines." *Sleep Review, The Journal for Sleep Specialists,* 7 Mar 2018, www.sleepreviewmag.com/2018/ 03/rural-diagnoses-sleep-apnea-911-2014-2017-finds-analysis-insurance-claim-lines.

Shane, Leo III. "Report: Wars in Iraq, Afghanistan cost almost $5 trillion so far." *Military Times*, 12 Sep 2016, www. militarytimes.com/news/your-military/2016/09/12/report-wars-in-iraq-afghanistan-cost-almost-5-trillion-so-far

"Sleep Apnea – Overview and Facts." *Sleep Education,* The American Academy of Sleep Medicine, www.sleep education. org/essentials-in-sleep/sleep-apnea.

"Special Section: Prostate Cancer." *Cancer Facts and Figures 2010.* American Cancer Society, www.cancer.org/content/ dam/ cancer-org/research/cancer-facts-and-statistics/ annual-cancer-facts-and-figures/2010/cancer-facts-and-figures-special-section-2010.pdf

Stiglitz, Joseph E. and Bilmes, Linda J. *The Three Trillion Dollar War: The True Cost of the Iraq Conflict,* W. W. Norton, 2008.

"The Institute of Medicine Report (IOM 2000)." *VA Guard,* Nov/Dec 2008.

"United States Military Casualties of War." *Wikipedia* (multiple military references cited), accessed Aug 2018, en. wikipedia.org/wiki/United States_military_casualties_ of_war.

Veterans and Agent Orange: Health Effects of Herbicides Used in Vietnam, Institute of Medicine, The National Academies of Sciences, Engineering, and Medicine, The National Academies Press, 1994, doi.org/10.17226/2141.

Veterans and Agent Orange: Update 2014, Committee to Review the Health Effects in Vietnam Veterans and Exposure to Herbicides, National Academy of Sciences, Engineering, and Medicine, The National Academies Press, 2016.

Wood, David. "Beyond the Battlefield." *Huffington Post,* 10 Oct 2011, updated 19 Jan 2017, www.huffingtonpost.com/ 2011/10/10/beyond-the-battlefield-part-1-tyler-southern 999329. html

www.benefits.va.gov

38 CFR Book C, Schedule for Rating Disabilities. U.S.Department of Veterans Affairs, Web Automated Reference Material System, accessed 6 Aug 2018, www.benefits.va.gov/ WARMS/bookc.asp

"VA's 2016 Annual Benefits Report," *Department of Veterans Affairs,* accessed August 2, 2018, www.benefits.va.gov/ REPORTS/abr/ ABR-Compensation-FY16-01262018.pdf

www.knowva.ebenefits.va.gov

U.S. Department of Veterans Affairs. *M21-1 Adjudication Procedures Manual,* www.knowva.ebenefits.va.gov/system/ templates/selfservice/va_ssnew/help/customer/locale/en-US/portal/554400000001018/topic/554400000004049/M21 -1-Adjudication-Procedures-Manual. (The entire manual is applicable to this book, with the most pertinent sections being *Part III – General Claims Process; and Part IV – Compensation, DIC, and Death Compensation Benefits.)*

www.va.gov

"2017 VA Agency Financial Report." *Office of Finance,* U.S. Department of Veterans Affairs, 15 Nov 2017, www.va.gov/finance/afr/ index.asp.

"Audit of Veterans Benefits Administration's (VBA) Income Verification Match (IVM) Results," *Department of Veterans Affairs, Office of Inspector General,* 8 Nov 2000, www.va.gov/oig/52/reports/ 2001/99-00054-1.pdf

Cory-Slechta, Deborah, et al. "Update of Health Effects of Serving in the Gulf War, 2016." *Gulf War & Health Volume 10,* The National Academies of Sciences, Engineering & Medicine, www.va.gov/RAC-GWVI/meetings/apr2016/A-Pres1-ermanGibb.

"VA Utilization Profile FY 2016." *U.S. Veterans Eligibility Trends and Statistics, 2016,* The National Center for Veterans Analysis and Statistics, U.S. Department of Veterans Affairs, Nov 2017, www.va.gov/vetdata/docs/ Quickfacts/ VA_Utilization_Profile.pdf

VA "FY 2019 Congressional Budget Submission." "FY 2018 Budget Submission" "FY 2017 Budget Submission." "FY 2016 Budget Submission." "FY 2014 Budget Submission." "FY 2013 Budget Submission." "FY 2012 Budget Submission." "FY 2011 Budget Submission." "FY 2010 Budget Submission." "FY 2009 Budget Submission." "FY 2008 Budget Submission." *U.S. Department of Veterans Affairs, Office of Budget,* www.va.gov/budget/products.asp

www.publichealth.va.gov

Agent Orange Review, U.S. Department of Veterans Affairs, Health Care, Public Health, 29 Volumes dated Nov 1982 to Summer 2017, www.publichealth.va.gov/exposures/ agentorange/ publications/newsletter-archive.asp

"Health Effects of Serving in the Gulf War." *The Institute of Medicine (IOM), accessed Aug 2018,* www.publichealth. va.gov/exposures/ gulfwar/sources/oil-well- fires.asp#s

"Oil Well Fires During Gulf War." *Department of Veterans Affairs, Public Health,* accessed Aug 2018, www. publichealth. va.gov/exposures/gulfwar/sources/oil-well-fires.asp#s

www.research.va

"VA Research on Hearing Loss." *U.S. Department of Veterans Affairs, Office of Research & Development*, accessed Aug 2018, www.research.va/gov/topics/ hearing/cfm.

www.nih.gov

"Noise-Induced Hearing Loss." *National Institute of Health's National Institute on Deafness and Other Communication Disorders (NIDCD),* accessed Aug 2018, www.nidcd. nih.gov/health/noise-induced-hearing-loss.

www.gao.gov

"Federal Workforce: Recent Trends in Federal Civilian Employment and Compensation." *U.S. Government Accountability Office,* GAO-14-215, 29 Jan 2014, www.gao.gov/products/GAO-14-215

"VA Disability Compensation: Actions Needed to Address Hurdles Facing Program Modernization." *U.S. Government Accountability Office,* GAO-12-846, 10 Sep 2012, www.gao.gov/products/GAO-12-846.

"Veterans' Disability Benefits: VA Can Better Ensure Unemployability Decisions are Well Supported." *United States Government Accountability Office (GAO), GAO-15-464, Report to the Chairman, Committee on Veterans' Affairs, House of Representatives,* June 2015, www.gao.gov/assets/680/670592.pdf

www.congress.gov and Federal Laws

Breslin, Patricia ScD et al. "Proportionate Mortality Study of US Army and US Marine Corps Veterans of the Vietnam War." *Journal of Occupational Medicine,* May 1988, journals.lww.com/joem/Abstract/1988/05000/Proportionate _Mortality_Study_of_US_Army_and_US.7.aspx

Code of Federal Regulations, Title 38 – Pensions, Bonuses, and Veterans' Relief, Chapter 1 – Department of Veterans Affairs, Part 3 – Adjudication and Part 4 – Schedule for Rating Disabilities. Elaws.us, updated 28 Jun 2018, federal.elaws.us/cfr/title38.part3 and http://federal.elaws.us/cfr/title38.part4

"H.R.303 – Retired Pay Restoration Act," *U.S.A. Congressional Record, 115th Congress (2017-2018),* www.congress.gov/bill/115th-congress/house-bill/303/all-info.

"H.R. 303 – Retired Pay Restoration Act." *U.S.A Congressional Record, 108th Congress,* V. 149, PT. 17, September 24 to October 3, 2003. books.google.com/books?id=7vNAyiK CBw IC.

"H.R. 303 – Concurrent Receipt of Retired Pay and Compensation," (also references H.R. 303, Retired Pay Restoration Act of 2005, H.R. 2076, S.558 and S.845, 2005), *U.S. Congress,* books.google.com/books?id=0dw3itGECN0C.

"H.R.556 - Agent Orange Act of 1991." *U.S.A. Congressional Record, 102nd Congress (1991-1992),* 6 Feb 1991, www.congress.gov/ bill/ 102nd-congress/house-bill/556.

"H.R.1961 - Veterans' Dioxin and Radiation Exposure Compensation Standards Act (Dioxin Act)." *U.S.A Congressional Record, 98th Congress (1983-1984),* issued in August 1985, became law on September 25, 1985, www.congress.gov/bill/98th-congress/house-bill/1961.

Kang, Han K. et al. "Soft Tissue Sarcomas and Military Service In Vietnam: A Case Comparison Group Analysis of Hospital Patients." *Journal of Occupational Medicine,* Dec 1986, journals.lww.com/joem/ Abstract/1986/12000/Soft_Tissue_ Sarcomas_and_Military_Service_in_Vietnam.aspx

"Revised Medical Criteria for Evaluating Respiratory Disorders." *Federal Register, The Daily Journal of the United States Government,* Social Security Administration, 9 Jun 2016, www.federalregister.gov/documents/2016/06/09/2016-13275/revised-medical-criteria-for-evaluating-respiratory-system-disorders.

"S.1094 – Department of Veterans Affairs Accountability and Whistleblower Protection Act of 2017." *U.S.A Congressional Record, 115th Congress (2017-2018),* congress.gov/bill/115th-congress/senate-bill/1094.

Schecter, Arnold et al. "Agent Orange, Dioxins, and Other Chemicals of Concern in Vietnam: Update 2006." *Journal of Occupational and Environmental Medicine*, 48(4):408-413, April 2006, journals lww.com/joem/Abstract/2006/04 000/Agent_Orange_Dioxins,_and_Other_Chemicals_of.10. aspx

"Veterans Claims Assistance Act of 2000 (VCAA), Public Law 106-475," *U.S. Congress*, 9 Nov 2000, www.congress.gov/ 106/plaws/ publ475/PLAW-106publ475.pdf

www.ssa.gov

"Disability Evaluation Under Social Security, 3.00 Respiratory Disorders – Adult." *Social Security Administration, Medical/Professional Relations*, www.ssa.gov/disability/ professionals/bluebook/3.00-Respiratory-Adult.htm

Disclaimer of Liability:

I have written the truth, the whole truth, and nothing but the truth, to the best of my knowledge and ability. I would testify in court to anything I have written herein. However, I am a human being, as fallible as any veteran or BVA member or Congressman. If any error or misrepresentation of facts is found in this book, please submit the details to me, sdprice248@gmail.com, and after verification, I will happily revise that portion of the text before further distribution.

The example cases identifying veterans as "Veteran X" are real, but even I have no idea who they really are, and I could not reproduce evidence of their claims in court. Any resemblance to yourself or to a veteran you know is purely coincidental, or in any case it would be impossible for VA or the fraud-police to find you, unless you turn yourself in.

S. D. Price